THE WAY OF INTEGRAL LIFE

The Wisdom of Three Masters

VOLUME THREE

The Way of Integral Life

THE TEACHINGS OF A TAOIST MASTER

By Master
NI, HUA-CHING

The Shrine of the Eternal Breath of Tao
College of Tao and Traditional Chinese Healing
LOS ANGELES

Acknowledgement:
Thanks and appreciation to Janet DeCourtney, Andrea Giambrone and Liza Hughes for editing and word processing, and to Karen Kristen for the painting shown on the cover of this book.

The Shrine of the Eternal Breath of Tao, Malibu, California
College of Tao and Traditional Chinese Healing, 117 Stonehaven Way
Los Angeles, California 90049

*Dedicated to those who live
with a goal of attaining
the complete growth of their life.*

CONTENTS

PREFACE

The content of a religion is the psychology of a society. It is also the manifestation of the intelligence of the people. In different ages, the intelligence of the general population evolved, and along with new developments in society, a new psychology was brewed. Despite these changes, some old questions still remain unanswered. Thus, although the dominance of the old religions fades, their shallow beliefs still find a stubborn root in present-day costumes and performances which impede the advance of human growth.

Truthfully speaking, different time periods and a deeper intelligence should produce new religions that would serve to parallel and genuinely assist the spiritual and psychological growth of people. Unfortunately, most people are too busy facing new frontiers of modern discoveries and knowledge to look into the deeper levels of spiritual reality. They have not developed their capacity to discern the unchangeable truth which underlies life; the simple essence of life within contains the truth, not any external establishment or religion. Each person has three complete spheres: physical, mental and spiritual. The conceptual means for understanding this has varied according to the religion and time.

With its immature leadership, the majority of the human world is still in an epoch similar to that of the middle ages. Religious dominance has nothing to do with individual spiritual development and modern science does not do very much for spiritual discovery either. The subtle spiritual foundation of all life is still quite outside the realm of modern scientific research and detection. The spiritual development of ancient attainment has been passed down to modern times, filling the gap left by scientific research. The tradition of Tao offers a method that reveals an individual's spiritual energy, a process unknown to modern science. This knowledge gives you the great direction of the Integral Way, which can unify the development of the three spheres. It embraces a complete knowledge of a balanced life and the nature of the universe.

The learning and practice of self-cultivation under the guidance of an achieved teacher enables you to experience your individual spiritual energy in a peaceful living environment. The wise student is able to utilize good knowledge offered by someone who has experienced difficulty in obtaining it. Those who are not in such ideal conditions will find it beneficial to learn and follow the guidance and knowledge of the Integral Path. This guidance is the fruit of the cultivation of the achieved ones and is beneficial to all.

It is important that such knowledge not be lost or escape the reach of sincere people. The realization of this knowledge in an individual life will provide the foundation for one's growth. It is also important to connect it with modern knowledge and technology for the improvement of medicine, lifestyles and relationships, society and politics. My advice to any student is to search and learn the methods and techniques that will awaken his or her spirit and spiritual energy, not merely at the conceptual level, but on the genuine spiritual level. After sharpening one's sensitivity, a person is improved spiritually and many channels of the secrets of life are opened. Such a person may be rejuvenated, but can no longer expose his sensitive being to a disturbing world. With good support, a person who is ready to learn such truth can establish his cultivation and spiritual exploration by himself, with the help of a teacher. If three individuals among ten were to achieve such important knowledge, the world would move towards a more balanced and harmonious direction. This is my wish for the world and the reason for publishing this teaching obtained from the cultivation of the ancient developed ones. It is in the greater interest of the world that I have opened the secret, not for myself. It has been my offering to share publicly what I have learned from the direction and conclusions of the developed ones of antiquity.

Compared to spiritual reality, conceptual activity is just a medium for telling the truth, but it is not the truth itself. Nonetheless, good thought and ideas still hold a very important value in human life. The works of Chuang Tzu and Master Hui Neng are being published separately as *Attaining Unlimited Life* and *Enlightenment: Mother of Spiritual Independence.* A number of students helped review them, and in the process, some questions arose. This book, *The Way of Integral Life,* answers those questions. In some ways, it is not I who is producing this valuable guidance; it is the response to the inquisitive modern mentality that this ageless truth of the correct way of life and faith is offered.

Ni, Hua-Ching
August 12, 1988
Orcas Island, Northwest Water Region of U.S.A.

CHAPTER ONE

TO BE OR NOT TO BE?

NO ONE can deny that our life is a matter of existence. Some events are routine, some special, some you like and some you do not like. By experiencing your daily routine and all events, you are existing. The broader your experience of life, the stronger your soul becomes. We create difficulties, however, when we unconsciously consider life as a group of events taking place in the world specifically for us, or relating to us primarily.

Each event, no matter how large or small, is a condition supported by many subconditions. Human life is a special event of nature because its specific existence involves the subjective mind. With effort and development, the mind can come to be trusted as an objective tool or guide. This discussion attempts to review the matters and events of a life, considering a personal life as an event in nature.

All things and events in nature are temporary phenomena that change. They disintegrate when the original conditions that brought them into being are removed. When conditions come together, they give birth to existence; when they separate from one another, that existence dissolves. The birth, transformation and dissolution of all matters and things contribute to creating new conditions and situations. The most subtle example is the thoughts we have each minute. Viewed objectively, the assembly of conditions that gives birth to an event or an object in one's life seems uncontrolled and totally beyond the reach of the mind. However, events can be influenced through the function of a properly managed mind. So, if you wish to change a situation in your life, can it be done?

There are some conditions that you can control and there are others that control you. Ask yourself what can be learned from a given situation and what you can do about it. Correct understanding can produce a positive, helpful mental attitude with which to face any situation. This suggests a comment on the subject of religion. Some eastern religions reflect a negative attitude towards life, saying, "Since we are controlled by our objective existence and external conditions, there is nothing much we can do about ourselves. It is just not possible to improve things in the short span of a lifetime." This philosophical passivity, as a religious belief, conditions the mind and limits it by taking a passive, helpless or negative attitude toward the normalcy of life.

If it is your understanding that life is nothing or that it is an accidental occurrence of nature, then your attitude, whether you are correct or incorrect, shapes your response to it accordingly. In the pure spiritual cultivation of Tao, life is neither recognized as something or not something. It does not establish a conceptual direction for the mind, or a mind-set, because to do that to the mind produces more trouble than happiness. If once you decide conceptually, for instance, that life is bitter and painful, your decision will subsequently affect you spiritually. Holding that view will separate you from life, which you now view as composed of conditions and relationships that cause you trouble. Spiritually you will withdraw. You will keep withdrawing and become smaller and smaller.

The pure spiritual cultivation of Tao nourishes the integral spirit of life and treats all events as equal. You responsibly take care of what is necessary, which establishes a more positive orientation toward life. Life is not a single element; it is the ongoing integration of all things in life.

When you look at life in general, you see it is made up of a number of smaller events or elements. When you look at your own life, you define it in emotional terms as happy or miserable, high or low, rich or poor. I suggest that you do not remain at the level of personal emotions when by going beyond it you can examine the elements of natural life itself. The further you go, the less sense of self is involved with the elements which are simply characteristics of some small events in your life. It is as though your life is seen as a single event in the universe; therefore, all achievement by an individual life serves the assemblage of the other elements.

There is nothing really higher, or more definite, because the assemblage of high/low, rich/poor is a condition quite different from personal sentimentality. The understanding of the conditions in one's life - or a situation in life - if produced by a deep examination of the different levels of elements, would show an insignificant material basis. What is there to be sentimental about? Your life? Your achievement? Your condition? You are acting out a scene on a stage. In spiritual practice, all things are dependent upon your deep view. By knowing your life is an assembly, there are no existing traces left of the self once the assemblage is dispersed.

Some religions promote total elimination or extinction of the self. They assert that once you have achieved extinction of the self, there is then no pain or misery to be felt in life. From this developed two very different kinds of spiritual attitudes, both based on the establishment of a pair of large elements: the world and the self. One view would have you surrender the self, accepting that external pressure is greater than one's capability for life. Stated simply, this is to accept the loser's role in worldly life. The other attitude is that the self is stronger and more capable, more powerful than the world. This sense of self generalizes into the sense that God, a creator or conqueror, is shaping the mind. One way is to surrender; the other is to win or conquer. Inevitably, however, struggle and conflict are generated by practicing either of these ways. The former attitude is represented by Hinduism and Buddhism; the latter by Judaism, Christianity and Islam.

A person of Tao recognizes the polarity of life and knows that natural life lies in the balance between the polarity of world and self. Taoist practice is not based upon either the spiritual attitude of passivity or the spiritual attitude of aggression. A natural life keeps adjusting its physical, mental and spiritual condition to reach a balance, because balance is the well-being of a natural life. *The Book of Changes and the Unchanging Truth* expresses this attitude of balance that makes up the path of continual life.

Let us look again at the root of spiritual conflict. Spiritual conflict arises because the thoughts and attitudes of established conceptual ideologies have conditions underlying their teachings, doctrines and religious practices. Under the conditions of a certain situation, a doctrine or spiritual expression was established from one person's understanding of the law that all things have a birth and an extinction. According to this law, all solid elements in the world, as well as all mental creations, are subject to the law of transformation or change. Once you understand this, you no longer insist upon following a certain religion or doctrine, nor do you limit yourself to observing one particular practice. To reach maturity and to liberate one's true nature from the confusion and entrapment of cultural creations, it is necessary to understand that all teachings, doctrines and religious practices are not something for a student to cling to, but to pass through. With maturity, one recognizes the true significance of the existence of both mental and material matters. This recognition can enable you to attain the original freedom of your true nature and avoid the pitfall into which generations of humans have fallen. The hostility and antagonism generated by the material and conceptual spheres are not real; truly understanding this could help you accomplish the great achievement of the ancient spiritually achieved ones. What did the spiritually achieved ones cultivate? This. What did they teach? This. If you part from this center of balance, you will be led into confusion or a negative attitude toward life. The purpose of my endeavors is to show you the spiritual balance reached by the ancient sages.

Any thing begins when all the conditions for it come together to shape its existence. It changes or dissolves because it does not have an independent self: those conditions, terms and elements which originally supported its birth and existence have now changed, departed or dispersed. Therefore, the length of the existence of something, whether short or long, cannot be determined by the thing itself. It is determined by all the conditions of its origin. For example, the duration of the blossoming of one flower cannot be decided by the flower itself. It is decided by the earth, moisture, sunshine, climate and protection from human hands. Some ancient developed ones taught people to recognize this assembling and also pointed out the impermanence of the assemblage. Impermanence characterizes the maintenance, changes and dissolution of everything and shows that from birth, all is temporary. The entire process contains impermanence within it, not only near its end but during the whole process. Even an end is impermanent. All things which decay must necessarily reach death because the elements which originally supported the freshness of their existence become weakened or dispersed. Therefore, a new thing will occur to replace it or something new will independently arise. This new thing happens because support is supplied by new conditions which gather together to manifest in a particular way. This is the fact of assembling.

This law of assembly cannot be changed by human will. What human will can create is leadership of oneself or of a society, to decide what will work, what needs improvement and what should be purified. Human will itself is an assemblage, a concurrence under the law of assembly of all the elements which make it appear as will. Is this will free?

Some ancient developed ones who observed the coalescence of elements called "will" said that it is not free, but that it is achieved knowledge. Achieved knowledge comes from correct cognition. Without this cognition, there is no achieved knowledge. If there is no achieved knowledge, no true decision can be made; in that case, one needs to decide what one is going to learn or what one needs to improve or purify. One's perceptions must be purified and impartial to gain correct cognition, which produces the possibility of choice. Further, one's perception is purified when the personal ego or self has dissolved. A person then becomes unbiased and impartial, and at that point there is the possibility of choice. Once there is choice, there can be the operation of the will.

The will itself is dependent upon different underlying situations. Thus, the term "free will" is not completely accurate and choice is also, in fact, a comparative opportunity; it is also not absolutely beneficial or detrimental. Even if free will were to be allowed to operate totally by itself, then what you may call a free life of choice is decided by wholly external and internal conditions of all kinds - big and small, solid and subtle - assembled together by forces beyond us. Thus, we need spiritual growth to improve ourselves even in decision-making. In the sphere of how to operate your mind, there is no outer, written law to follow, but people of spiritual development can discover that there is a subtle law which controls the formation, transformation, change and interchange of all things. Your further development is needed before you can determine what is truly higher or truly better, what should be followed and what should be avoided in your life.

There is fundamentally one thing we need to know. If we agree that the existence of life, events, things, facts, governments, societies, relationships, marriages, etc. are each an assembly of supportive elements and conditions that bring a thing about, and that the dispersion of conditions and terms dissolve its existence, then we are only seeing the external operation. We have lost the vision of the internal operation. Can you say that all is external operation in your life? It is not. Allow me to offer a different view.

Life itself is a latecomer in universal nature. The mind and the spirit are also latecomers, although they are so very important in a life. Please consider this: at the beginning of the evolution of the universe, there was no recognition of will, purpose or significance. It was not until the latecomer evolved, followed external laws and slowly obtained inner awareness that the spirit grew within the shape of a human life. Knowing that the mind is a latecomer, you can see that the world has managed under its own law, not ours. This law is not written; the law is subtle.

Now I would like to talk a little more about the strength, power and capability of an individual's cognition. Our eye is conditioned by the nervous system, muscles and the special equipment with which we are naturally endowed. There is no way for us to decide what each of us should get. It happens naturally. We also do not say that it is the coordination of elements and systems that allows us to function as a whole. All organs always function at the level of instinct. Although different organs produce different things, it is our recognition that is unified; all the recognizing, cognitive organs and senses serve a subtle organ called the mind. One may say that the mind has a material foundation because there is a brain; however, at the level of the brain one cannot find a way to improve one's thoughts. A doctor can operate on a brain without finding different thoughts there. A tool from the outside is needed for the expression of thoughts, such as writing. Thoughts are the production of the association and coordination of the many elements within a person. Recognition is of the material level of color, texture and other categories. Recognition serves the subtle organ of the mind. Behind the mind there is another subtle agent we call the soul.

People think that common sense is gathered at the physical level of the senses and is communicated to the mind. But sometimes the knowledge a person gathers from the outside causes an internal conflict because the subtle agent that is behind or above the mind knows differently.   The existence of the subtle agent can be proven.   It can cause things to happen on a different level and in a different way.   While material reality can be proven materially, spiritual reality can be proven spiritually, with one important condition: highly achieved spiritual energy can discern realities far beyond the perceptual reach of our physical organs.   For example, there is a difference between knowing a person and feeling or experiencing a person.   There is a difference between knowing a thing and feeling or experiencing it.   If the capacity to experience deeply is unified with knowledge, the spirit of the person is balanced and strengthened.   Sometimes, however, a person's spiritual level might be much higher or lower than his mental capacity.   Or his mind will sometimes do foolish things, especially if it has been trained by an education stressing intellectual development, because it does not properly recognize resistance to the feeling or input from the high spiritual level.

All knowledge, subtle or intellectual, serves the substance of life.   If the substance of life is the coalescence of all things, then what is the fundamental element?   What is the nature of the smallest unit of the assembly?   The answer to this question has been disputed and researched for many generations, and antagonism still exists between those who take sides for either idealism or materialism.   Neither view is complete, however, because both of them are just smaller units or fragments of the whole.

The ancient developed ones with the most advanced spiritual achievement thought of the universe as a tai chi.   This is a diagram with two areas, one side dark and one side bright.   Within the bright side there is a dark point, and within the dark side there is a bright point.   This describes the integration of everything. Even the smallest element of the greatest assemblage contains the integration of both.   The smallest cannot be defined as material or as mental.   It is both.   There can be further development, until a point is reached where nothing more can be expressed; but from there development proceeds again slowly from the subtle level to the apparent level. A dispute has arisen as to whether or not there is non-existence. Looking to the spiritual development of the ancient developed ones, we do not blindly accept what they have taught but go further into the matter ourselves.

When we live as an equal with all the assembled small elements, matters and conditions, there is no existence of unified mind. Spiritual birth, or the birth of mind, is the awakening or awareness by an individual existence to its surroundings. In other words, when we follow and live our lives according to immediate experience and react to personal elements, matters and conditions, there is no existence of a unifying mind or higher awareness. Spiritual birth is the awakening of the unifying mind. It is the birth of awareness within the individual existence. Without this awakening, there is nothing that can be called mind. Without this awareness, you cannot know you are spirit that has attained this growth. In connection with this revelation of assemblage, the teaching we need to hear is that we should not be proud or stubborn or opinionated. One should especially not become monomaniacal and insist upon certain beliefs or ideas. This leads to trouble in the world.

The awareness of spirit is an achievement of consciousness, but it is not your creation. It is the natural development of life. True knowledge develops from the realization of the impermanence of all things. Spiritual growth or awakening helps us to break away from religious, spiritual, material or conceptual stubbornness. The impermanence of the assembly of all things is the most trusted ultimate truth of life. Whenever an existence forms, it must give birth to its opposite. If there is the birth of this, there must also be the birth of that. Once one dissolves, its opposite dissolves as well.

This knowledge can be confirmed by the understanding that to know a thing is to establish the existence of that thing, subjectively. The knowledge that things arise together can be confirmed by observing one thing establish another. No matter what the nature of that establishment, whether material or conceptual, it must be the assemblage of a group of connected things, thus, all existent things are a temporal assemblage. Whether the nature of the things established is material or conceptual, they are the assemblage of a group of objects or forms of temporary existence. And if something no longer exists, it is because the formal assembly of the matter has dissolved. Therefore, one way to begin breaking up mental obstinacy through subjective effort is to know that the existence of all things is subject to the law of gestalt or the law of impermanent assembly. One can apply the knowledge of this law to begin breaking up one's mental obstinacy, bit by bit, through the same way: first a thing is established by one's recognition, and then dissolved. This law governs everything from the lower sphere, that is describable, to Tao, the ultimate subtle law. Tao is not someone's creation. It is the path of natural development. It can be subtly recognized, yet it cannot be established. It is not subject to the operation of the mind. It is the unanalyzable subtle unity of the integral universal life.

With this in mind, you can observe the external world of the mountains and rivers and earth, and observe the internal world of conscious mechanisms. It is like an object that you are going to examine in the dark; the dim light, the eyes and the object make a new configuration. In this, you may find the fact of assembly. You cannot decide the most important element in this event, but by working on this longer, you attain true knowledge. You become wisdom itself. Finally you can be liberated from the mistake of subjectivity or personal consciousness and reach the truth of everything. What is the nature of this mistake? The mistake of subjectivity is the result of making the self the center of the world. This means that being subjective is the result of insistence upon the self. When this becomes externalized we have the belief of a God as the dominating power of the world.

Further, there are two ways to view the self. One way is the common sense approach to self-existence. For example, "I think, therefore I am." Another way is developed from a refined sense of self. You become subtly aware that the universal mind is behind everything. Similarly, there are two ways to see this. One is that the universal mind is reachable and knowable, that it is the orderliness and harmony of the existence of the universe itself. Another way will lead you to think that behind all there is something never to be known, a God who manages and controls everything.

Here we must be very careful. Is there a universal authority who takes care of the world and each individual's life? Or is there only a subtle universal law which can be discovered by the spiritually achieved ones and learned as a guideline for one's life, a law of balance, symmetry, gentleness and patience that contains all kinds of positive virtues for the world? The subjective attitude would lead one to believe there is a strong, powerful, forceful head or leader somewhere who manages the rations to provide for our life and fortune. We also learn from this special being to manage our life, put everything in our dominant control and management and ration the provisions to our relatives and surroundings.

The objective way leads to spiritual achievement; the other, the subjective way, to spiritual pitfall. However, we do not need to talk about spiritual achievement. We need to see how to correct the mistake of subjectivity. Because if you learn to insist on the self, then you emphasize your personal attempts in life which may not be in accordance with universal rightness or with common agreement or benefit. Then, also, you cannot be satisfied or achieve your goals because all achievements brought about by subjectively insistent hard effort are subject to the impermanence of all assemblies. You push yourself and impose your personal will and expectation over the "foreign" units, conditions and terms, all for your own purposes. You suffer setbacks which produce pain. Practically, you

brew bitterness for yourself and create misery and
ugliness, all of which starts from the insistence of self,
especially the controlling self.   Such trouble does not
come from the objective self, which looks only for harmony with all the assembling elements.   Once you
understand that this insistence of self is an assembly,
you will want to learn to practice the universal law for
balance, symmetry, peace and constancy, instead of
generating violence, force and willfulness, which do not
work.   Therefore, it is important to understand the law
of assembly, to thoroughly know that all assembly is
impermanent; then you can reach the stage of selflessness and be liberated from the bondage you gathered
about yourself.   The achieved one learns the universal
self, the universal law.   Sometimes it is called "no-self."
The universal self is no self.   The small self is an assembled tendency toward insistence or attachment.
Once you brush away the insistence, you can not only
see the truth, you can live with the truth.   The truth is
that there is no self!

To dissolve the self is to implement the universal
self.   Your inner wisdom leads you to the embrace of
the entire universal life.   The path from unachievement
to spiritual development leads us to know that what
we think of as ourself is not that at all.   The things
that we think connect to ourself actually connect to no
self.   There is no self.   With the correct recognition one
can rectify the twisted understanding caused by the insistence on subjectivity, and dissolve all unreasonable
pain and trouble, moving from darkness to light.   For
an ordinary being to go from undeveloped to developed, the mind must unite with the universal mind.
What in yourself is universal self, the true God?   Although the mind is the latecomer in universal nature, a
learned and developed spiritual capacity, truth, and
growth can come to be harmonized with all beings and
all things of the universe.   Peace is not attained by
giving up the world or withdrawing from all relationships or situations; peace is achieved by learning to
operate your life in accordance with universal law.   Be

familiar with and adapt to this universal law and demonstrate it in your individual life.

Ironically, when this recognition is reached, sometimes people become more selfish. By understanding the impermanence and selflessness of life, they sometimes decide to retreat somewhere and not be bothered by the world. They conclude that high achievement is to be self-centered, so they wait passively for the extinction of the body. They simply do not know that something above all assembly is permanent: the subtle law. Everything changes and moves, but it all circles around the center of the subtle law. The impermanent assembly of events follows that law. It is the extension and impression of the subtle nature of the universe. You cannot do anything about your life. You can only achieve yourself by embracing the subtle law. In that way, you can enjoy enduring life with an enduring soul, quite apart from the impermanent assembly of the social and material phenomena of life.

In this way, you will have the permanent virtues of patience, kindness, tolerance and love for all the positive supporting elements and all the relationships established in the positive flow of nature. Practically, you cannot live alone and think only about the importance of your single self. If you are afraid of pain, suffering and agony, it is because you think about yourself too much. Once your spiritual awareness is transformed or allowed to develop to the high spheres, you will be able to embrace the entirety of universal nature because you will have become the truly divine. You love people because you love yourself. If you hate people it is because you hate yourself, since everything radiates from inner awareness and inner attitudes. This is the decisive factor of your true life.

The conception of experiencing either trouble or happiness is due to assembly. The experience of beingness itself is assembly. Therefore, one may think that through non-being one can dissolve all trouble; not necessarily, because non-being also is assembly. From being you know non-being. From non-being you know being. Therefore, it is not necessary for happiness or trouble to become fixed states in the mind, because these are phenomena in motion or emotion. The occurrence and dissolution of everything is conditioned. You might like to, if you can, work positively to change some element within you. It is hard for a person to change the world; it is easy to change oneself. You do not have to bend yourself or damage your spiritual integrity in order to change, or to correct and adjust a sentimental or negative temperament.

Therefore, to talk about self or no self, assembly or no assembly, does not mean too much spiritually. Practically we are all individualized: we feel pain, we feel trouble, we feel happy. Surely we need to learn how to manage our minds. More importantly, we are limited in the improving of our minds, but there is no limitation on improving our spiritual powers. If we improve our spiritual condition, it is possible to attain what is divine. If that becomes the way, even if on the physical level we do not see how, there will be hope for the majority of people. However, we can, with developed special knowledge, avoid and correct troubles. For example, psychic ability is now popularly recognized. The power above psychic power will also be recognized. Psychic ability can enable one to see things under the ocean or underground. It can also be applied to human life, either destructively or beneficially, depending on the management of something higher like the substance of universal and spiritual awareness.

The practice of the I Ching during the Zhou Dynasty was not begun by one person alone. A group movement by the assembly of mind was looking for the best judgement or wisdom. You see, human life is a matter of assembling or gathering and it can bring happiness and joy to society provided that the right decisions are made by our leaders. It can also lead a nation or society to the edge of danger. The development of spiritual energy has a positive contributive value in human life. The master of strong psychic capability should develop himself still higher. (It is said that Hitler was an example of having psychic abilities but no spiritual development.)   Human life can be foolish as a result of its spiritual or mental condition. To confirm the value of spiritual development, it is necessary to first correct the conventions or obstructions in our life.   Then we can live spiritually, scientifically and with balance.   To live spiritually does not mean to be stubborn, superstitious or biased.   It means living life at its most effective: life lived with spiritual clarity. That is the true eye or vision, higher than the third eye in the development of a human being, and it can guide us to the further development of the entire human society.   If a nation would gather together a group of highly developed psychic people willing to offer their vision as service to the decision makers of that society, at least 90% of the waste could be eliminated by using their high spiritual clarity.   But be careful.   Psychic vision is still partial vision.   It is still beneath the integral vision of attaining Tao.   Psychic energy can never be higher than Tao as the integral spiritual principle.   It is important for each individual to develop this spiritual clarity above his psychic function.

What we abstractly call assembly or existence, and disassembly or death, causes all phenomena in the world.   The occurrence of a thing or matter, its transformations and its end, are natural, which means you cannot control them externally.   But you can subjectively manage a balance and you can see how to best achieve well-being under the given conditions.   That is spiritual achievement.   So we need to correct the mistakes resulting from a negative mental approach, whether religious or intellectual.   We also need to attend to some naturally balanced guidance and lay down a foundation that will enable us to take further steps in our life.

In the learning of Tao, the Integral Truth, naturalness is the best policy.   Nothing is adopted and nothing is given up at the conceptual level; it matters only what service is given to the substance of life - all life - in any moment, unmotivated by any conceptual establishment or pre-conceived ideology.   This is why

Tao is the path of openness. Ask yourself: are you open?

This has been a long talk on my part. Your brain now is filled full, and for the purpose of releasing this congestion, let us return to the beginning of our long exploration.

We have roughly touched upon the matter of existence. Each event, no matter how large or small, is a condition supported by many subconditions. It is necessary to look deeply into this and thoroughly explore it to reach a correct and useful conclusion.

We know that all things and occurrences are temporary phenomena that change and disintegrate when the original conditions that brought them into being are taken away. When conditions come together, they give birth. When they part from one another, existence is dissolved. Birth, change and dissolution of all matters and things contribute to new conditions or situations.

The thoughts we have each minute, the assembly of conditions that give birth to an event and objects in our lives seem to be beyond our control, beyond the reach of the mind. If we wish to change a situation, can it be done? Is there any subjective substance to the mind? In answer, the function of good management of the mind can produce assembly as well.

If we are only passively controlled, managed by and subjected to conditions, we can control some but we are also controlled by them. We cannot control some but we are still controlled by them. What is the right thing to know and to do about it?

The right point of view about the way things come together, are maintained and dissolve can produce the right mental attitude with which to face any condition. This is the matter we are talking about, not just saying that everything is something and that many small elements come together. How things come together and disperse is not so important; the important thing is what we can do about it or what kind of mental attitudes or policy we should have. This could generate a limited philosophy or intellectual view of life, or the development of a passive or aggressive religious expression.   Let us have something more truthful and serviceable in our lives, something from the factual background of nature.   This is the principle of balance, which was discovered by the true sages.   "To be or not to be" is not the question: the question is whether or not we have attained the natural balance of our life being.

CHAPTER TWO

LIFE IS NATURAL

Discussion between Master Ni and some students

Student: Master Ni, does life have a purpose or is it accidental?

Master Ni: Life neither has specific purpose nor is it accidental.   It is natural.   I believe you are very serious in this question.   If I say life has purpose, you would want to know what is the purpose of your life.   Believing in a purpose, you would then become religiously fixed in your attitudes and thus increase the conflict between your ego and the world.   If I say it is accidental, you would think your life is not your business.   So let us review the achievement of the ancient natural developed ones; this will help to answer your question.

The discovery and spiritual achievement of the developed ones is a spiritual method and practice by which one can achieve or mature oneself and become enlightened through means that are self-evident.   Life itself is a convergence of natural energy.   This means that life is a formation of different energies that occur through a specific process in time and space and converge.

It is this convergence of many subtle and apparent elements and conditions that comprise a life.   Once those elements and conditions, both subtle and obvious, are disassembled, life no longer exists.   The cessation of life is the retreat of all supportive elements and conditions.   The unnatural death of a human being is the same as the dissolution of any other event or object which is an assemblage of a group of conditions.   Some of the conditions which assemble are apparent and some are hidden, but the event still comes under the law of assembly and disassembly.   It is simply an aspect of the process of disassembly.

The entire universe is an assemblage of all matter and is subject to change.   All units of the universe, such as galaxies, stars, planets and the earth keep shaping or forming themselves; there is a correspondence to this in the smaller life of a human being.   All are subject to change.   The understanding of the basic pattern of changes of all things has been abstractly described by *The Book of Changes*.   During any moment of the convergence or integration of the conditions that comprise an object or event, its significance or meaning is established.   Once it is dissolved, no other important or unimportant significance or value can be added to it. Therefore, watching and valuing this moment of life and not the next moment is the correct expression of the existence of life.   This means that the integral path of life is right in front of you!   It is where you walk. Movement and activity in a life are what present the reality of life.   There is no future reward that can dignify or sublimate the essence of life in the reality of this moment, because the next moment will be a new assemblage of many conditions.   In other words, life is a process, and truth is also a process.   Life cannot be caught or captured in the moment of self-presenting by any force aside from itself.   Any attempt catches only the change and not the permanence of a situation.

From this understanding, and through spiritual cultivation and discipline, one can strengthen and fortify the integration or convergence of different energies in a life by changing one's patterns.   One must first have correct understanding, which involves subjective proof (experience and knowledge) that life, whether in the subtle level or in solid form, continues to integrate, reintegrate and refine itself by the growing and increasing subtle essence within.   Different physical and spiritual elements comprise your life; you are constantly organizing and reorganizing yourself.   You are born in this moment and continue in each moment to have a rebirth of your life.   Spiritual reward is not brought about by externals; it is accomplished internally.

Because spiritual reward itself is internal, this very moment is what affects the next.   This moment gives birth to the next moment.   This section of time in your life grows the fruit that you will enjoy in the next section of your life.   What you sow spiritually, you will eventually harvest.   No awakened soul can afford to damage himself spiritually by doing evil.   Evil actions are equivalent to a person cutting his own throat with a sharp knife; however, he cannot see what he is doing because on the spiritual level it is invisible.   When a person commits evil actions, perhaps no one has seen what was done, but the person himself knows what happened.   External religions can serve as a metaphor for this spiritual truth, as in one's waiting for judgement or reward and in being a good person.   However, realistically, reward or punishment is in this moment: are you watchful in coordinating your movements and activities with your developed intellectual mind, which cooperates and associates with the developed spirit of your being?   Whoever neglects this fundamental discipline will have no spiritual future, and the spiritual foundation they have built on religious forms is not real.

Therefore, it is important to understand this moment.   When you are aware of the truth of life, you establish yourself in this moment and you recognize the value, significance, dignity and spiritual position of your life as completion.   The next step of life with its new circumstances is just that: new.   You need new integration, new adaptation and new refining; you go one step further into new spiritual evolution.

Perhaps this leads you to think, "Physically we become old and worn out after reaching the peak of life."   This is true.   All life follows a pattern of growth and decline.   But the one who is subjectively aware that his life is on the channel of correct spiritual evolution will know that he is not going to become older and worn out.   He is renewing his life all the time.   He will transform his physical energy into a higher spiritual essence that can bring him to another, more enduring life. This choice is made by those who have a different understanding of life than most people. The most fundamental thing you need to understand to make this choice is that life is the result of the convergence of many different supportive elements. If even one element is not supported, especially with regard to mental or spiritual elements, a fall will occur. Higher vision most profoundly serves human life, especially in mental and spiritual aspects, which are closely associated.

Since life is a matter of convergence, then what is its purpose? One viewpoint holds solely that life is a function of material things with different pieces and parts together forming the machine of life. Eventually one part or another wears out. When the life machine cannot be repaired, the life machine is finished. Given this mechanistic point of view, there is no higher purpose to life. An opposing metaphor, however, describes life as a piece of music composed from the organization of different notes. In this view there is a super-mind or master plan behind the organization of the music. If this is the case, then each life must have a purpose.

Confusion also arises because of certain teachings. On one hand, people are taught that there is karma and reincarnation and that peace can come to a person who has understood the emptiness of life and nature. This way of thinking implies that life is a reincarnating essence, and that the karma accumulated in past lifetimes is the reward or punishment for the new life. This way of thinking teaches people to become more responsible for their actions and their lives and to recognize something higher than predetermined destiny or physical reality.

On the other hand, there is a different way of thinking. Some people are taught that life is merely an accident; that everything is meaningless, and nothing is worth thinking about. This negative teaching implies that whatever you do is right and helps you relax about the circumstances you are in, whether lofty or lowly because, after all, everything is an accident. So what is there for you to worry about? Why be anxious about anything? Not only is your life incidental, but all human, animal and other life is incidental and has no purpose. My friends, if you take this view that life is accidental, then life will indeed be a big accident. Why bother taking responsibility for yourself or anything else, for that matter? Where is the music of life and spiritual dignity? Is there no God, Buddha or any being higher than greedy or aggressive people looking to restrain other people in a world devoid of meaning? Is that what life is all about? Allow us to probe more deeply into this.

Life can be expressed in many different ways. You might take the view that life is conditioned, i.e., that the environment determines the species. For example, it is only in trenches that mosquitoes are produced. It is only in trees that birds are produced. Different kinds of natural environments produce different forms of life. Thus, it would follow that people born of a good family would have a higher level of education, better manners and a greater opportunity to be achieved, etc., and that people born into ordinary family environments would tend to have more struggle and suffering in their lives.

However, in the human sphere, which is a complete triangle of physics, mind and spirit, life does not work this way. It is not always true that people born into a good family are good people or can make positive use of their opportunity to achieve themselves. Quite the opposite can occur. Different levels of background provide different freedoms that allow the development of life. While this holds true in both the social and material spheres, supportive conditions are especially obvious in the material sphere. When, for example, there is the establishment of a new relationship or behavior - except natural ones like blood relationships - its occurrence has been conditioned beforehand. You might believe the new relationship or behavior to be accidental; but if you look deeply into your inner being, the attraction or behavior has long been in existence, but only now manifests. The behavior or attraction has been waiting a long time for the ripeness of the situation and conditions to come together. The deepest understanding reveals that an accident is not an accident. It is a necessity; it is purposeful. The movement of the entire universal nature has a subtle law above it which governs all movement. Without deep vision, one does not have the understanding that any movement by itself is both an event and a spontaneous occurrence. It takes deep understanding to realize that any movement in the world is both previously arranged as well as spontaneous.

The fact is that in one way life is conditioned, which leads to things happening of necessity; and in another way it is accidental, which leads to randomness. In one way it is mechanical; in another way it is haphazard. How can a human mind adapt to these diverse situations with distinctive understandings? By developing the third aspect, that's how: developing the spiritual growth of nature to evolve from the mechanical, physical sphere to reach freedom. It takes a million years to develop life or consciousness a little bit. Freedom is a gift of achievement, on whatever level of life, given the limitation or bondage being dealt with. We, through living wrong and doing wrong, cause our own souls and the souls of other people to suffer sickness.

Our organic being was originally endowed by nature. Although all life is endowed by nature, human life resembles nature in completeness with all three spheres: physical, mental and spiritual. We must learn how we can use the freedom of the more subtle level, i.e., the spiritual, to assist the levels of lesser freedom. It is valuable for your life and well worth looking into.

The ancient developed ones understood that life can be both conditioned and also accidental. It was not necessary to define it one way or another. For example, a peach tree gives peaches in the late spring. It can give good peaches in a good season or in a good natural cycle, with correct warmth and moisture, air and nutrition from the earth. But in the same peach garden, some trees will do better than others. Some need more care than others. Human life is just like that. Some do better, and others do not do as well, but the human mind reacts differently than a tree. A peach tree does not have a developed sense of itself. It is not bothered by doing better or worse than another tree, or by doing better at one time and worse at another time. It follows nature, so it does not have anything like trouble in the mind. Humans are different. They have feelings about themselves. They watch others, and they can be jealous of others who do better or feel dismayed if they cannot do as well. They can also feel pride that they do better than another. But they cannot objectively look at themselves as natural, which is a condition starting pre-natally. There is not much about your limitations that can be changed. The thing to do is to live naturally and change what you can. Some people, however, develop or follow religions instead of realistically improving themselves and their lives. They steep themselves in deep meditation or invent profound ideologies which cover their failures and only serve to keep them from taking responsibility for themselves.

The achieved ones know what the nature of life is, not only outside but also inside. The most valuable thing is to follow the life-nature inside and harmonize with the outside. This is the teaching and achievement passed down by our spiritually developed forefathers. It is not a psychological approach that transfers one's focus away from the pressure of day-to-day living or the immediate environment. It is the self-truth of taming one's own evil temper and ambitions and turning them into a life of spiritual well-being. Spirituality cannot be separated from life itself. The subtle, essential sphere of life is still associated with the general patterned life of eating, sleeping, working, etc. Big and small grow equally under the light of spiritual health. There is a great need for the spiritual development of

all people. The best thing you can do for the world is
to develop yourself spiritually.

People ask about destiny.   Destiny is internal.
What you grow inside is manifested outside. You can,
however, look at the general external conditions to see
how your destiny is manifesting.   Let us take, for
example, a person who lives in China and a person
who lives in the United States, both born at the same
hour but in different societies.   Their fortunes and lives
will be different, not because of geographical differences, but because of the differences in the political
systems.

The personal destiny that people are sentimental
about is changeable.   In order to characterize the small-
ness of an individual life being, the science of astrology
originated.   By using the rotation of the sun, earth and
moon along with other information, astrology meta-
phorically illustrates a personal destiny or energy formation.   In reality, a natural life needs to be aware of
its true relationship with the heavenly bodies.   Heavenly bodies are used as illustration of the combination of
energies in an individual life.   The objective value in
seeing a life externally through astrology is to adapt
yourself better to the conditions affecting the circumstances of your life.   However, the outer circumstance
cannot be sufficiently or accurately described in a book,
because each individual will experience it differently in
their life.   Some people spend many long years studying astrology.   It can truly tell one something about the
external conditions of a person's life, but the benefit of
its service depends on how you use the information:
whether you face it or run away from it.

We have talked about astrology, religion and spiritual development.   To avoid the complication of too
much conceptual activity, I want to return to the basic
recommendation of following nature.   By nature, I
mean the virtues of nature.   Astrology, religion and
spiritual development all arrive at the same point:
they each tell you to follow nature, to attain natural
health in all three spheres of your being and to grow

or develop your own vision above all of them.   Give up all the mental contamination and cultural pollution which is self-generating.   Gather essence from all your external learning.   A peach can grow well when it is exposed to sunshine, wind, air and warmth.   If, however, we wrap it up and take it away from the garden, it will not grow well.   Human nature is already enveloped in too many layers of plastic; even now you can be nursed by glass tubes.   The new lives in the future may be brought in through glass tubes, but the basic life still needs to respect its natural health.   It is not enough to merely respect the health of nature; we also need to respect and harmonize our healthy natural life with the harmonious order of universal nature. Our life nature is one with the universal life nature. The troubles of a family, an individual, a group or different nations are basically the same disharmony; they reflect a conflict with the basic nature of life.   The problem is created by people themselves and sometimes others.   Disharmony is created by lack of understanding about nature, by many false concepts which stem from incorrect teaching and thinking.   One who cannot remove the false concepts cannot enjoy either himself or nature.

People who deeply observe the human world know it is pulled by the past, which keeps human society from further development.   If people wish to develop further, they must first restore their knowledge of natural health which is the essence of natural life. People's moral well-being is natural in the beginning. Immoral behavior, such as stealing, is a poor solution or adaptation to handling one's own needs in society. Once a person's original health is lost, healing is then applied.   Support is given from the spiritual medicinal systems when a person is sick, weak, too old or undeveloped.   Religious teachings are important only when you are morally, emotionally or intellectually sick.   Although they are not unnatural, they are for sick people in a particular stage of evolution.   But if you stay with these conventional religions, you cannot grow any more.   Do not continue to take their poison.

A healthy being does not need to rely on medicine, because the spiritual self-cultivation of the integral way develops and covers all spheres of one's well being. The integral way is for people who achieve their spiritual independence from the mass treatment offered by the big religious hospitals for the sick.   Once you restore your strength, you come back to nature.   Only natural vitality can cure all wounds and grow new flesh.   There is nothing better to pass on to your sons, daughters or good friends than to support them with nature, follow nature and enjoy nature.   You need look no farther than the universal nature which resides inside us.

Nature is health.   Nature is normalcy.   Even if we live in the natural world, we still need to guard against abnormally timed natural cycles.   When people lose their sense of humor in life, they can become stiffly religious.   People of spiritual self-cultivation do not stiffen their minds by using previously programmed practices which support their well-being only at certain times or are used for spiritual amusement.   Religion may be a good tool to teach children through bedtime stories, but all children must grow up.   The world cannot be managed by bemused children.   It needs to be guided by people who have reached spiritual maturity and independence, who can keep guiding themselves by the natural subtle light.

When people are children, they marvel and wonder about spiritual phenomenon without attaining true knowledge about it.   They do not know that the subconscious level of the mind gives off a spiritual response like echoes, such as in dreams and unconscious reactions to external stimuli.   All the marvelous or terrifying spiritual phenomena that you see in the world comes from you: your enhanced or intimidated soul.   The value of your self-cultivation is in knowing how to remain in peace and in one piece: mind, spirit and body together.   Can you practice that?   We are most powerful when these three partners are together. There are small partners among them too, but most of the time, the mind wanders away.   It is marvelous what the mind can do, but people do not understand this.   Mistrust and conceptual images cause one to think that outside forces are what make things happen in a person's life.   People do not know the strength and power of the inside harmony which can alter outside circumstance to create phenomena in the spiritual sphere.

If personal spiritual experience makes a person more superstitious or self-indulgent in spiritual pursuit, it is because he does not understand that the balanced mind, spirit and body is the brightness of universal nature within his life being.

Even after this long discussion, this may still be an inadequate answer.   However, all of you have the opportunity to prove these words and what is between the lines and find your own answer: Is life with purpose or is it accidental?   Can anyone answer me now?

Student: Life is natural.

Master Ni: No matter whether life is with purpose or accidental, there is tea and refreshment on the table in the next room, so please enjoy them and give yourselves the real answer from the enlightenment of a healthy tummy.   Now let us take a break.

CHAPTER THREE

THE PURPOSE OF LIFE

A gathering in Malibu

Master Ni: What shall we do to entertain ourselves today?

Students: We would like you to talk further about the purpose of life.

Master Ni: This is a serious matter. It is, of course, a philosophical subject. But it can also be a personal spiritual focus, because after a period of intense experiences in a person's life, a reflection shines out from inside to ask: what is the purpose of my life?

In ancient times, the church taught that priests were the representative of God or the go-between of God and people; religions taught that the purpose of a person's life was to serve God. Later, people realized that this doctrine was untruthful and that it was the invention of the churches and the priests, who were then benefited by it. Thus, new light started to shine on them; little by little, people were on their way in search of the purpose of life. It became a definite need to know what life is.

There was a similar experience in Chinese cultural growth involving the relationship between human inner strength and external establishment. Buddhist teaching came from South Asia and over-expanded during the Tang Dynasty (618-906 A.D.). The direct teaching of Zahn (Zen) Buddhism, still maintaining the form of a religion, received support. It was not separately established, but rather was a new deep awakening to the indirect religious teaching of Buddhism. Then, during the Sung Dynasty (960-1279 A.D.), the neo-Confucian school arose, which is the further developed teaching from the original teaching of Confucius. This new spiritual understanding taught that God or Heaven is your own conscience, and the purpose of life thus is to serve your personal conscience. But what is your personal conscience? It became defined as developed moral and ethical knowledge. So instead of pursuing religious fantasy, scholars of the day began to pursue the discovery of moral and ethical knowledge. Their focus was on the substance of the natural mind as the source of this knowledge. However, as the intellectuals developed their knowledge of morality and ethics, they limited their effort to the scope of scholastic probe and study. Although the scholars and intellectuals knew that it was each person's moral obligation to defend their society, few offered their lives for this moral realization. The knowledge of spiritual reality made great progress, but it did not help defend the security of the nation from the invasion of the northern tribes.

In the Ming Dynasty (1368-1641), a great scholar, Wang Yang-Ming (1472-1528 A.D.) corrected this spiritual mistake of evading the realization of moral knowledge once attained. He understood that the truth of spiritual development lies in unifying one's developed knowledge of spiritual morality and ethics with one's personal realization in life. This means to bring the knowledge into existence, to manifest or activate it in the world. He taught that the purpose of an individual life is to serve the truth of life, which is the meeting of knowledge and actualization. He promoted this principle among his friends and students as "The Union of Words and Deeds, of Knowledge and Behavior," and he realized this principle in his personal life. He was not merely a scholar of words, he was also a person who carried out his moral duty to defend an endangered society. He became a general in wartime.

Following his example, you might think that all Chinese intellectuals, who were the influential class of their society, became wise. However, most of them still attended to their own life's pleasure at a time when their society was exposed to the calamity of war and other dangers. The scholars at the end of the

Ching Dynasty (1644-1911 A.D.) were deeply aware of trouble in the country; this awareness opened the door for revolution to come. The calling for intellectuals to be responsible for the improvement of their society became widespread and intense among young scholars, preparing the way for Dr. Sun Yat-sen's revolution. The sense of social morality among the members of the national party and communist party was much greater than that of the ancient scholars, but, unfortunately, the formulas they adopted to cure the disease of the old society of China were not truly appropriate. Their approaches were either ineffective or too extreme. New problems were created; specifically, power struggles between parties and within one party arose, which nullified any positive improvement brought about through the sacrifice of many intellectuals' precious lives.

My point is to use the example of the slow intellectual and spiritual progress of China to describe the slow progress of human society in its entirety. So far, spiritually, we have nothing to add to Wang Yang-ming's principle: the purpose of life is to live with the developed knowledge of morality and ethics and directly realize this attained knowledge. It has brought forth my spiritual appreciation, and so I would like to recommend application of the principle of the union of spiritual knowledge and personal life to all of you.

This discussion brings us to the principle of equality between spiritual and secular life, and the equality of all good, high spiritual teachings.

When a person attains spiritual maturity, he treats everything (human, as well as spiritual or conceptual matters) equally. Equality is a good quality to attain through spiritual achievement. By attaining spiritual equality, one can recognize that different spiritual paths are equal. All are meant to serve people and the growth of human life by expressing the healthy side of people's spirit. Although different spiritual practices have different functions, a correct or rightful spiritual practice is a healthy expression if it explains, promotes and supports the healthy direction of human nature. Some practices are meant to support human emotion, some help people attain psychological maturity and some are for spiritual advancement. Others are a social discipline. Although they are on different levels, their purpose is the same: to serve the growth and harmony of the individual being as well as human society. As long as they do not bend or distort human nature, they are beneficial.

The existent fragmentary or splitting religions and spiritual practices adopted by most people serve a self-limiting purpose. They function within their own conceptual structure. For example, some function to support emotional peace; some help to attain psychological maturity; some help to improve the moral condition; and some promote spiritual mellowness. However, each is incomplete, and may be restrictive, especially when they extend control or protection over their followers. In over-protecting, they cause trouble by dominating the growth of individual believers or followers. Many well-intentioned religions or spiritual practices can also produce this limitation as a negative side effect. These religions are different from the pure Direct Path, which offers a broad healthy spiritual education in the form of a school supported by some individual's spiritual strength, rather than a religious enterprise or business. Religions would best be maintained in this way, as different schools that allow people at different stages of spiritual development to learn from them as one part of life's learning voyage. Religions would be best not extending control over their participants. Once the ambitious nature of religions is corrected, a useful and objective contribution to human growth would be found.

Unfortunately, most spiritual practices and religions express an incomplete or immature stage of spiritual growth. They are unable to function as a true help for human life, moral conditions, lifestyles or emotional patterns. Instead, they become obstructions in the way of further advance. Leaders of those religions should reform them to offer their true essence to the world; otherwise they can be destructive.

What was attained by the ancient spiritually developed ones? Their spiritual achievement was carefully expressed in the work of Lao Tzu and Chuang Tzu. Today's modern people and the spiritually developed ones of later generations who expect to attain spiritual growth are mostly affected by the teaching of conventional religions. Maturity comes through breaking away from both overly-negative and overly-positive, but narrow, influences. It is easy to observe the contemporary spiritually developed ones; those people are versed in several religions through reading and objective observation, and they try different spiritual practices without becoming attached to any of them. They gain their spiritual independence and balance through their study and experience of different religions and different spiritual practices. If one maintains a spirit of liberty, study and research into different religions can be of benefit, and one thus does not become entrapped at a limited level before attaining full growth.

Some religions and spiritual practices originally were organized to assist our spiritual growth. They help teachers and students develop themselves and reach a peak where they can see the roads that have been previously traveled, as, for example, in Chinese, Japanese, Korean and Tibetan forms of Buddhism. All of them are featured in Zahn (Zen) training practices, which are the pure yoga practices stripped of the colorful costumes of Hinduism and the Chinese villagers' Taoism. Religious customs should be pushed aside and forgotten when you study pure yoga practices. You do not need to wear colorful costumes or follow the rituals practiced by Chinese villagers in the pursuit of Taoism; it is more important to learn the essence. This can help broaden people's spiritual vision and the spiritual situation of society in general. As for people who are interested in developing their natural capability of life, in contrast to having such total confidence in modern technology, energy transformation exercises from the tradition of Tao are worthy for one of spiritual aspiration. They will help one to attain a practical and useful achievement: fulfillment of one's spiritual ambition.

Please keep something in mind. All religions somehow, accurately or inaccurately, are an externalization of the inner spiritual reality of human life. Thus, if one's enlightenment is attained through religious study and learning, it is the internalization of external religions. This is the main difference between today's spiritual students and the ancient developed ones. In ancient times, people grew directly from natural spiritual inspiration. It is the people of later generations who see the reality of truth through the written work and rituals of different religions. Most become confused or stop at the shallow, superficial level, without truly immersing themselves in personal spiritual growth. The direct spiritual attainment of the ancient ones was development in the tradition of Tao, Mohism and some open-minded Confucian scholars.

The spiritually achieved one knows that universal spiritual nature cannot be conceptualized because it cannot be reduced to being thought of in one way or the other. The spiritually achieved one also sees through all names and terms which attempt to describe universal nature. Universal spiritual nature can be either broadly termed or narrowly termed, known as God or as any name with a conceptual definition. If it is narrowly termed, it is for a special function. If it is broadly termed, it is for broad integration. Universal spiritual nature can be strong or it can be soft. Spiritually undeveloped people fix their vision or belief in only one direction, which brings limitation and can cause trouble, sometimes more trouble than a developed one can have the capability of dissolving. It is important to develop oneself enough to know the depth and profundity of universal spiritual nature overall as well as in small, specific, useful ways. In ancient times, spiritual development was simpler than what is now required. Later generations have learned by the classes, reading, joining, sharing, expressing and through much research and study. Anyone who is successful, who does not become entrapped by a particular section of his studying journey, can achieve himself and regain his original spiritual freedom, independence and dignity. This way he saves himself from falling into the attraction of a certain small practice or religious dogma.

It is important to understand the principle of equality in all spiritual practices. Different practices bring about different spiritual qualities. Once blended, they lose their spiritual distinction. The principle of equality of all spiritual practices means all religions serve you differently. In truth, each religion has its own way of expressing the same unique spiritual reality, but through a different set of circumstances. The differences of circumstance may be overlooked in order to follow the one spiritual truth. In other words, all religions function equally by expressing a part of the integral truth. Do not let them bring forth conflict within the organic being of your natural life. If conflict is seen among any two practices or religions, it is the limitation of the conceptual definitions that is causing the problem. It is important to discern these secondary religious conflicts as deviations from the great path of one truth.

More importantly, spiritual development in modern times is not only for oneself, but also represents a stage of spiritual growth of the entire human society. One needs to help not only oneself, one needs also to help the world see through the barriers of race, the wall of different rituals and the compartment of varying spiritual practices and religious concepts. Seeing through these culturally created barriers would help harmonize all of human society. If we would allow ourselves to become integrated through spiritual development, it would diminish the difficulty and hostility caused by our own conceptual creations. This is a fundamental spiritual achievement. Higher than that is attaining personal spiritual enjoyment, the pure joy of spiritual fulfillment. As modern intellectuals, you might like to take a free spiritual sightseeing cruise through different spiritual studies. This is more for personal enjoyment than to meet the emergent public need for inner harmony and the healing of our modern, but fragmented, human mind. A person who is aware how to work to develop himself and to help in his surroundings can see the benefit of spiritual growth and the attainment of spiritual truth. He does not impose himself on others, but knows how to yield; he does not insist on conceptual conflict or physical strength or engage in prejudicial, hostile warfare, but refines his own gross energy into high spiritual clarity.

Please understand that the work I have delivered to you comes from years of progress by many individuals who have attained universal mind throughout numerous generations. Any of you who can open your minds briefly to join the universal natural flow of life is blessed. You can avoid the mistaken sacrifices that result from past narrow vision, racial prejudice and jealousy. The individual who has attained spiritual development will not be greedy for impractical enlightenment. Some of you may read my books containing the great spiritual attainment from countless generations, which are reproduced and augmented through my own absorption and learning, and you might feel enlightened. Once you have enlightened your thoughts or understanding, the achievement becomes yours. If the next time you study them you do not feel enlightened, it is because the teachings have already become part of your being. Someday you must study further to confirm your understanding, confirm your mind and spirit and discover new things. One of spiritual development knows how to manage his mind and his spirit to continue to attain higher and deeper achievements. With universal spiritual nature, once a better version is reached, the old copy is thrown away. People should live for new life and refresh their minds, and not stay with the stagnancy of past creations or descriptions. One who can break away courageously from narrow descriptions of the great spiritual truth can sail in the vastness of the spiritual ocean and reach the boundless future with Lao Tzu, Chuang Tzu and all the ancient natural developed ones. A believer follows a partial expression of the spiritual truth; the student of Tao follows the Integral Truth and makes all religion a part of the explanation.

CHAPTER FOUR

WHO CREATES US?

Discussion Between Master Ni and Students

Student: Master Ni, many times you have described the universal spiritual nature as creative.   Is this what is illustrated by the Book of Genesis in the Bible?

Master Ni: Yes, as long as you do not insist on any particular set of words, the Bible can be considered a means of expressing the creativity of universal spiritual nature.

Student: I wonder about the four different versions of the Bible that I have studied.   One is the King James version, another is called The Living Bible, then there is the American Bible and the Catholic Bible.   The translation of each one stresses different things.   For example, one says that the Earth was chaotic and void in the beginning.   Another says it was shapeless and empty.   As for how the Earth became shaped, one translation says that the spirit lived high over it, while another says that the spirit brooded over it.   A different one says that the spirit watched over it.   Which way did spirit really work on earth?
    Also, I have read that the world was dark in the beginning.   If God and the world both come from darkness, then darkness is the mother of God and the world.   Or if in the beginning the world was chaotic and void, were chaos and the void the mother of creation?   Is creation the result of external pressure or of internal creative nature?   How did the world start exactly?

Master Ni: The original shape does not matter as much as the subtle law to which all things are subject and which persistently keeps the world transforming. After one's mind becomes developed, and with mature observation, the subtle law becomes describable to a certain degree, revealing itself through its creative and destructive activities. This was the discovery of the ancient Taoists, the people of natural mind: from the original whole - Tai Chi - yin and yang are manifested. All manifestation then follows the law of change, with its cyclical transformations and movements of polarity, in the search for fitness and balance.

Without knowledge of the subtle law's operation within all the creative activities of nature, a different vision might be produced. The point of view of an undeveloped mind might be that creation is the result of blind impulses in physical nature. An undeveloped mind does not see that the universe in its entirety is one interrelated network of energy, and that it is through the internal changes in this big field of energy that different things, beings and realities are expressed. The truth is that all manifestations of universal existence follow the subtle law in the relative sphere which can be seen in the great pattern of yang (positive) and yin (negative) movement as it unfolds.

By observing the migration of birds, for example, one can come to understand the working of the internal system of the birds. They know beforehand the arrival of the different seasons without consulting calendars or reading books. This system of knowledge cannot be made apparent to the eye the way an organ can be exposed through anatomical dissection. The migration knowledge of birds is one expression of the natural and normal function of life in its healthy, wholesome and original condition.

Some fish swim thousands of miles to locate the exact warm current in which they were born for the purpose of laying their eggs. Again, this does not depend on physical organs of sight or the reading of books. They have a special internal system that functions above their physical organs.

Student: Master Ni, isn't instinct just a matter of genetic codes in the molecules of the body?   It seems that if something is a system, it is formed and could be observed.

Master Ni: With or without form, once natural energy is made into a life by nature itself, the corresponding internal system of the life is built into the life-being. One might think that all lives in the same species would be the same or equal, but this does not occur in a mechanical way like industrial mass production; some individual lives in a species will have a better chance for natural development than others.

Cats and mice and birds will suddenly disappear from a place that is going to suffer a natural disaster such as a fire, earthquake or tornado.   This, too, depends on an internal system at the basic level of life. However, people's pursuit of knowledge at the controllable human level is not a useless endeavor, as long as what lies beyond the visible foundation of life is not denied.

The internal system I have been describing is the spiritual function.   Before becoming intellectually developed, human beings behaved naturally.   Naturally means spiritually.   If we suddenly dislike a place, or certain people, if we really want to be in another place or with a specific person, it is the guidance from our own internal system which is informing us, providing that we are not being emotionally or intellectually prejudiced.   We do the right thing without having to know why.

The function of the mind in life seems to be to ask the question, "Why?"   People habitually look for a solid, tangible answer to this question.   This is one direction and in many respects it is correct.   Above it, however, lies the spiritual function, which is confusing to the mind because it cannot be put into a test tube and examined.   Some people whose minds are incomplete will therefore deny the existence of the spiritual level of life; but someone with an objective mind will appreciate these principles and seek the complete, not partial, knowledge that is truly serviceable to all mankind.

What is the reality of Genesis concerning the beginning of the world? All the different translations are correct; it can be one way and all ways and even none of these. This is because it is, at best, an indirect description. It is not the direct spiritual function itself nor the internal system of nature itself. If we are looking for accuracy and precision in discovering not only the beginning of the world, but the beginning of spirit, we turn to the knowledge of the ancient developed ones. They said that the existence of spirit and the beginning of the world happened at different times, that spiritual energy is a late-comer, the result of natural evolution.

Any existent thing must have the quality of beingness; thus, it must be a being or a thing. On the conceptual-perceptual level, when once the existence of a being or a life is established, the existence of the being can be known or witnessed by other beings. If God exists, then he must be a being. Being known by other beings, he is thus one among other beings, although his deep nature could be as complete as the universe itself.

In the beginning, not all levels of beingness or small unities within the great composition were known, because life was a whole, without an overly intense sense of individualization. Nonetheless, all kinds of energy and potential were self-contained in the simple fact of being.

To be is to live. To be is to exist. To be is to be the world. To be is to be spirit. Once the sins of the world are eliminated, the sins of the spirit are eliminated, too.

To be is to be in a state of no separation. To be is to be all. To be is not to be a single phenomenon in the world. Any individual being can be seen and recognized as it presents itself in a relationship with all other existence. If it were otherwise, the single being would not be distinguished.

We have just jumped from the beginning of the world to the phenomenon of human cognition; the world's beginning and the philosophy of human cognition can be made intellectually into separate subjects because, historically, cognition is a much later development of being, although it is a capability of life; before it was expressed, it was contained in life's nature.

When we were children we lay in the cradle and our capability for recognition was weak. Although we could not recognize one being from another, we always spiritually discerned our mother from other beings. Seals and sea lions use their double-function fins as legs to climb up the rugged shore in order to enjoy the warm sand in the sunshine. Thousands of seals and their youngsters fill the shore. The mother seals go down to the shoreline to catch fish for lunch or dinner, but when they come back they know which among the thousands of baby seals are theirs, and the babies know which is their mother. They do not talk or have any system of reuniting mother and child; it is totally dependent on natural means or spirit.

In the beginning, being and spirit are undivided. There is no distinction between body and spirit; it is one whole. After a long, long time the human mind develops and asks, "Why?" A human being knows to eat when he is hungry, but he will also eat when he is not hungry: now both natural and unnatural are given expression, two different sets of behaviors. So there are things that are spiritual and natural and things that are unspiritual or unnatural. At the beginning there is no such distinction; there is only natural.

When unnaturalness begins, the body may respond by physical illness, and spiritually there is a very subtle internal warning system that stops you or tells you in some way not to do something. Those in whom this internal system is strong we recognize as sages. Most people do not have a strongly developed internal system, but it can be developed and cultivated. For example, when a person's mother and father pass away, there may develop problems arising from the deceased ancestors, and it takes spiritual discernment to know whether this is, in fact, the case. Because most people are not in touch with this level of spiritual truth, religious systems of understanding became established.

The Bible is one way of expressing the dimension of dualistic mind which arose long after the oneness of being had been destroyed. After engaging in dualistic thinking for a long time, people began to assuage their doubts about their own internal systems by a belief in, and a worship of, external spiritual systems. We must understand that it is very easy to become confused.

From the ancient achieved ones in Tao we know that a human being is a small model of the universe and that the great universe is a large model of individual life. The healthy internal spiritual function is always useful in individual life. Just as the large universe is an expression of its own spirit, individual human life is also an organic expression of its natural internal system or spirit. Communication between the large life and the small life can occur because individual life is one part of universal life. This is how the ancient developed ones discovered self-government and self-development in order to go from a small life to the large life. But there is not much to discuss about this; they did not say that the large life would govern, rule or save your life. One's own internal spiritual system, however, can be externalized; conversely, each individual can internalize the organic spiritual nature of the universe. Each individual is complete with a communication system to the entire universe as a large individual life.

If someone blindly follows an external spiritual system or the artifice of religious ritual and is overly superstitious, one will damage the wholeness of one's spirit by expressing partiality. You see, the spirit of the individual and that of the universe are initially united as one life. By over-externalization, one cuts oneself off from the original reality of sameness. The first thing we do in our spiritual development is to develop spiritual awareness, so that we can know the difference between the mind and spirit. The intellect and the internal spiritual system are two different systems which need to be reunited before we can become spiritually achieved.

Earlier I mentioned that to be is to be spirit; to be is to be life. This means that to be is to be all, to be the whole thing. Without a body, the spiritual function cannot be known; without spirit, the physical level cannot be recognized. There is also a need for the mind.

Let us review the matter of the creativity of nature, or, speaking in an idealistic manner, God. As has been seen and experienced, the world of things and beings is the creativity of organic nature. The first reason of the universe is expressed through the creation of nature. We say the universe itself is an alive reason; its continual creation is the exposition of the first reason. Nature has defined itself precisely by its creativeness and its creations. The first reason defines itself by continual reasoning through the constant unfolding of the universe to the human mind; the human mind is not separate from it. It joins the reasoning of the natural creativeness. The subtle law is neither the creativeness of nature nor the reasoning of the first reason. The subtle law which governs all is called Tao. Through learning the subtle law, truth can be known and thus understood. Nature can be controlled only partially by the developed human intelligence; it cannot be controlled in its entirety.

The creativeness of the world is most easily understood as coming out of the impetus of nature. Others believe that the world is the creation of God. Let us suppose God is the first reason, or the first reasonable being; if this be the case, then his creation must be reasonable too. Unfortunately, the world was created somewhat unthoroughly. Some deep human minds can probe through the roughness of the surface to know the subtle reason, which is deeper and needs the human effort of self-discovery. The discovery by the students of Integral Truth is that the creativity of the universe continually unfolds; thus the first reason of universal life keeps unfolding, too. It is not something that is ever accomplished, finished or done. The thought of general religion, however, is that the world is waiting for graduation by someone, perhaps the creator himself. This is a religion of a dead world.

On the physical level, the creation of the universe seems to be a blind physical impulse that continues to push and push and push, mechanically without end. However, when you carefully examine the world, you see that it is an organic life; the universe is not the way of total blindness. Human life, for example, has gone through stages, beginning in caves. Primitive man did not know the difference between who was a sister or mother and who was a man or a woman. But the species has grown out of that stage. First came spiritual capability, then intellectual explanation. Some people developed a spiritual function strong enough to control impulse and transform it into the impetus which can correctly express creativity in a healthy way. This expressed one step of human spiritual growth and does not mean that only God is creation or an extension of the growing human mind. Nor does it mean we should stop the continual spiritual development of all people. Development cannot be replaced by a belief-structure formed thousands of years ago.

In a spiritual sense, creation is the expression of the creator himself. For instance, if you create a mess, then you are the creator of a mess. If you create order, then you are the creator of order. If you steal, you are a thief. If you create benefit, then you are the benefit, and if you create trouble, you are the trouble. It is direct. There is nothing in between. Is it that the great creator as God is a creator of a mess and continual disturbance?

In Genesis, God created human beings and animals. When he created human beings, he became human. When he created animals, he became animal. There is no difference, because they are both physical shapes; a natural spirit starts to 'flesh itself' differently, seen as its creations. Today some women object to woman coming from the rib of man. Can man issue from the rib of woman? Surely! The creator is a trouble and a trouble is the creator. God created the rib bone; God is the rib bone. Since God created woman, God is also a woman. Each entity of creation is the creator itself.

This is one way of describing the physical impetus which brings everything into the world. When you attain spiritual development, you can put everything in your life in correct categories without becoming confused. Then your internal spiritual system - developed as a microcosm of the universe - can handle the different functions and uses of all things without conflict. If you only study about creation and seek to understand it as knowledge, it will not be enough. Going only half way with spiritual development will bring you to see there is conflict and dispute within your own life that cannot be overcome. Only complete spiritual development can put all differences into a perspective which supports the whole being of life, and then you can live a life which is harmonious both inside and out.

This is a rough sketch of the beginning of the world and the beginning of spirit as seen by the ancient developed ones in the tradition of Tao. A person makes a good conclusion based on assembled facts; however, even with the same facts, different levels of mental development will draw different conclusions. The spiritual knowledge of an individual internal system of spiritual functioning was passed down from the ancient developed ones. Once we learn about it and prove it for ourselves, no one can confuse us with a concept. The reality of the entire universe, the reality of nature, cannot be totally described by language. Nor can you be satisfied by someone else's conclusion; that is only intellectual pacification.

To be is to be the whole, to be is to be truth. When you live life as naturally and completely as an integral human life can live, then who creates whom? If you make someone your son, the son makes you a father; this is pure conceptual activity. People confuse themselves by conceptual mud wrestling. The reality which expresses integral truth has never been confused!

CHAPTER FIVE

IS GOD EXTERNAL OR INTERNAL?

We are already aware of the similarity between the spiritual reality of individual life and the spiritual reality of nature itself. When spiritual reality becomes overly externalized as religion on the general level, whether it be Judaism, Islam, Hinduism or Buddhism, people cannot attain it within themselves. Believers took external teaching to be the truth during the time when the popularity and dominance of external worship was overwhelming. Internal teachings, such as the schools of Lao Tzu, Chuang Tzu and the true teaching of Zahn (Zen) Buddhism, were also respected at that time. External worship is actually derived from the truth of the internal spiritual system. The externals of Buddhism were infused from the teachings of Tao; it is the pure teaching of Tao which is the teaching that I continue.

External religious worship should be recognized as a method established for each individual to learn to respect and strengthen his internal spiritual energy. Most people do not know how to respect and honor their internal spiritual system because they do not respect themselves. Such a person is not responsible or sensitive to his own spirit. Spiritual teachers of different traditions in past generations tried to find ways to educate the masses, so they developed external systems. An achieved one knows that external religious education is a trick that can be confusing to people and has no real possibility for success in teaching them. This is because the externalization of internal and subtle truth cannot be understood unless internal truth is taught at the same time. It is difficult to educate undeveloped people about internal truth, because they do not respect themselves and they are not delicate or subtle enough to recognize that they have an internal spiritual system that is as real as the physical, emotional and mental aspects of their being.

Attempts at teaching internal truth developed into two kinds of external systems. One type of system works to organize society under the rule of a particular spiritual banner. The other kind of system tries to teach internal spiritual reality by using an external approach. For example, in the beginning, Buddhism was a kind of philosophy initiated by Sakyamuni, who was dismayed by the helplessness of people in the face of life's troubles. In the beginning, Buddhism maintained a basically philosophical attitude. After he attained himself and straightened his thoughts from his conventional teaching, he taught differently; it became an internal practice, even though it retained a certain degree of ideology. So later, the new Buddha was not a philosophical leader, but had become the spirit of Buddha. Through externalization, however, Buddhism became another system of worship with two basic steps. The first is externalized as religion and takes a psychological approach based on immaturity. The second step of external worship helps a person reach maturity and recognize the emptiness and voidness of all ideological activities. Thus, the approach of externalization comes back to internal enlightenment, especially for those who are overly attracted to worldly pleasure and material expansion. It is one good approach, but it is still limited to the mental level, especially in so-called 'esoteric Buddhism,' which is organized with complicated rituals and practices. Its purpose is to help the student achieve a normal life.

In the traditional teaching of Tao, a student remains intellectually and conceptually quiet. Internally, after directly experiencing and developing oneself to know the entirety of the spiritual system within and without, one reunites man and God into oneness again. A newborn, red-skinned baby is the symbol of this oneness, of that which existed before the divergence of the two. By two, we mean the realities of life and mind which, through internal cultivation, then reunite to form one's original nature. The body, mind and spirit of a student slowly attain unified growth through a practical, disciplined, healthy life and through the development of the mind. Spiritual reality is attained by a system of spiritual cultivation which proves the existence of spiritual reality to him. Then the three spheres of one's life being can be rejoined into one, as they were originally.

Different religious systems of worship have different goals. I do not deny that the overly externalized systems like Christianity, Judaism and Islam can be used as a model for internal development; however, it requires individual development and maturity to utilize these external systems as a source for strengthening the internal spiritual system. In this case, there is no difference from the teaching and learning of Tao which uses any external situation to increase inner awareness and strengthen one's own internal system to function in harmony with nature.

Religions always emphasize belief in something external, without promoting spiritual awareness. To believe without awareness is to be blind; it is a weakness and will not lead to fulfillment. The ancient developed ones usually kept their mouths shut about external religions, because these ordinary religions do help people in that they serve as reminders that spiritual reality exists, even though they do not know what or where it is. They can, however, recognize the temple, the statue, and the book. But once the external trappings and layouts become habitually accepted by a person, the truth can hardly be learned from them. Did Jesus not suffer persecution from his attempt to help people transfer their external belief to internal truth? No external system can ever replace an internal system. The combination of the two can be a fruitful marriage if the rightness of the external practice has been discovered from the inside out. If such a discovery is fulfilled externally, it becomes the Union of Tao and Man or Union of God and Man. Otherwise, religion over-emphasizes external belief without teaching individual spiritual awareness.

The problem is that external beliefs have been utilized to control people and direct them away from their natural spiritual understanding. There seems to be no correspondence between what is naturally right in life and conceptual beliefs established by religious authorities. Many sins were committed under the names of "worship" and "belief." Religion has, therefore, become an obstacle to true human spiritual growth.

Healthy spiritual teaching always fosters a balance between internal achievement and its correspondence in the external world. If external teaching is merely book learning, without self-achievement, cultivation or enlightenment, it is limited to the mental sphere of conceptualizing about spiritual reality, expressing only then the sickness of a segmented soul cut away from a re-union with the universal spiritual reality.

Student: Master Ni, I understand now why you suggest that your students have a personal, family and group spiritual shrine.   The simple shrine at home or in a personal place is a reminder of the sacredness of our inner life.   Before people can be achieved, they need reminders to search for the harmony of their internal spiritual shrine.

I also understand your language better now.   Sometimes you use the words normalcy, ordinariness or naturalness to describe the standard of achievement.   Normalcy seems to mean truthfulness, goodness, beauty, wisdom and holiness all together in one, not like the ordinary segmented way of separate things.   If you attain one, you attain all.   If you lose one, you lose all.   The completeness of these qualities is the reality of high achievement.

You have also said that the universal divine nature is formless.   As I now understand, in the East - China, India and other places - people experience spiritual beings in their dreams and visions.   Most popular among these is the God-dess of Mercy, Quan Yin.   To Western Christian believers, however, the spiritual shape of that energy appears as the Holy Mother or Virgin Mary.   In the Middle East, people have still different spiritual images.   Spiritual energy itself is formless, but the human mind forms it. For instance, we believe that Moses had a sound mind when Jehovah contacted him, but it was Moses' personal experience that made God tell him that he was Jehovah, the ancestor of Moses' tribe. The same experience would be interpreted differently, in terms of language, through the mind of another individual in another culture. We must accept differences and realize that different systems express the same truth in different ways. Once formless spiritual reality is given a description, differences are created. Even so, the reality of the spiritual level is still One: true, beautiful, good, wise and holy. Total and complete with these five qualities, it resides in all different customs and languages and is the sign of spiritual development. Its absence is the mark of spiritual undevelopment. Those who are spiritually developed will ignore differences of interpretation and directly experience the truth which is indescribable.

Different versions of the same book all describe the beginning of the world in different ways, but no one can accurately describe the beginning of the world. Also, though they all describe the same thing, none of them necessarily relate to the actual beginning of the world. Spiritual achievement is hardly contained in external expressions. The danger of overly externalized teachings is that they may destroy the reality of spiritual purity. Those who are undeveloped insist on a specific interpretation of reality and are stubborn about holding onto their personal opinions. The education they offer thus becomes detrimental to people's natural spiritual sensitivity and keeps them from knowing the actual truth.

Student: Master Ni, I also understand now what is meant by the subtle law. It does not matter whether you are talking about the divine or physical level, all things and lives obey the subtle law. Although the subtle law is not dominating, no being can evade it.

The subtle law expresses health and wholeness in normal existence. Anything that violates its natural balance is soon finished, extinguished by extremeness. No matter how strong anything or anyone may be, if they do not follow the subtle law they will always meet with punishment and have to eat *the bitter fruit of their own internal sowing. No one in the world, whatever his religion, can evade the subtle law. A person can express his spiritual energy in different ways and worship God. Or one can say that there is no God and organize his or her emotions and life and mind differently, and it would not necessarily violate the subtle law.*

The subtle law is distinctly expressed in both the Tao Teh Ching *and the* I Ching. *It is the highest common reality of the universe. It is the non-ruling ruler. Its ancient name is Tao, the path, the way. All people follow it. I hope my understanding is correct.*

Master Ni: Both of you have expressed your understanding of the Integral Truth.   Your achievement is priceless to your own life and the lives of others, which will contact you through different relationships.

I need to confirm that normalcy can be expressed as complete or whole virtue which includes truth, goodness, beauty, wisdom and holiness.   At another level, you must understand that in normal healthy situations, normal spiritual energy is always present, but externalized religions express it in different ways.   For example, in the East, people worship the Goddess of Mercy.   Among her most popular names are: The One Who Can Save People From Misery, The One Who Responds Promptly to Those Who Suffer and The One Who Wears a White Robe.   This goddess enjoys great popularity in Asian countries.   The Holy Virgin is exactly the same in the West.

However, in both of these cases, first a person needs to have misery before he can pray to someone to come help him.   Only when a person is in trouble does he need help; therefore, spiritual reality is only recognized when there is trouble present.   We must recognize the normal peacefulness and health that is already supported by the presence of our own spiritual energy and that of the natural environment.   Similarly, external religions need trouble and sins so that they can look for a messiah to deliver them from their miseries.   They do not know how to respect life without misery.   Truthfully, it is not the God or Goddess who helps you in times of trouble that should be specially worshipped. If you are going to worship something, it should be the God or Goddess who supports you in times when nothing difficult is happening, when things are normal and there is no trouble. You may feel dull and bored, but those are the times when you should extend your gratitude.

An achieved one does not make trouble in his life. He puts his energy into purifying himself and preserving his sensitivity to the spiritual reality within and without. This is the true standard of spiritual achievement and the direction which the ancient achieved ones pointed out to their descendants who wished to learn the depths of spiritual reality in the operation of everyday normal life. The tradition of Tao dedicates itself to this.

Normalcy is not limited to truth, goodness, beauty and so forth. Generally, in a culture, segmented concepts and figureheads of authority, beauty, power, etc., are exalted; for example Mao Tse Tung, Hitler and Stalin, all of whom earned their positions by personal charisma, intelligence and effort. They were able to organize people and thus rise to power. There must be goodness, beauty and power in such people to attract others and make them obey their personal ambitions and desires. Even a notorious gang leader must have something that attracts followers to him, such as generosity or taking care of friends. The virtues of such people as these, however, are fragmented, and others are trapped by the incomplete education of general culture.

Spiritually, a good thing must be healthy; a beautiful thing must also be good. In general, however, good is not understood as healthy or virtuous. We need to recognize the value of integral virtue and see the fragmented, conceptual establishment of the world as the ancient achieved ones saw it. From our study of the teachings of Lao Tzu, Chuang Tzu and Master Hui Neng, this understanding can be deepened. No one can do a complete job and attain growth through individual effort alone; it requires the effort of all sages, but most important is your own effort in absorbing their wisdom and your sincerity to attain the integration of your new life.

CHAPTER SIX

LIVE WITH THE SPLIT WAY
OR THE INTEGRAL WAY

August 1987 in Malibu

Visitor: What is the spiritual benefit or disadvantage of the learning of Tao or other religions?

Master Ni: I have answered a similar question a number of times before. This time, I would like another friend in this meeting to help me respond to you by his learning and achievement.

Student A: As I see it, general religion stays at the conceptual level of thought and is active within the relative mental sphere. It is accompanied by a dominating ego and aggressive, strong emotions. Its focus is not to support people's spiritual development but to group people with strong emotional convergence by using a fixed image. Such religions reject any individual or group that expresses something different. The dominance of this emotional and spiritual immaturity blocks the spiritual growth of the majority. Such religions are characterized by promoting superficial spiritual faith without encouraging spiritual awakening.

Examined on an individual level, it is normal that people have religious or spiritual ambition. However, because they have become stuck and annoyed by everyday life, they would like to establish another life in which they can live differently and have no trouble or annoyance. They would like to have a spiritual life path that does away with anything causing worry in worldly life. If they do this, they emotionally establish a separated life which is more idealistic than honest.

It is not serious spiritual truth that after death people need to stay in the tomb for a thousand years, waiting for the heavenly king or god to come to judge them, deciding which soul should be punished and thrown into the fire and which can ascend to heaven for enjoyment. It is not serious spiritual truth that people need to reincarnate life after life to suffer before they ascend.   All these statements, however, function as postponed promises; you believe the heavenly kingdom or reward is not for you today, but in the unreachable future. Instead of realistic achievement in the present, it teaches that people must give up their good life now to look for a life in another time.

Meditation and prayer have been established as two important religious and spiritual practices. Some people in everyday life feel bad that they do not have time for prayer or meditation all day long, because they believe that they cannot become spiritual without lots of time to meditate or pray. So they think they are not spiritual people. Or, they think that only people who have time to spend praying in a church or a monastery are spiritual or holy and that those who do not have time for this kind of activity and live in the world are not spiritual. But the ultimate truth is that it is not high spiritual development to remain in a religious establishment away from general, ordinary life.

In this regard, the mind becomes split. People who stay in monasteries make vows not to participate in worldly life. Whether Christian or Buddhist, people stay in monasteries because they have learned to disrespect worldly life. A student of Tao cannot hold the same expectation. Tao is not about learning something different from your normal life or only enjoying meditation; it is not about living in quiet, avoiding a troubled mind or being away from the world. This is not the real way of learning Tao. Tao is the absolute and the integral path. It is not a relative religion, but it is alive in our every breath.

Master Ni: Let me confirm the understanding of the student.   To learn Tao, you cannot postpone your realization and achievement until the future. You need to realize the Heavenly Kingdom in each moment of your life. Tao, as the integral truth, does not require that you take many lifetimes to cultivate yourself to become stronger or luckier, or that you must wait a thousand years for the last judgement and justification. Tao is not that. The Way is to rectify your own mind and heart, each moment. Sincerity is Heaven. Honesty is God. Righteousness is the true authority of every life relationship. In each moment, you may judge yourself. You are the one who is the judged, and you are the judge. Each moment the Heavenly Truth is the truth of your life! Cultivation and real life are not a separate business; you cannot be heaven this minute and be a devil the next minute. You cannot think that only when you are praying or in quiet retreat you are holy and, when you do other things, you are not. If you think that managing worldly life and taking care of problems and hardships is not holy enough, then you are always on a seesaw. You need to be on one side, but you are pulled to the other side at the same time. You are constantly experiencing one side up, one side down, up and down. By never settling your mind and resolving this conflict, your achievement can never be completed.

The absolute truth is like a sharp sword which allows you to cut through the middle of the so-called secular and holy ways, and so finding the exquisite, all important center. Without the balance of inner spiritual essence, both extremes are wrong. If one can attain one's spiritual essence and live within the spiritual light, there is no difference between left or right, up or down; the only way is straight and centered, because you cut away the detours. The most important thing is that you maintain the goal to cultivate, nurture and strengthen your spirit. Having such a goal sharpens your awareness in the midst of the reality of everyday life. Each moment of normal, positive living is your achievement; you are fully and positively living each minute. It is not the same as living with a deceptive mind or emotional escapes. The achievement of living is the having of a good life itself. It is realized in the quality of one's life. Bravely living, without being evil-minded, is living in the light. To live in the light is to live as God, the son of Tao. It does not mean you have to get away or escape from your worldly problems before you can embrace Tao. Living away from the world, there is no Tao. There is no other spiritual reality than whatever comes together to compose this moment; it is the constant reality of your individual life and the reality of the entire world.

Do not expect a savior to come from outside. No savior is real enough and handy enough, other than yourself. Achievement comes in each moment by seeing the difficulty and correcting it. Do not expect a messiah from a different world to come to save your life after your life is trampled. The messiah is you. If you identify yourself as a sinner, you are a person of sin. If you identify yourself with the divine beings, you are a divine being. It is not a matter of defeated or swelling emotion; it is a matter of conscience. Conscience means awakening, spiritual awakening inside, which enables you to see, to do and to be right.

So living an earnest and balanced life is to live with the Heavenly Truth. Each minute in the normalcy of an individual life is the Heavenly Truth. There is no other Heavenly Truth greater than the truth of everyday, ordinary life. This is the true religion. This is the absolute, Integral Way. It is not like ordinary religion, which separates a person from the Heavenly Light and offers an emotional balm in its place; this is a spiritual by-path. People do not know that their growth needs each good moment, no matter what happens in it. One's growth depends on how a person makes use of each moment, all of the time that he or she is given. If you make each moment a poison, it will poison you. If you turn it into a healing tonic, it will support you. Worldly life is the real nutrition of the soul. Worldly life is the school of the soul. It is the ladder which leads to all the angels and the angelic life. The result depends on who you are and how you use each moment that you are given. To live artificially in the ideas of religion is sick. The sick soul finds the hospital whose medicine is group hypnosis. This is an important message to the healthy souls looking for well-being.

So on the other extreme, does this mean that we should not meditate? That is not what it means; go ahead and meditate. Does that mean that we should not do all the helpful things that support us? You still need to engage in constructive and life building activities for yourself apart from what is expected or demanded of you by the world. You need to take action, because otherwise, if you are only talking, "I realize my every moment to be exactly as the revelation of Heavenly Truth," it is just talk and remains superficial. Deeper reflection and realization are also needed. Reflection is seeing the truth; realization is being and actualizing the truth. Do not be partial - instead of complete - by only talking. It is valuable for each person to do his self-cultivation and self-discipline. Keep learning from the wise spiritual teachings and use them as the light guiding your steps; otherwise, you might fall back into the darkness of the undeveloped soul.

Realizing or actualizing your spiritual life does not come from escaping to the mountains, living in rural places or monasteries, and going to churches or temples. Yes, you can go to a teacher, if the teacher is compatible with your level of balance and you are not looking only for material benefit. After you learn this principle, you can use your realization to see whether you are being pulled from one side to another, or if you are learning to keep your focus straight. By being centered, you keep advancing in your righteous way of life with universal moral nature.

Visitor: Does it have to do with keeping positive?

Master Ni: You can utilize that teaching to support your balanced life. I, myself, have written eleven books which are not intellectual; rather, they unite spiritual energy with intellectual capability. Everything in them can be utilized in everyday life, with every moment's thoughts, to cultivate your mental attitudes and practice your spiritual integration. All my written work as well as my personal spiritual achievement was accomplished at the same time that I was working and living in the world. My parents and all the great

masters have accomplished it in the same way. One
does not need a specific time and space away from
worldly life to accomplish this. Once you realize what
you must do, do it every moment; then your achievement is already there. You do not need to wait another thousand years or many lifetimes to be enlightened. You cannot be sure of the present; how can you
be sure of the future? You can only stand firmly now.
If you are driving on the freeway, you cannot allow
yourself to drive carelessly today, saying that tomorrow
you will drive more carefully.

Let us talk about methods of cultivation, meditation
and practice. The right practices are very important.
For example, people use leather to make shoes to protect their feet. Shall we instead use leather to pave all
the roads you walk on, or is it more convenient to use
it to make shoes for your feet? Leaders of different
social programs wish to spread leather over the entire
earth for everybody to walk on without hurting their
feet. Their motivation is good, but their plan is ineffective, because their extremeness would destroy the
living organism of the world. Spiritual people both
need to protect their feet and help the world. Assist in
the good goal of taking away big sharp stones from the
road and, at the same time, wear your leather shoes
when you walk on the smaller sharp stones in the
road. Your cultivation is the action of making and
putting on your shoes everyday! Guide your mind
and spirit away from any possible downfall or stumbling that could cause you to brew a negative attitude
toward life. A person may speak about high moral
principles with his mouth, but he must practice living
the good principles day by day for them to become his
truth. Both practice and philosophy are needed. It is
important to respect and practice maturity as well as to
enrich and revitalize our organic moral nature by embracing the simplicity of the integral way of life.

People who stay in the mountains and rural places,
cultivating themselves in order to keep their moral
nature away from temptation or evil, are performing a
small practice. It is agreeable to the world, because

they do nothing to interfere with others. People who perform religious practices in everyday life, going along with the established rituals and routines that confirm the community's emotion and spirit without actually extending undiscriminating love to people of all races and religions, are considered, mistakenly, to be doing a broad practice. In either case, people doing any spiritual practice correctly are known for their great tolerance. However, people who do the broad practice tend to be more shallow, lacking spiritual depth; and people doing the small practice tend to care only for themselves. Both practices are defective because they do not bring a person to the point of true balance between self-responsibility and service in the world.

It is helpful for each individual to understand that he is born a unique and individualized being, and it is necessary for him to learn and combine different kinds of practices rather than limit himself to just one. They are for his protection and nutrition in his spiritual and integral life; they will help him maintain his integral nature. The reality of life is the real spiritual path that we live each moment. Well-balanced living is the fruit of this achievement. Heaven or hell do not come to you tomorrow; they come in this moment, and it is you who invite in one or the other by how you live. That is what is important.

Visitor: How does the practice of living a well-balanced life differ from doing certain practices such as Chi Gong?

Student B: The practice of individual energy fortification and transformation, popularly called Chi Gong or Chi practice, has many purposes at all levels. Generally, at the physical level, energy transformation exercises are used to improve your health by rectifying circulation and secretion functions. It improves your emotional balance. We value the gentle way of energy transformation exercises. There is no problem with any practice if it is correctly taught and well learned. Some types of religious practice are useless to people. Some people think too much of themselves and decide

they need a special spiritual practice to achieve a higher level
than others; but those thoughts will pull them down.   They
think they will benefit by being lofty and staying at the tip
of an imagined pagoda in their spiritual ego, cold and unen-
thusiastic.   That is wrong.   In worldly life, one finds the
right, positive thing to do in life, and it is rewarding in
itself.   If one does not find the right thing to do, it is not
rewarding and makes one negative.

Many religious practices are unreasonable.   For example,
in the Catholic religion, they make the followers repeatedly
imitate the suffering of Jesus.   Through hundreds of years,
what spiritual achievement can believers attain from such a
practice?   Some other practices are a special spiritual train-
ing.   For example, students of Buddhism buy fish or birds
and set them free in the water or the trees.   The fishermen
on the waterside laugh about this.   The teaching and be-
havior is really laughable, but it is one way to teach in-
dividuals to have a kind heart and to love life.   If a person
can learn to love life by throwing fish back into the ocean
and releasing birds back to the trees, perhaps in daily life he
can learn to be kind and not hurt himself or other people.

People need good religious education, but they also need
to develop their vision and understanding in order to know
the value of what is available.   It seems to me that the
integration of different spiritual approaches is the direction of
the new epoch.

Visitor: If you do those practices such as Chi Gong with the
motive to develop yourself to help other people, is this a good
motive?

Student B: Yes, this is good positive learning.   Everybody
needs to learn something and maintain it in everyday prac-
tice.   People do many things; why not take a few minutes to
do energy transformation exercises, Tai Chi or any other
effective practice?   People play cards, watch movies, etc.; why
not do something to help your health directly?   The wrong
thing is when you value the spiritual practice more than the
work at hand.   You learn energy transformation exercises to
help your health so that you can live your life and work
better.   When you do not consider the good work before you

as meaningful, but you would rather go to learn Chi Gong, you have already lost the vision of true spiritual practice. It is not hard to organize a personal schedule to do all your important practices and those things that support your life. Those good practices can be considered an important part of your life alongside eating, sleeping and working; but do not be like the people who endorse spiritual teachings that devalue worldly life and practical matters.

All people need to understand their spiritual goal clearly. Every moment, whether you do spiritual practices or general work, all things that are of positive meaning are holy and sacred. Whenever you have respect toward each moment of your life and the work you are doing, you are happier and more productive and do better than others. If you are rushing about, remaining rough and unrefined about your life, or if you are more serious about one part of it, you lose your balance between practical life and those auxiliary practices.

Spiritual practices are not bad unless you use them as an escape. Then you become like someone who is overly fond of make-believe or acting in plays. Acting is someone running away from one's own self. Acting in a play can be compared to believing in the illusions of general religions; they both carry the reality of running away from oneself. Religious followers do not like to live their own practical lives. They wish to live like somebody else, a person of a different place, and not be connected with their own reality at all. Why does the actor need to go away from his real life? Because he cannot stand the truth of his discovery that his own life is empty. He has not attained any spiritual essence in his real life. When on stage or on the movie set, he acts so well it looks like real life, but it is the life of someone else. He plays many roles, but he cannot stand to play himself. Everything passes through his mind so quickly that no spiritual essence is attained. Spiritual essence can be expressed in one's external life, but it also can be maintained at the innermost core of one's being without showing outwardly. People who cannot find their real selves go from one stage to another, searching and searching. Just like a good actor, you are cast first in this role, then in that. Your life changes more often than an ordinary person's life does.

But none of these roles are deeply satisfying nor is it the real you.   You wish to make each role so real, and indeed, you have the capability to make them seem real outwardly.   But none of them hold the spiritual essence of life, which is too deep to be touched by the busy mind.   The experiences of life the actor performed on the stage make him more skillful in acting, but he does not become enlightened by the experience. He has merely been an actor in it.   People who have a noble spirit are usually not in a noble position.   Most people who are in a noble position have no spirit of nobility.

So why do we need spiritual development?   What the integral way teaches is to express the Heavenly Truth in each moment of our life.   Instead, most people are escaping each moment or wishing it to go away; looking for the next episode, wanting to be something else.   Or they hypnotise themselves with novels or television or movies.   They keep escaping and escaping, skipping and jumping, running and avoiding.   You run away from the real moment, the real life, the real truth that you cannot stand, because it is plain and maybe boring, but it is truthful and holy.

Visitor: It seems like every time I do find myself, something from outside comes along and pulls me away.

Master Ni: That is because you have not achieved how to live in the present and to set your mind in the moment now.   When something from outside pulls you, you cannot immediately see both yourself and the real meaning of the pull.   People are pulled away - escape subjectively or suffer from outside annoyance, temptation or enticement - because they cannot stay spiritually centered.   If you could realize the Truth of Life in each moment, you would be complete in each moment; you would not be pulled outside, nor be smoldering inside emotionally.   You are not somebody else and you are also not the shallow sense of self that you think you are.   You are a developed spirit in human form.   It is only a matter of learning and un-derstanding; becoming one with reality.   Achieving a goal and the spiritual learning and practice it requires is one.   You feel unhappy when you are yourself; you feel unhappy when you are not yourself. The problem is that when you feel yourself, you do not enjoy the moment of being yourself; and when you do not feel yourself, you feel unhappy too.   You think you can enjoy; but what you enjoy is what you do and not what you know. When you know it, because you are spiritually centered, you are in the quiet.   In other words, even though there are pulls and enticements, you still remain in the moment of complete being and spiritual centeredness, able to enjoy the new composition.   In that way, you can be in any situation and react correctly, and still be responsible to the world.

The entire world is connected with you. This is what you come to know with spiritual achievement in the integral way.   And this is the point that demonstrates the difference between religions which separate you from life and the Integral Way which unifies you with life. The separating religions are afraid of pulls and enticements, so they encourage living apart from the world. The guidance of the Integral Way is to encourage you to live wherever you are and to move forward without fear to meet the challenges and experiences that will bring you to a new spiritual range or new Heavenly Realm. The Integral Way of spiritual achievement is a more developed stage of life. It encourages you to know that in this moment you are achieved by directly being aware of it. It is not living only for your personal interest or receiving payment for the work of other people's interest, because these attitudes come out of the negative mind.

The Integral Way does not present any conflict, because when you help the world, you help yourself, too. If you do not help others, you also do not help yourself. If you always put the physical self above the physical world and the physical world above the true spiritual self, you are split. If you are unhappy, it is because you think that every moment you have to be dominant over the world, that you must be the boss of your relationships. Nobody can do that. Others live for you, and you live for others. The entire world, the entire universe, is one being; the entire span of history, no matter how long or short, is one being. You make trouble by thinking about self. That is not spiritually centered; that is self-centered. When self-centered, you worry, you are unhappy or upset because things do not go as you wish. This is a habit you establish after you are born into the world and you feel pressure from your surroundings. You make your self-protective shell stronger and stronger. As you continue to separate yourself from the universal nature, you make yourself smaller. You antagonize the world, even while you think that the world is antagonizing you.

For example, if a young person feels that her parents have not treated her well, this is because she holds a standard about how they should treat her as their child. And love has no standard and is not measurable. Once you establish a standard, there is a separation and you withdraw more from them. Only when you are not with them do you feel happy. Surely, naturally, people have different energy constructions. You may be with some people who feel like a beam of sunshine; while others may make you feel chilly. Choose your company well in terms of this and other more important factors.

If all your experiences are only psychologically smooth, filled with good feeling and good thoughts and soft emotions, this can actually become an obstruction to your spiritual growth. Spiritual growth is simple. The difficulty is that people have too many negative habits built up from their practical experience, such as always needing to watch out for the aggressiveness of others. This is why you shrink back from the world and try to live like an island. You cannot open yourself any more, because of your experience says that, once you are open, you will immediately get hurt. Spiritual achievement means that you can be open to being hurt and are able to survive the difficulty and grow. If you shut yourself in, you will never grow. Spiritual training enables you to live in the moment you have right now. You do not need to wait another thousand years for someone to come along and take care of your worldly problems and straighten out the wrongs that others have done to you. You need to attain your spiritual achievement and live with the spiritual truth unfolding in each moment. Good spiritual life happens now. Right away. No postponement. Postponing is psychological, not spiritual. Although the spiritual reality cannot be expressed perfectly through language, we must not be afraid to use language to discuss it, as we have done so far.

From meditation one can obtain calmness, mental clarity and non-impulsiveness (self-control). But it is wrong to stay in a meditative life just to indulge in the good feelings. It is only correct to use the spiritual qualities and capability you attain from self-cultivation to give back to life. In this way, spiritual achievement will be useful for all life and not become two separated and unrelated things. The early religious leaders who had not yet attained spiritual maturity designed this separation between spiritual and everyday worldly life. This fundamental conflict, stressed throughout generations, prevents the benefit of spiritual achievement from ever being realized. No spiritual realization can be obtained by living rigidly in one side of life while wishing to benefit the other side. It is like a cat chasing its own shadow, pouncing on the shadow as if it were a mouse and in reality, catching nothing.

The real heaven must not be outside of a person's life. Heaven is the experiencing of the real world without gathering its poisons which come to you through maintaining competitive habits of greed, prejudice, stubbornness, aggressiveness and jealousy.

Material achievement is a part of spiritual achievement. It can support your spiritual development so spiritual benefit can be extended to all aspects of your life. This is the way of fulfillment of integral life by following the path of integral truth. Being on the path means to use one's spiritual development to assist and direct practical life and material achievement to support further spiritual development. Thus both, hand in hand, help to bring about the total improvement of an individual and his surroundings.   Spiritual cultivation and practical life go together to follow the integral path, marching forward into the endless future of conjoint internal and external development.   This means that a person can follow along the path to enjoy the wholeness of being.

Tao is full of life.   Religions present life as twisted in duality.   Tao is deathless.   Religions exalt death with beautiful hidden terminology and call it Heaven, or being at the side of God.   It is life that should be exalted.   With its normalcy and health, it is an endless path.   People can learn to live positively by living a life with complete virtue.   In this way, they can transform the basic energy of their life-being through the direct experience of a normal life.   The extension of the normalcy of life is wisdom, compassion, righteousness, bravery, faithfulness and balance.   When the natural foundation is right, such virtues can be produced; but when nature is distorted, these natural virtues become difficult.   Spiritual self-cultivation aims to adjust one's personal inner nature to universal nature.   Nature is sweet and it produces virtue, which is also sweet. Trenches with dirty water are the homes of mosquitoes; backward religions offer the darkness of the trenches, so what sort of life can they bring about?   Let us live with the oneness of universal nature.   Is life not the complete expression of universal nature?   Or need it be twisted by our own human conceptual creations?

Where should we go, to where do we return, and how can we live fully and completely?   Please answer me with your understanding.   It is not hard to earn confirmation from the teaching of the ancient achieved ones.   It is hard to confirm the truth of life by oneself. Let us live this moment fully and completely as it should be; do not live on the surface of thought and emotion, because that would be a waste!

CHAPTER SEVEN

APPLYING THE INTEGRAL TRUTH

An interview with a New Student in Seattle

Student: Master Ni, I have read all of your books and now I want to check some things out with you to see if my understanding is correct. When one learns the integral truth from you, the application of what one has learned is to have no discriminating mind and, thus, not establish a dualistic vision. This seems to be the total application of integral truth. Am I correct?

Master Ni: I think there is more to it than just this. It is easy to misunderstand the integral truth as a combination of everything and to deny the different functions of all existence. When this happens, we see the phenomenon of the undeveloped spirit which regards everything as the same. Such a person does not know whether a woman is a mother or a daughter or a girlfriend. Such a person also thinks that all forms of worship and religion are the same. If this were the truth, then there would be nothing to learn, and we could all lay back and become beach bums!

The integral truth can be considered an important spiritual and philosophical approach that views any individual object as part of a whole when we handle the matter on the same level. Individual human life, for example, has eyes and ears and limbs and organs, but all these things do not exist by themselves. They are all connected as one being; and, although each part makes up the whole being, everything still functions differently. The mouth takes the food into your body, but another kind of work happens in the digestive system. After the absorption of the essence of the food, the transportation and distribution of that essence are handled by another organ which also cooperates with the entire system as a whole.

The person who follows integral truth, therefore, does not blend everything together. One who truly has precise, keen discernment knows the differences among things and the relationships among their specific functions. The ability to recognize distinctly different functions, qualities, uses and values is the result of spiritual development. If such a developed person were put in a new environment, he would immediately be able to distinguish where he was. His eyes, ears, nostrils, skin and subtle organs would all become active together and gather information. Actually, a person's entire body is totally communicative, especially the skin of the forehead, the pores of the scalp and the bones of the skull, which immediately begin absorbing or refusing the invasion of new energy from the new environment. A person who develops such sensitivity cannot be cheated by what looks good to the eye alone, nor can he be fooled by any other single organ or sense. One who is integrally developed immediately knows where he is and what the problems are, directly, without having to make any judgement or decision by means of a complicated intellectual operation. The whole body immediately starts to communicate with, or reject, the new energy in which he finds himself.

From this example, you can see that spiritual achievement is not a matter of the mind or any single organ. It is the entirety of the life-being of the individual. The teaching of integral truth is not going to require you to eliminate the discernment of your healthy sensory functions nor mix everything together. Nor does it require you to delude yourself that all religion or all worship are the same and not harmful in some cases. If that were true, then you would not need to go in search of development.

In the great tradition of Tao, you are asked to maintain your childlike heart. Consider this an important message and regard your childlike nature as holy. This does not mean that you should die young before you experience anything! A true saint, a true holy being, is someone who can restore his or her natural integrity, maintaining this original purity without being cut to ribbons by worldly experience or being broken-hearted and soured at the end of his or her life. The true saint, or whole being, can maintain his integral original nature through all life experience.

After coming in contact with, and learning, prejudicial teachings, people become prejudiced and jaded themselves. An integral being, however, does not become soured or embittered or salty because of his worldly experiences. Is this not important? You have continued searching for truth in order to confirm your innate understanding of the original clarity within yourself. It was your mind and heart and integral being that guided you to break through the clouds of culture and the smoke of confusing religions.

Do you believe what I have told you is the integral truth? If you truly believe it, you are misguided. If you do not believe it, you are also misguided. If you do not believe it, you are misguided by yourself; if you do believe it, you are misguided by me.

What, then, is the integral truth? Such a thing cannot be expressed or described sufficiently merely by illustrating a few circumstances. The key to understanding the integral truth is to take information such as what is being given here, examine it and see if it holds true in your own life over a period of time. It needs to be experienced.

Student: What do you think is the integral path or integral truth?

Master Ni: In your situation, I would say that having no preconception is the integral path. In other circumstances I would say that practicing non-split mindedness or wholeness of mind is the integral way.

Student: Because we understand, because we know, we can connect ourselves with the integral path. How can you say "no preconception is the integral path?" If we don't learn the integral path, how can our training and learning be correctly applied to the circumstances of everyday life?

Master Ni: My friend, please understand that as you develop, through your life and even at different times during one single day, your path will appear to change.   What you need to learn now and what you will need to learn ten years from now is different, although it is the same path.   The integral path cannot be established by a name or a concept, for your mind would be entrapped by the name or concept.   It is called the integral path by virtue of correct application of the mind.   If the mind is correctly applied, then the integral truth is also revealed and expressed.   The correct use of the mind, however, is only correct in relation to a circumstance; it cannot be forever formalized or fossilized in one way or another and still remain correct.   Therefore, all conceptions are responses to different particular situations.   Knowing this, how can we establish something called "the truth," to separate the reality of changes?   All names are temporary; a concept applied to a reality.

Student: Master Ni, do you think the existing body and the responsive mind are the integral path?

Master Ni: No matter what the situation - friendly, hostile or neutral - is it easier to find completeness and harmony in all things before we even recognize the existence of a personal physical body and mind?   Do not apply any artificial separation by a mind educated to a way of habitual splitting and the Integral Truth or the original oneness can be found.   You may doubt the use and value of the Integral Truth and find it hard to gather back into its complete, natural and flexible wholeness.   This is the trouble with people in general who do not know how to correct themselves spiritually and thus attain well being of mind and spirit.

Student: From what you say, I have understood that no preconception is the way of the integral path and that the body and the mind were originally the integral path. This sounds contradictory. Please help me with this point.

Master Ni: To have no preconception is the integral path. Once all preconception is dissolved, the mind becomes quiet and you are living the integral path. To talk about the natural mind is to talk about the integral path; they are one. The natural mind holds no preconceptions. To have no preconception, therefore, is the integral path. The natural body and natural mind are the integral path, because the integral path is the life-being itself: the body, mind and nature. Consciousness of the original body and mind cannot then be held; when the conceptual mind has no existence, it is the entirety of nature.

Student: The body and mentality of an individual being is small and shallow. How can they cover or hold something as vast and profound as the integral truth of the universe?

Master Ni: Usually people see only the figure or shape; they do not see the shapeless, formless essence behind the shape and form. They do not know that all form is supported by the unformed truth behind it. One who can see the unformed truth behind all differently formed things and beings, behind all formed life, can see the integral truth. One who holds the formed as the totality of truth throughout time cannot see the integral truth.

Student: Now, Master Ni, I am asking you to explain the formless.

Master Ni: In this stage of my personal spiritual exploration, there is no single master over nature. The master is nature itself which is in a state of continual development. Neither can anyone or anything be master over your bodily life and mind. If you can dissolve your self-opinionatedness, you will then allow yourself to grow. You are then one who follows the integral path.

There is one road to reach nature, and that road is you - your non-conceptual self. Unless you follow this road, although you may live to the end of time, you can never see the integral truth. Reach the organic being of nature by living like nature and being nature. The organic being of nature can be harmed by what is unnatural. Thus, to learn what is natural and avoid what is artificial is the natural way to preserve one's organic life being.

Nature is like water. In integral spiritual practice, one recognizes the existence of the rough circumstance and the free response of his own internal nature. Thus he does not accept that a circumstance has absolute force over his nature or over his internal essence. Nature has the ability to alter those impermanent circumstances. Although circumstance is the external force, the natural is the internal essence. External form can affect the shaping, but form cannot control the content. Like water, nature can express itself in any form or circumstance without losing its essential nature. The mind of most people only recognizes nature by the form, but cannot see the subtle nature beyond the circumstance or form. Thus, people only see the verbal and vibratory nature, but do not see the non-verbal and non-vibratory nature. People see the force of circumstance, but most of them do not know to cultivate their own natural spiritual organic being. It is similar with an individual's struggle between personal ambition and personal destiny. Destiny shapes you in a rough sketch, but you can change it by filling in the fine details. There is nothing that can stop your spiritual vitality.

Student: If you say that having no preconception in using the mind is the Integral Truth, then bubbles must be a fine expression of the Integral Truth. Bubbles have no substance. Bubbles have no heart or essence. We can't be bubbles. So why should we bother to learn? You mentioned that the body and mind are originally natural.   If that is so, why do we need to learn anything?

Master Ni: You learn to undo what is unnatural.   My friend, your understanding of the truth is based on what you can hear, see, feel, etc.   Thus, you learn to keep separating yourself from the integral truth.   You are not looking for the integral truth of the great organic being of natural life within you; you are looking for a special idea or doctrine that can be written or heard and which can attract your mind.   You think that is the truth.   You do not think that what is beyond writing, hearing and thinking can nonetheless exist as the Universal Truth.

There are six senses: seeing, hearing, smelling, tasting, touching, and knowing.   Knowing a thing includes knowing it intellectually and knowing it intuitively.   One knows both through feeling and through thinking.   All senses are functions which respond to external circumstances.   You must understand that there are some things which cannot be seen, but they still exist, no matter whether you can see, hear, taste, smell or touch them, or not.   Do you have any experience of what lies behind and beyond the seemingly concrete reality of your senses?

What are your senses and knowledge based on?   They are subject to change; they are not always the same.   How, then, can any of them be the eternal truth?   If you do not reach the subtle essence of nature, you think your seeing is truth, your hearing is truth and your knowing is truth.   However, your senses can perceive only changeable circumstance, but not the truth of the universal common reality.   People generally relate only to a part of nature, rarely the whole: they call truth what is not truth, or at least not the integral truth.

So yours is the life of seeing, hearing, feeling and knowing, which holds you back from unseeing, unhearing, unfeeling and unknowing.   Most people create obstructions out of the things they see, hear, feel and know. They cannot see, yet see the unseen; hear, yet hear the inaudible; feel, yet feel the unfelt, know, yet know the unknowable.   By insisting on what they perceive, the obstruction remains. If one can break up the obstructions, then one's mind can serve to reach the truth of the Integral Life.

To learn nature is to learn the whole, not just a part. What is humanly established as knowledge takes a fragment of the whole and calls it truth.   Truth cannot be separated from the greater continuum of its unfoldment and still be considered truth from this limited perspective. People do not know the difference between limited conceptual knowledge and the integral truth.   One of integral truth is not entrapped by any thing, emotion or force that could keep him from living a life of full organic growth.

If your mind spiritually responds to a circumstance without any preconception, then you are living the integral truth.   For example, you did not wish to see the weeping face your girlfriend presented to you last night; but the next morning is another day, full of sunshine and warmth, and she is not depressed and crying now.   If you let your mind be controlled by past experience and hold a preconception, you may walk away from a person who is pleasant company.

Student: Master Ni, does one of great spiritual achievement have a heart that loves and a mind that knows right from wrong?   Are the highest achieved beings and the integral truth one or separate?

Master Ni: One of great spiritual achievement has a heart that loves and a mind that knows right from wrong, because these are organic functions of nature. Such a heart and mind expresses health. It is different from a mind that holds preconceptions or a heart that holds resentment. When healthy, they are not affected by a difficult circumstance, person or object for any length of time.   They have developed the natural capability to discern the truth that is beyond any matter or object; thus they remain free.

Student: The highly developed one who teaches people must have a motive or ambition. But I have read that the integral path does not involve any obligation to teach others and is thus not preconceptual. If the Great One is not without preconception, then how could he have a motive or ambition in his life in giving teaching? There must be two separate entities.

Master Ni: The highly developed one who teaches people has no personal motive or ambition. He or she helps people from his or her nature, like a sweetly-scented flower that gives its delightful fragrance, not asking anything in return. The Great One can cover the small one. The small one cannot cover the Great One because of its nature. The Great One is a spiritual teacher who awakens the spiritual nature of all people by the integral truth. He or she promotes non-doc-trinal teachings by encouraging the growth of the heal-thy, organic spiritual being of each person. Thus, the Great One is someone who helps deliver people from a life of untruth to a life of truth. The integral truth helps all people, not specific people. Thus the "Great One" and the "Integral Path" are natural functions of universal mind and universal spirit. They are direct truth itself, not the play of names or conceptual ideas, which function when the organic being of a human mind has become separated, sick and confused. The truth is a reflection of universal nature, not a separated creation of the mind. Ideas are tools that can be used to guide a fragmented conceptual life back to whole-ness and a split spiritual life back to the indescribable, indefinable one truth.

Student: When the integral one and the integral path are named, who is the one to name them? If there is someone who names them, how can you say there is no separation?

Master Ni: The integral one and the integral truth are the saviors of a self-damaged conceptual mind. They are the natural salvation of nature itself. If we can reach to the capability of the natural mind, we find that the natural mind is a function that responds fluidly to circumstances. A healthy natural mind does not hold onto the intellectual knowledge or emotional response that goes along with any circumstance. It responds, then moves on to the next thing.

In human culture, many rigid conceptual ideas are established by partially developed people who have not yet reached truth but who insist on the validity and solidity of their ideas. This has inflicted tremendous damage to the organic being of human society. But what concerns us is how people who have a special awakening or calling to the Integral Truth can cultivate the integral path in their lives. The integral nature of the universe is not apparent. When a person is healthy, he is not particularly aware of his health, but when he is sick, then the importance of health becomes apparent to him. After we have learned the importance of the integral nature of our life being, how then do we cultivate it? Many people who wish to be spiritual are supported by adopting the belief of a religion. This is like someone sitting by a fireplace, using a stick to stir the ashes, looking for a water bubble. You are fooling yourself. You receive no growth by doing this. Spiritual development is attained by facing all of life's circumstances and being aware that all circumstances are conditioned by something, and all those "somethings" are also conditioned by something. When you examine all matters of life more and more deeply, you see that at any particular time in your life, whatever you have been holding onto as a support or rationale for your emotions and suffering has been like the strings pulling a puppet this way and that. It is your own spiritual darkness that causes or allows the situation to happen.

The life activities of an individual are exemplified by the movements of a puppet; they are controlled by something or someone behind it who pulls the strings to make it perform in a certain way. The something or someone is also controlled by someone or something else. Chuang Tzu presents an example of this with his illustration of a cicada singing in a low branch of a brush in the meadow.   A praying mantis behind the cicada is ready to seize it, not knowing that an oriole (yellow bird) is waiting behind the mantis.   The oriole does not know that a child behind it has aimed an arrow on his bow at it. Chuang Tzu is watching, and when he nervously screams, the child's attention is distracted, the oriole is startled and flies off, the mantis is disturbed and the cicada also moves away.   No one knows what happened or why.   Can we awaken in time to avoid exposing ourselves to the interrelationships of dangerous chain reactions?   However, our focus is that the activities of individuals and society are controlled, moved this way or that, by the strings of multiple factors, such as financial, physical, emotional, psychological and conceptual pulls.   The Integral One learns to be aware of living in a chain reaction affected by a number of factors.   The integral one sees to the core of a situation.   Each moment of his life is directed by the subtle light.   In everything people do, in every syllable they speak, there is a relationship between the factors behind the action and the action itself.   This is the bondage.   No one is free except those who have broken through the obstacles of their spiritual darkness.

The simplest actions and the simplest language are needed to develop ourselves spiritually and present the whole truth.   Our lives are not lived out in order to fulfill the chain reaction imposed upon us.   If you know this, you will not waste your time learning something that cannot enhance your spiritual independence or something that cannot be applied in your healthy life.

Student: The integral one and the integral truth, as you say, are ways of living. All the secondary teachings are not the direct truth itself. Why don't many spiritually achieved people practice the cultivation of Tao or the integral way?

Master Ni: One who has achieved the integral truth does so by not doing anything in particular.   By doing anything special, anything other than embracing the Integral Truth itself, you move away from the integral truth. The truth itself needs nobody and nothing extra or special to complete it. By living naturally, the integral one does not do anything extra to make special things happen. There are people who are learning from the spiritual truth, however, who keep making things happen all the time. As a result, a vast deviation is brought about.

The integral truth does not require you to know anything, but some people who learn the integral truth force themselves and others to know many things. The learning of Integral Truth is a process of self-discovery. The teachers are teachers of self-discovery. The truth does not belong only to one person; the truth is yours, too. One who truly achieves the integral truth never blocks another person's vision by establishing false beliefs.

The Integral Truth requires no special discipline. If you can live correctly and naturally, if you are simply one with the integral truth, you do not need any special discipline; you are one with the integral truth. Pay attention to what is subnormal and abnormal in your life. One who starts to make progress in spiritual truth overcomes something by forsaking the obstacles that already exist in life. One of integral achievement concentrates on spiritual development by harmonizing his or her individual self with universal spiritual nature.

Student: What do you mean by "Integral Truth" and "Great One" in all the books you have written? Are they to be considered just as tools for helping people? If these are not the truth, though, what else can you call truth?

Master Ni: We avoid making the same mistake as other religions, which is establishing something to look up to as greater and more important than your own life.   The written work I offer provides direction and proof of your own spiritual self-cultivation.   It offers pictures of a true dragon.   They are not the dragon itself.   Thus, your own spiritual cultivation is the direct way to develop yourself to be the true being described in my works. If people could trace deeply all things which are not based on nature in their lives, identify and uproot them, they would not need to look for the suchness of truth. The true and the false are like medicine and disease; neither are of significance to those who enjoy health. Maps are for people who are on a road. If you see deeply into reality, you can see what is important and what is wrong. Nobody should die for external conceptual establishments. No sacrifice should be made to support prejudice.

Student: You have already mentioned which teachings are diseases and which are medicines, but if this system (the Great Path) does not stand for the ultimate truth, then what is the ultimate truth?

Master Ni: I do not want you to just hold onto something conceptually, believing that concepts are what is most important, because both the conceptual expression of the teachers and the understanding of the students can themselves be further developed. From one point of view, it is not the teacher, but the student who harms the truth. Viewed another way, it's the teacher who harms it. The truth is alive; we need to keep it that way. It is not the teachers' way of saying it or the students' way of understanding it that makes the live truth become dead. This is also the mistake of philosophers and the effect of philosophy. For example, once a young man learned from his teacher to keep his word: he was told that one's words should be as good as one's life. Later, he had an appointment with a girl. The meeting place was a bridge over a stream. Unfortunately, at the time of the appointment, the stream became swollen and the water began to flood. Since he had given his word to wait for the girl, he did not run away from the forceful rushing water; instead held onto the stone pillar. He drowned in order to keep his word.

You are looking for the truth, or you are looking for some conceptual definition: some shape, figure, color or other particularity, but I cannot respond to you in any particular way, because the integral truth cannot be expressed by particularities.   I am not that kind of teacher.   You should not be that kind of student.   In teaching the Integral Truth, there is no comparison or single way of expression that can define it.   Even when we say that truth is beyond language and conception, truth is still not so far away from language and conception.

When birds fly through the sky, they leave no trace, but there are still birds and sky and the route over which they fly.   There is just no trace.   You cannot hold the bird which flies over as the real life of the bird.   Neither can you look for truth in the route of the bird.   Thus, looking for the unshaped truth, you must dig to the very bottom of existence, examining everything that is false.   No single truth based upon a conceptual description or teaching can be held as eternal.

In looking at yourself, do not lose yourself in what you have created conceptually; instead, watch the creative self, the creator and the productive mind that cannot be bothered by its own creations or the lack of them.   If you find the source, cultivate the pure productive energy of the mind more than its creations. You should be able to do this when the mind is at peace.   Why should one keep disturbing or negatively abusing it?   Once the fish is caught, the net is put aside.   Once the thought of truth is reached, the thinker rests.   Neither the catching nor the net, the enlightened thought nor the mind is the truth.

Student: Master Ni, we know that the truth is profound and subtle; that, within it, both the true and the false are dissolved.   It neither establishes a comparison nor is it separately established.   In the entire universe, the truth continues to unfold through changes.   Since all people are conditioned and formed, how do we stop the root of good and evil in individual life which affects all human society?

Master Ni: Good and evil are conditions of different stages of development.   The root of good and evil is created from having perceptions of the individual self. These perceptions only appear in confrontational circumstances.   The root of all lives is good; circumstances cause people to appear to be differently.   Thus, good and bad are conditions.

When you respond to situations with your mind and your actions, if it is a correct response it is called good; if it is inaccurate, or if you overreact, it is called bad.   What we should pay attention to is the fact that in this free society, for instance, there are many people in a poor condition, but not all of them are thieves. Conditions may be the same, but personal reactions to a difficulty are different.   Each new condition brings new possibilities.   Thieves do not necessarily change the condition of poverty.   Honest work brings about a broader opportunity to improve a life condition.   However, humans can be conditioned and one's choice of reaction is the expression of a person's inner situation, developed or undeveloped.   Life can be changed, because conditions can be changed.   There are negative ways a person can effect change through external pressure, but there are also positive ways to change conditions through a person's inner development.   You might wonder why some people are wise and some are foolish.   You also know the answer: wisdom and foolishness are still conditions that can be changed.

What, then, is the integral truth which helps all people?   It is clear that the one who practices integral truth does not preconceive good or bad, making a prepared response to each situation.   Through the practice of spiritual discrimination, he does not engage in creating any confrontation.

Student: It seems to me, though, that someone who avoids confrontations can never overcome problems or achieve anything.   How, then, is such a teaching useful to all people?

Master Ni: The answer to this can be found in the study of *The Book of Changes and the Unchanging Truth*. The different positions of the lines of a hexagram express different energies.   In general life, actions are only appropriate or inappropriate momentarily.   No one should make hats that people have to wear for a hundred generations.   Many spiritual leaders in the world hold onto hats and suits that were made generations ago, using them to cover the undeveloped reality of humans, which, in turn created a great amount of conflict and confrontation.   Do you think the Integral Truth of no confrontation is useless?

The application of Integral Truth originated as a great spiritual achievement of ancient Taoists.   In general religion, divinity is something that exists separately from your own life-being.   With the Integral Truth, things cannot be judged because you establish a self aside from the object and the world, which means, you should *not* establish a self aside from the object and the world.   There is no confrontation, no separation between the spiritual nature of the universe and that of your own life-being, your life and the life of nature.   It is one.   It can also be understood that with the Integral Truth, there is no separation of self.   Because you keep thinking of a separate being at a certain level, you resist joining the being of oneness.   You can never achieve the spirituality of oneness by dualistic establishment.   In the application of general religion, God is God and you are you, forever.   In the application of Integral Truth, spiritually you have absorbed God or God has absorbed you.   There is no trace of two different beings.

Some Zahn (Zen) masters of an earlier time are exemplified as great practitioners of the Integral Truth. We know this because they left a trace through their records.   Many of those who practice Tao directly leave no trace.   As Lao Tzu says: Tao is the traceless path.

Is this practice less developed than the dualistic practice of general religion?   It is amusing to see the achieved Zahn masters who still live within the external religious frames they spiritually rejected.   If the external exhibition of Buddha statues is extinguished, what then can they contrast with such subtle teaching as the Integral Truth in teaching the students?

CHAPTER EIGHT

THE MYSTICAL PEARL

You have a mystical pearl
    which exists in your spiritual life.
Sometimes it appears,
    and sometimes it disappears.
It rolls along on the journey of life with you.
This pearl has great power;
    it is neither too big nor too small
    for different situations.
However, it can light you up both day and night.
When you look for this pearl, it shuns you.
In reality, it follows you closely
    whether you are moving or still.

A long time ago, the Yellow Emperor was traveling
    on the Red River looking for his pearl,
    but all his efforts were unsuccessful.
Only the one who focuses with no dualistic mind
    finds it easily.

It can see and it can hear.
It can know the true and the false.
Thus, the developed one calls it a mystical pearl.
Many people look for it far from the shore of the ocean
    of great truth.
Too often they fail, mistaking a shiny bubble
    for their mystical pearl.

The wise teacher says, "In the composure
    of your own life-being,
    you shall find it."
It is so bright and so distinguishable
    from all other things of the universe.

It can dissolve all your problems and worries.
It provides you great convenience.
It burns away the rush of complexity
    in all different circumstances.
It conquers sadness.
It removes the mountains of difficulty
    and exhausts the ocean of troubled water.

This is the treasure under your flesh.
It wakes you up in the morning
    and lights up your darkness.
It has no particular form.
It enlightens you by establishing no teachership.
It treats you no less than any of the developed ones.
This treasure can be possessed
    by the delicate use of your mind.
This mystical pearl of yours
    has unfathomable profundity.
It is linked with the universal nature.
What it can produce is like the morning sun.
It pops out from among all the shining stars
    and gives out an unsurpassed flow of golden light
    to fill up the cavity of the sky.

It does not learn teachings with the limited mind.
It does not like to be a name
    among all the other established names.
It does not fall to any side or create sides,
    nor does it maintain itself in the middle.

When your eyes follow my pointing finger
    to see the moon,
    forget the finger.
When you have reached the destination,
    set aside the map.
When you have attained the truth of life,
    there is no need for any other description.
There is no other truth greater than the truth
    under your clothes.

Student: Master Ni, is the mystical pearl my mind?   My mind does not have such great power.   Is it my soul?   My soul is usually suffering.   Is it Tao?   Am I not deep enough?   Kindly explain to me what it is.

Master Ni: If I tell you, there is some danger that you may become stuck by what I say.   However, I can try if you promise that you will not do any part of what I tell you.

Student: I promise I will do my best to reach what you say directly, to catch the essence and not hold on to the wording as you have carefully warned me.

Master Ni: What the ancient developed ones called the mystical pearl, on one level, is the inner being of individual life.   By inner being, I mean the composition of the mind and the spirit and the emotional level which lies between the mind and the physical body. The inner being, once gathered into a whole, in a well-balanced condition, is like a pearl rolling on a silver tray, smoothly and without obstruction.   In everyday life, when we get stuck or upset by different circumstances, have all kinds of reactions, and become angry, worried, disturbed, etc. - all these feelings keep our inner being from rolling smoothly along its way, and it is damaged.

We know, objectively, that in practical human life no one is without any emotional or conceptual obstruction.   Thus, how one manages a situation depends on the development one attains from one's cultivation. Spiritually, "to manage" means to utilize the developed internal strength and gathered energy which can empower one to surpass and overcome external obstacles occurring in the form of different circumstances in one's path.   No one has a life that is trouble-free and completely smooth.   One who purposely cultivates himself, however, can smoothly navigate through all circumstances that would ordinarily hinder one's emotion or mental activity without being harmed or deformed by the external situation.

This valuable mystical pearl illustrates the condition and level of an individual's spiritual development. Sometimes people lose their mystical pearl or self-nature when they look for external things to support their mind and spirit and engage in conceptual or religious creations on which they come to rely. Faith and confidence are thus the performances of a rigid mind; they are not natural or true. Instead of looking at or overcoming the real difficulties of a situation, they create a false solution.

The learning of Tao and the cultivation of a mystical pearl is different from the practices of general religious belief and from the conceptual comfort and emotional feeling of being supported by these false creations. One who is powerful and cultivates his own mystical pearl can shed light upon the right way and save himself trouble and confusion in finding the right way. He is able to live effectively.

At this level of your development, you should understand the mystical pearl with no difficulty. Nevertheless, we cannot narrow the mystical pearl down to just wisdom or intelligence, or a balanced mind that is reached by overcoming external circumstances in life. The mystical pearl describes something unformed and unformable, something indefinable, but something which can be applied in each moment as the essence of the contact between two opposites. The mystical pearl, itself, is the unique, absolute substance in the universe. It can be your own, but, at the same time, it is the truth of others and of circumstances as well. In the lower, physical sphere, there is always confrontation and conflict. When one reaches the mystical pearl, there is nothing which cannot be dissolved; no hostility or prejudice can exist in those who attain the mystical pearl.

The mystical pearl which you defined as your achievement is one way to define it. Sometimes the unobstructable universal spirit defines it as divine nature, but that is also just one way to express it. In learning the integral truth, we recognize the nature of the universe as integral and not divisible. It is simply the essence of all lives, the essence of the universe, above all disputes.

Student: Master Ni, how do I nurture my mystical pearl?

Master Ni: Intellectually, it can be described with the purpose of helping someone like yourself who is interested in nurturing their mystical pearl.   The eight virtues of the mystical pearl can, thus, be discussed as follows:

1. Direct observation   Observe with your spiritual eye all different phenomena that appear externally and to where they disappear.   Maintain yourself in quietness to recognize a thing or a thought clearly and see its continual unfolding.   Direct observation is the combined result of direct experience and examination.

2. Awakening   If the truth cannot be seen by you, it is because it has been covered by your own emotion and attitude; thus you are unable to distinguish truth from untruth.   In quietude, awakening begins to grow; once it grows enough, it is accompanied by deep discernment.   It pierces through the solidity of all untruth to reach the boundless profundity.

3. Composure   This means you do not hurry to make a point of your understanding that you would call truth. Once you are not struggling for the truth, then falseness will fall away from your mind.   From the preliminary reaction of all the sense organs, from the activity of all the senses and thoughts, composure helps you to see the transformation of all things and to live in the deep root.

4. Wisdom   Through concentration one attains composure.   Through composure one becomes wise.   Wisdom dissolves the stagnation and stubbornness one creates.   Calmness is different from the stagnant mind. The mind should keep rolling, like the pearl on the silver platter. The plate is not still; however, the pearl can move freely and remain still itself.

5. *Clarity*   The conjunction of composure, or calmness, and wisdom produces clarity which enables you to see all things; nothing can escape your transpiercing vision, which responds like a strong ray, without establishing any emotional relationship.

6. *Smoothness*   This exists in most relationships that enable you to smoothly move along in your life journey.   By wisdom you have attained clarity.   With clarity there is no more darkness; there is a power that can carry you through all obstacles. The mind, when it does not create any more obstacles for itself can, therefore, fully exercise or move without further obstruction. However, the un-nurtured mind creates obstacles by its activities and thus, loses its freedom even in looking for freedom.   The mystical pearl, if achieved, has the capability to pass through any obstacle and attain freedom without the need of creating the name of freedom.

7. *Usefulness*   The mystical pearl helps you to bring about changes in yourself for the better; but the changes are themselves subject to change.   The mystical pearl responds to the universal subtle law and guides you correctly.   The gentleness of the universal divine nature begins to unfold in you.   It is helpful to you when you have problems and can be useful in tackling these difficulties in a way that sets you free from creating more problems and difficulties.

8. *Forgiveness*   Forgiveness can help you when you are emotionally stuck somewhere.   All troubles express what has been gathered together by an undeveloped mind and ineffective being.   Opportunities would be able to bring help to you.   However, the help you receive is not a permanent protection.   Your life can only be delivered by continual self effort and spiritual

achievement. The world can only be improved by the conjoint effort of individual spiritual achievement in all members of human society. Even so, the mystical pearl will still be useful in your life or in the world. It cannot be used up or exhausted by anything, because it does not create anything negative. To keep your mystical pearl rolling is to forgive all the wrong someone has done to you.

These eight virtues of the mystical pearl are the virtues of true mastery. The true teacher cannot pass his mystical pearl to anyone, but he can teach the eight virtues of the mystical pearl to many. The achieved one recognizes his spiritual affinity by reflecting the eight virtues of the mystical pearl in his life. This is the true recognition and appreciation he gives.

To teach is to directly transfuse one's achieved spirit to one's students. Students can be recognized by being the "reflection of the teacher." The eight virtues of the mystical pearl shape you like the spiritual influence from an ancient developed one. This teaching has been passed down through generations and generations. Its spiritual resonance can be found everywhere in people's lives.

The flow of life has no return.
You can never command yourself
    to go back to the origin,
    to return to the source.
There is nowhere that you can call home.
You can choose anywhere to be
    and anything to be.
The trail through the forest
    is hidden by heavy snow.
The mountains are all covered by clouds.
You are the host and you are the guest,
    all become quiet.
What, is the truth still not expressed?

Student: Master Ni, I am interested in the eight immortal virtues of the mystical pearl. Are these something that can help me achieve myself, or do they merely express a state of spiritual achievement?

Master Ni: You can eventually achieve yourself by cultivating them.   Human beings are born with a divine nature.   Once they are born into the world and experience worldly life, they develop and extend themselves in extreme ways which cause the mystical pearl to be lost.   The developed one who experiences worldly life can sharpen or strengthen these eight divine qualities.   Some people may attain one or two or three different qualities of high spiritual stature, but only the one who attains all eight divine qualities can recover the mystical pearl and restore his own divine nature, thus accomplishing divinity above all ordinary lives.   It can be understood philosophically and will help one in the sense of knowing that this is precious to have. Practical realization can be achieved by serious personal spiritual cultivation.   The eight virtues, in reality, express one's own nurtured and developed strong spiritual energy.   Spiritual cultivation is done by practices in all three spheres.   The practice of the sphere of mind should be separately taught.   In general, meditation and personal cultivation make the eight virtues the goal and standard of direct personal pursuit.

In this practice, the eight divine virtues can gather the Divine Energy of Benevolence and Great Understanding, the Divine Energy of Development and Blessings, the Divine Energy of Virtuous Power, the Divine Energy of Universal Love and Truth, the Divine Energy of Penetrating Wisdom, the Divine Energy of Breaking Through All Obstacles and the Divine Energy of Stability and Security.   With these eight divine spiritual energies, one can accomplish the cultivation of the Great One of Divinity to become the Great One of Divinity.

In daily life, if you have faith in the mystical pearl which encompasses all eight divine energies, you will find them to be one with you and they will help you overcome the obstacles in your life.   You will be able to see clearly whether the obstacle is of your own making or is from the external world. It completes your achievement and is not, therefore, just a one-sided psychological demand.

When people live in the physical world, there are three main ways to help them reach the well-being of a natural life. The first is to have faith. Some people foolishly suffer for an artificial faith, yet at the same time their faith supports them in facing the suffering. This application of faith, therefore, is a waste. The second important practice is patience. If you do not have great faith, but you have great patience, this can also enable you to tackle worldly troubles. Patience without development, however, is negative and wasteful. This is also a passive approach of partial benefit. The third way is direct wisdom, which confirms your healthy faith and enables you to have the patience to achieve your goal of a great life. One who holds all three keys - faith, patience and wisdom applied together - has the master key to all the checkpoints and difficult circumstances of life.

Without wisdom, faith is blind. Without wisdom, patience is wasted. One who has wisdom without faith is cold and cruel. Wisdom without patience lacks the perseverance to realize something that you can see. These are the three legs of the cauldron, a symbol from ancient times expressing this great union.

In the past, most religions emphasized single elements of spiritual practice or faith without realizing the dangers of such partial practice. One must learn the complete practice to know where one is going.

CHAPTER NINE

MODERN SPIRITUAL PROGRESS

Human growth is slow. When people started using their intelligence to establish ruling systems and such, the mischief of the world began. Then, after long suffering, people awakened and started looking for democracy, equality and independence. This wisdom developed from experiencing the setbacks and short-comings that resulted from the unnatural development of human society. Has their goal of a great, happy life been attained? Not at all.

Natural spiritual harmony has been too long ne-glected as an important element of individual life. All people should learn to respect the existence of other people before talking about democracy, equality and independence. One cannot respect others if one does not respect oneself. People can only learn to respect others from the example set by their close relatives. If sons and daughters learn to respect fathers and moth-ers, students to respect teachers, and subordinates to respect instructors or supervisors, etc., all kinds of conflict among people could be reduced.

Without spiritual achievement based on self-respect and respect for others, without people looking to fur-ther develop themselves, democracy, equality and in-dependence can prove disastrous. They can bring trouble to individual lives. However, with respect, you can observe effectively and learn from all things and enrich your life. With respect, you can learn from your father, mother, brother, neighbors, teacher or anyone else. Even if you are more capable than other people, you still need to respect others by willingly offering help; sharing what you can give and what you know in a good way.

The purpose of democracy is to promote social morality and to eventually attain the progress of human society. Independence from all authority and social equality has been achieved to the detriment of many generations. It is not achieved for the sake of expressing individual differences. We have mentioned that human beings grow very slowly; they attend to one thing while ignoring others. Most of the time, individuality is overemphasized and the essence of democracy is forgotten. Without respect, equality encourages people to demand their rights before removing their own obstacles to supporting the system correctly through moral obligation.

If you do not respect your important learning, you can never attain correct achievement from it. Spiritual learning needs respect and devotion. Your spiritual achievement is important not only in your personal life, but also because it affects your surroundings. Other people and your environment are either benefitted or harmed by you according to the true measure of equality, independence and democracy you and other people enjoy. Equality, independence and democracy are your personal responsibility. You cannot abuse this good foundation by creating problems through expressing nastiness in your personal and social connections. Thus, spiritual development is important to anyone who lives upon a well-developed foundation of human society. Would a person rather go back to being a slave or learn to watch his own moral condition, helping thereby the development of all things?

Sometimes someone of one gender is more capable, knowledgeable and reasonable than the other as a natural fact. However, people, whether of more intelligence or of less, are eager to use the principle of democracy and equality to extend their personal will in all areas; they forget about respecting each other and choose only what is best for them. They look only for personal preference. In that case, there can be no harmony or true benefit, and this is why wars, visible or invisible, keep happening. This even occurs between brothers and sisters, different groups and communities, and especially different schools of belief or thought. Democracy results from all people in one society wanting to be the boss or leader. Given a new, healthier political approach, its influence can be extended in areas where a different focus can be considered. In a family, children should learn from the parents and not compete with them, and the parents should also not compete with their children and not teach them things that are destructive. In school, teachers should be respected. Nothing positive can occur if young ones do not respect their teachers and teachers do not even respect their teaching work. Once humans stopped learning how to respect people, the world began to suffer from the multiple ways people have found to mistreat each other.

Not long ago, all the power in a family or a community or a country was centered around one or several special individuals, and whatever they said and did was right. No one else could be right. People suffered from such darkness for a long time, but they accepted the errors of authority established in this way. Now they have awakened and changed to a new direction that is much better. Instead of having so many battles or wars, there is more discussion and argument; however, people mistreat themselves by disrespecting each other and overemphasizing their individual independence and freedom. Without right development of each individual, liberty and equality are ill-formed. The value of such a system is harmed when people do not present universal righteousness. The tool for seizure of political power is still the exertion of someone's selfish will at the expense of other people.

What we have discussed here is human spiritual achievement. There is no need to add anything to its importance. We know that insistence on party principle cannot be a substitute for wisdom. Wisdom is not something you can establish rigidly, but its application can always be improved. Wisdom is based on the spirit of unobstructed development. This is the healthy spiritual function which can help an individual and the world attain a higher, better self.   Stiff and inflexible religious prejudices that stand in the way of the harmonizing of human society are unhealthy.

Without spiritual development, no amount of progress, however modern, is sufficient.   With everyone's spiritual development, the virtue achieved can promote a much better society, which may approach the condition of Heaven.

CHAPTER TEN

QUESTIONS OF SPIRITUAL CULTIVATION

Discussion Between Master Ni and Students

Student: Master Ni, I request your guidance for my discipline. As I understand it, one's discipline in the learning of Tao has seasonal differences. It is now winter. Is there anything special I should do?

Master Ni: Before and around the Winter Solstice is the time to stop all sexual activity until the late warm Spring. Similarly, after the Summer Solstice, strong food and drink should be stopped. People are children of great nature and should follow its cycles in order to nurture their lives. Your health is a manifestation of your spirit. In the learning of Tao, therefore, life itself is a holy subject. Since life is integral, no single aspect can be held as unholy.

Student: Master Ni, I feel that since all of us live in the world, we are always being influenced by our environment, family and friends, in the job we do and the people we contact.

Master Ni: We call this subject the environmental "smoking and dyeing of an individual." When people live in the world, they are "smoked" or "dyed" emotionally, psychologically, intellectually and spiritually with different "colors," rather than maintaining their original pure person. How much depends on the social closeness to which they expose themselves. It is important for people who are looking for spiritual integration and achievement to limit the amount of smoke they breathe and the color they are going to be dyed. Sensitive people should make only necessary contacts with the world and, even with very little contact, must still purify themselves daily from the smoke and dye of society. It is important to make friends only with those who follow the right direction of life and who have good habits. Even if you unconsciously converge energy with someone of low character, you will be pulled down. Thus, spiritual awareness is your own teacher.

As for the question of whether to isolate yourself or be part of a group, the answer is that human beings are social animals and only in a special situation would it be right to seclude oneself totally from others. You should, however, try to give yourself the time and space to look at the influences in your life and the effect your friends and society have upon you. It is always good to set aside some time for retreat, either to your room or a forest or a mountain or the countryside, where you are away from the environments in which you live and work, in order to examine how you need to guard yourself from their influence. This is practical instruction for those of you who have already suffered from being "a smoked and dyed soul" because of contact with your family, friends or society. Often, even this is not enough. A more effective approach is the good choice of someone who can give you the right influence, such as a teacher, friend or the right group of people, who would help the growth of your upright personality and effective living. A good educational system is also an organized system that can influence a student in a positive way.

Student: On most occasions, I feel my personal will power is not strong enough. Thus, I cannot fulfill what should be done, or keep myself from doing what should not be done, when following my personal knowledge, either intellectual or intuitional.

Master Ni: It is important for all of us to strengthen our personal will. People make many resolutions, but they keep very few, if any. This is because they have not attained enough knowledge and because they are not objective about the matter. For those who have attained truthful knowledge, this discussion of how to strengthen your will power will be helpful.

Suppose you wish to do something in your life. You first need to evaluate what you want to do. For example, if you want to do meditation or quiet sitting for five minutes, then, once you have made the decision, you must do five minutes. It does not matter whether it is a sitting or a standing position. Do not make any bargains with yourself unless your knowledge of such practice is changed. Some people do the standing position for the cultivation of chi for two hours. Will power is built up in small circumstances, then it can be applied to bigger things. If one has no will power, there is no strength of personality and the foundation of spiritual cultivation is lacking. The first thing to cultivate, therefore, is the power of life; will power is the power of your life being. You do not need to bend the world about you; you need to bend all impulses within yourself, such as intolerant temper, impatience and self-indulgent scatteredness. If you can do that, you are a spiritually organized and fortified person. If you decide to wake up at 5 a.m. in the summer and 6 a.m. in winter every day, then you must by all means try to do that. This is called will power.

It is not hard to make a decision or resolution; it is hard to keep it. In practice, at the beginning you need to force yourself. You cannot be a baby. You have to be a growing baby. That is the difference. A baby that does not grow is a dead baby; a baby that grows is alive. Students of Tao are growing babies, so we need to be exposed to different experiences which are the strength and power of life. If you stay in a monastery or a cave, you are not building the power of life. Such activities are only for specific purposes when correctly guided; otherwise they have no real significance.

If you wish to take a forty minute walk each morning, you have to take it, because you are the one who made the decision. Surely there will be circumstances in which you may do something else, but in general you must guide yourself directly and correctly without failing to carry out the decision you made. If you do not do it, there is no spiritual cultivation. Spiritual achievement is the attainment of something that did not exist before: from nothingness to something. Spiritual influence is on a very subtle level. If you do not have strong resolution or will power, nothing can be attained in your spiritual cultivation. On a practical level we train ourselves and build our strength through the simple matters of everyday life.

Student: Master Ni, how do I concentrate my spiritual energy?

Master Ni: In answering your question, I would like to talk about concentrated spiritual power. We already know that each individual has his own personal spiritual energy. Some people's spiritual energy is scattered, so nothing can be felt or seen. Those who concentrate it through an effective system of refining, or a system of belief, can express spiritual energy and experience so-called miracles. Miracles are always associated with human beings and their own spiritual energy. If a person has refined their spiritual power, or if ordinary people have a strong faith in something, their own spiritual energy makes the "miracle" happen. For example, in some places in Italy there are celebrations of the bloodshed of Christian martyrs. They take it as an omen every year if the dry blood kept in a metal container turns liquid. What happens is that a gathering or collection of spiritual energy makes the event happen.

An individual's spiritual energy can move a mountain or empty the sea. All good or bad things happen through developed or undeveloped spiritual energy. It is important to know that miracles require an external medium to awaken a person's spiritual energy. This could be a teacher or a spiritually developed one who can help a person release and awaken their spiritual energy. Through self-cultivation one can attain even higher, correct spiritual guidance. You can make flowers grow in the snow or fountains flow in the desert; it all depends on your personal achievement and how you have trained yourself and gathered your spiritual energy. You can make money, succeed politically, achieve yourself spiritually, intellectually or scientifically. These are all different directions, but behind all of them is one who has concentrated his own spiritual energy.

Whether you know that you have spiritual energy or not, whether you believe in God or not, everything still happens as a result of your personal spiritual energy and the response of external spiritual energy. When two sources of spiritual energy meet each other, then beautiful or ugly things happen.

At this level we are talking about demonstrable, expressible spiritual power. For example, by your thoughts you put a piece of paper in the paper burner on your altar. Your mind can light a fire by your deep meditation. At this level, you can apply your spiritual energy correctly or incorrectly; but it is still not the highest spiritual achievement. This is only one form of proof that you are gathering your spiritual energy well. True spiritual development enables you to see the right direction in which to apply your spiritual energy: in a fruitful, creative direction or a negative, evil direction. We need, therefore, the quality of the godly level of spiritual energy. This is what is most needed in today's world. People have attained intellectual development and can find all kinds of knowledge, but they have not correctly guided their energies toward universal spiritual oneness. If this harmony can be found within an individual as well as within human society as a whole, then a good, harmonious society can become a reality. Heaven can eventually be realized on Earth, or wherever human beings live. It is totally the responsibility, however, of individual spiritual achievement and the development of human society itself.

One shapes one's own destiny and, at the same time, society forms and shapes its own destiny.

Student: Master Ni, what is the right way to meditate?

Master Ni: The superficial meaning of the word meditation is to think deeply.   The meditation of a student of Tao, however, is not a philosophical matter of thinking.   It is the spiritual cultivation of quiet sitting or moving with the purpose of directly observing, experiencing and uniting with the spiritual nature of the universe.   It may also have the purpose of realizing internal harmonization.   Within time, refinement will happen as a natural process.   When you meditate, therefore, it is important to understand that once you sit you start a manufacturing or production system or establish a process like a nuclear reactor in your body. Most importantly, you should keep yourself natural because the internal work will happen by itself.

Usually most people sit in meditation like a dying cabbage.   They slow down their circulation and secretions and emotions and breathing.   This kind of meditation is devitalizing; there is no real benefit.   The correct guidance from the learning of Tao is that when you sit in meditation your job is to nurture the spirit of joy.   You are not defeated by society, you are not troubled by your life companion.   Many people who are disappointed in something sit in a corner meditating and call it spiritual practice.   In fact, they are defeated by life and use the shell of meditation as an escape.

If you meditate, you should nurture the joy of natural life.   Most people need a reason to be happy, but that is not true happiness.   True happiness is joy from internal and external harmony.   When you sit as a student of Tao, your face should smile and your whole being should radiate joyful energy.   Yet this is only part of it; good energy should be embraced within, and then it shows through the envelope of the skin as an aura of peace, joy and harmony, not confusion. At the beginning you can utilize mantras and visualizations either for a specific purpose or to enter a state of composure.   Once you can concentrate well, you should give up all tools that guide you in meditation and directly nurture pure spiritual joy.

During your meditation it is important not to brood on negative thoughts or emotions, or dwell on sorrowful events in your life. If you do not take care of yourself, the whole world may mistreat you, but only because you are the one who mistreated yourself in the first place.

Collect your thoughts and nurture the joyous spirit within yourself. Ignore whatever nuisances and disturbances occur. Practically speaking, you can fulfill your well-being by using this special guidance in your meditation.

Student: I feel the most difficult thing is my emotions. They are so fickle everyday. I would like to know how to manage my moods, without being managed by my moods.

Master Ni: Often, when people are frustrated by some transition, they declare that it is "not their day." But actually, every day is the same. With or without sunshine, every day should be a good day for one who has not damaged the youthful spirit within himself. A person becomes worn out faster when he is psychologically entangled in worldly experiences. This is especially true of the mind; when the mind is worn out, your youthful spirit is damaged.

In the learning of Tao we worship the spirit of joy, the spirit of peace and the spirit of happiness. Accordingly, you produce and feed your inner self with spiritual joy, spiritual peace and spiritual happiness. In a word, we also worship the spirit of youthfulness. Worship is not actually the correct word because of its religious connotations. "Embrace" and "cherish" express it better.

You need to practice embracing the spirit of joy, peace, harmony and youth every moment of every day. If you ask me what a student of Tao worships, I would say it is the universal spirit of joy, the universal spirit of peace and harmony and the universal spirit of everlasting youthfulness. You may say this is not possible. Sadness, misery, trouble and tragedy are sometimes facts of life. Negative religions are based on these things and offer only hope and faith as a remedy. If you choose to worship the universal spirit of sadness, go ahead and test it out. If you think that life is meaningless and filled with suffering, then go ahead and test it out by worshipping the spirit of meaninglessness. Tragedy and misery can then be your god and goddess, the dominant facts in your life.

If you are wise enough, you will realize that whatever spirit you hold is the spirit you are. Many spiritual masters of Tao seem like hopeless and helpless optimists, but you cannot say that they are shallow. They have simply exercised their spiritual freedom to choose between one direction and another. They know that there are such things as tragedy and misery, and they also know that tragedy and misery are the result of stubbornness. Because you are obstinate in your sadness, you do not like to welcome a sunbeam into the darkness of your bosom.

If you say, "It's not my day," it's because you are aware that everything is going wrong. Some days things do just go wrong, but it is a question of whether you are going to complain about the day or take responsibility for your mistakes and try to do better. If you complain about the day, you transfer the responsibility to the day; that's not helpful. If you just accept the day as a day like any other, but recognize that your energy is low, then you put yourself on the right track.

Even sages have "bad days." The difference, however, is that a sage takes responsibility for the trouble. He does not blame it on the day. When you say, "It is not my day," you should not look at the day, you should look at the night before. If the night before the bad day was filled with poor sleep or bad dreams, you have already been told what kind of day it is going to be. It would be better not to be too active, then. What you can do is manage yourself; you cannot manage the day.

*Student: Master Ni, what about the people who work rou-
tine, nine-to-five jobs every day and cannot stay home or
change their job situation?   How can they be less active or
better manage their day?*

Master Ni: I think everybody should start to learn to
better accommodate their different situations and find
their own specific way to absorb some useful guidance.
If the pressure of your job is high and your basic
survival needs it, then you should not establish a special schedule for your spiritual cultivation.   Just rest
enough and eat correctly to support your good
strength.   There should be no conflict created in your
way of correct survival.   You can, on weekends and
vacations, do what is needed to be done to assist your
positive and productive life.   Though it would be not a
great life, it is a life of spiritual dignity.   All else is of
secondary importance.
      In those precious days you have, no day can be a
"not my day."   Every day is a beautiful day.   Once
your energy is low, be careful.   Stay calm and be cautious in everything you do.   That's all there is to it.
      A great general can make a poor decision and
suffer defeat because of one "bad day."   A great in-
vestor may lose his whole fortune by making a bad
decision on one "bad day."   It is important, therefore,
to utilize all the signs in your environment, your body
and your dreams to cultivate yourself so that you can
be like the achieved ones who are hopeless, helpless
optimists.

Student: What does an achieved one look like?

Master Ni: I mentioned the ancient Taoist masters.
Actually, they did not use the word master, but
"shien," a happy person, a free spiritual individual,
which I usually translate as "integral being," because
their spirit is original, organic and complete, unlike the
spirit of general people which has been damaged and
twisted by life experience.   The ancient achieved ones,

just like you and me, experienced the bitterness and sweetness of the world, but their spirit remained integrated and whole without being harmed and twisted by those experiences. People become sour and selfish or narrow and withdrawn because worldly experience teaches them to be careful in a negative sense. They are always smooth in handling small matters although they do not usually display great wisdom. I used the word hopeless to describe the ancient achieved ones, but they are not really hopeless; they just do not extend their hope to others and the world. Their natural life contains great hope. The expectant feeling of hope, as generally understood, is not the same as the natural hopefulness of an achieved one. Their nature is hopeful, but they do not expect anything. Life is a string of circumstances; altogether, it is called "your life." It can be this way or that. If you have expectations, things may not happen the way you would like, and you will be dismayed. This is why I used the word hopeless to describe the ancient achieved ones; they did not expect anything of the world. They fulfilled their lives from the inside out, not according to how the world treated them.

I also used the word helpless to describe them. That is because they cannot be helped; they did not look for help, but they were still in a position to help many people and to be helped by many friendly energies. They did not look for help, however, the way external religions do. Ordinary religions establish the expectation of help from an external source, but the ancient achieved ones had no such expectation of the external sphere of life. They had natural hope, not hope in some powerful image as a result of their own emotions. If they were otherwise, I could not call them ancient achieved ones.

The ancient achieved ones managed and guided their lives by their nature. They were naturally happy, naturally optimistic; they were not dismayed or defeated. They maintained a childlike heart, so I call them hopeless, helpless optimists.

When some people encounter happiness in their lives, they become wild and crazy. That is craziness, not true achieved spiritual optimism. Spiritual joy is very harmonious and peaceful. It does not need to be expressed. An achieved one does not argue or interfere with the thoughts of others, either.

We should always remember the inspiring example of the ancient achieved ones who fully enjoyed life. The facts of their lives are not any different than the facts of ours; materially, they might have been even worse off given what we enjoy in modern life.

Student: Master Ni, you have talked about ancient achieved ones. Can modern people achieve themselves in the same way?

Master Ni: It depends on the individual. There is a difference between the nature or ways of ancient and modern people. In ancient times, if something important happened, a community would choose a group of six people to obtain divine guidance from *The Book of Changes*. This group would fast for at least three days, and each individual would do the I Ching to discover the subconscious reflection and extension of the matter to be decided. Then the different views of all six were compared to see what the majority discovered. There might or might not be a majority. If the views were equally balanced, they would then use another natural method of divination to determine whether the original casting of the I Ching among all six individuals was correct or not. Such an objective way of decision making is a far cry from the way of modern life where argument is the only method. Argument has become a synonym for modern culture; democracy and equality mean that you can yell and I can yell, while each denies the other's opinion and thoughts. Nothing is harmoniously, productively resolved, and so much time is wasted.

In any individual life, as long as one looks and works for harmony between the levels of apparent consciousness and subconsciousness, there is no internal conflict. With the guidance of the highly-developed spirit within, I have used a community to exemplify the life-being of an individual.

In daily practice, achievement is more an attitude than a fixed reality. For instance, any fact is complete or incomplete, depending on who views it. Achievement does not mean that you are the one who has the most complete information or the most facts. The degree of completeness is related to the level of one's achievement. An achieved person has a broad view that can encompass many aspects of a situation. Someone who is less achieved can only see some of the facts rather than the big picture. This is not the stage that the learning of Tao calls true achievement. Spiritual achievement means openness to all aspects without denying the opposite side of anything. What is called opposite is just a different way or approach that can help a developed one see the picture more clearly. One should always keep an open mind rather than argue over what is already known.

Achievement does not involve argument or confrontation at any time. Generally, people associate achievement with conquest over something, or a state of superiority or authority. Not at all! Such attitudes deny the position of all other people. Achievement is always related to the search for truth, not to the ambition for seniority or authority. This is important. You will not find an achieved one who is short tempered.

To come back to your question about ancient achieved ones and modern people, there really is no ancient or modern time discrimination. I use those words, but they are not meant to belittle modern people. Hopefully they will uplift those who study them in search of the truth. We should learn the attitudes of the ancient achieved ones, not the content of what they knew. Intellectual knowledge is secondary. The essence of their approach was detachment from all emotion. The ancient achieved ones were not self-opinionated; they were people of self-development who always looked to see if they were being truthful and open.

Argument is never productive. If you are right, why do you need to argue? If you are wrong, the argument is a waste. Why do you not just state it without claiming it? Conceptual confrontation and conflict are signs of undevelopment. In other words, we are allowed to be innocent and ignorant and yet be achieved. It is not shameful to be ignorant of something; it is shameful to be ignorant, stubborn and self-superior. Lower religions are based on the principle of denying the truth of each other. Spiritual truth is a matter of constant striving for completion, without stopping at any single point to establish a religion.

Do not worry about who was an ancient achieved one. Look at whether you are a modern achieved one.

Student: Master Ni, how do I develop myself to not suffer from the world?

Master Ni: *The Book of Changes and the Unchanging Truth* outlines the principles of development. Basically it shows the different stages of a matter in a person's cycle. A trigram is divided into three stages; a hexagram expresses six periodic stages. Change means the experience of different stages of a situation. You cannot expect things in the material universe to ever stay the same. The fact is, every event and every life is at a different stage of its individual accomplishment.

In terms of religion, people south of the Himalayas take a different view from those living north of the Himalayas. They overly exaggerate periodic destruction in individual human life. Some times are going to be good and some are going to be bad in the totality of human growth. Destructive periods are the initial stages of further growth; to overly exaggerate them is to introduce the doctrine of life as meaningless suffering. Suffering and joy are both realities of life. Life, in the relative sphere, can never be only one way or the other.

Natural movement does follow certain stages: observing the life strength of vegetation, or the prosperity of a society, you still see within it destruction, which is the negative stage of growth or development. People who are objective in spirit see this periodic destruction as a part of normal growth in life and a time to take things easy. Some spiritual people see it as a time of disaster, and they make each unit of time a unit of being robbed by either natural or artificial destruction. Teaching spiritual students this description alerts them to experience the changing times and different circumstances in their personal lives. An achieved spiritual person, however, does not see a low cycle as being a destructive, disastrous robbery because he knows that it is a natural part of life. Instead, he accepts it and sees how to use it to his benefit, not as a robbery. If one is not spiritually centered, all life experience may prove to be a kind of robbery that takes one's spiritual energy away, or damages it.

As we undertake our everyday lives, in each moment, each experience and each contact, we must maintain ourselves in the right spiritual channel in order to avoid suffering the spiritual damage created by ugly experiences.

No one can hold onto only one stage of life growth; at all times we are experiencing stages which are shown to us differently - physically, mentally and spiritually. An individual's lifetime is a composition and combination of all smaller periodic changes. Good luck will always make some people over-confident and too self-assertive. Those people should recognize that special treatment is a spiritual robbery of that period of time and become more objective about what these periods of time mean to them. It is incorrect to view a different stage of a person's life experience and decide that periodic changes are disastrous; nor is it necessary to receive periodic destruction. I do not think that predestined fate is really the absolute truth. For example, during his growth, a young person will encounter illness or hardship. But by virtue of his strong vitality, he will do better and better each time once he overcomes the illness or problem.

We should recognize, therefore, that low cycles are signs of further growth. At the same time, we should also recognize the potential for vitality or spiritual robbery when we experience different events and in our relationships. If your inner being does not remain calm and balanced, then your spiritual energy is robbed and your balance damaged. This can help a person of self-cultivation understand external circumstances better: utilize the circumstance to help your growth, but do not let it damage you.

I once lived in a place where two long rows of eucalyptus trees lined the walk to the house. Whenever the wind blew, the walk became covered with branches and leaves. This is like periodic disaster. People notice the loss of the branches and leaves, but they do not notice the trees constantly growing stronger. In your personal or business life, you sometimes suffer setbacks, but they may just be a sign of normal growth. So-called periodic disasters, like the falling leaves, are also signs of continuous growth.

One time, with the help of my students, I made a Tai Chi design in the garden out of special grasses and flowers. It was very beautiful, but at that time I travelled often and no one cared for the Tai Chi diagram in the garden while I was gone, so the lovely garden became a wild place again. When I looked for it and could not find it, some students said that the Tai Chi had been destroyed. But they did not know that Tai Chi can never be destroyed. Any creation, important or otherwise, is a Tai Chi, the result of the harmonization of two kinds of forces: one is the initial idea and the other is the realization of the idea's energy. Tai Chi itself is the reality of harmony between two kinds of energy. Once the two energies cooperate, something is created which becomes an extension of their Tai Chi.

The real Tai Chi, therefore, is not on the ground and cannot be destroyed.   It is behind all creation as the subtle law.

Student: Master Ni, I would like to know how to live with my family and other people.

Master Ni: Living with family members or other people in life can help us to accept people different from us, to let them be just the way they are.   You may sometimes feel irritated, disturbed or provoked by another person.   All human beings are born with different natural cycles, and their personalities can be described in terms of stars by astrology, or by different elements of natural energy (the stems and branches). The purpose of all the different systems of description is simply to tell us the differences of each person. Because differences are a reality, you cannot become used to being treated in one particular way.   You need to make yourself ready to accept whatever another person, or group of people, is.   Unless a person has an evil or immoral motive, you should always make yourself ready to accept them the way they are.   Some people are rougher in their attitudes, approach and communication.   You may not like their style, but someone else may like it.   If you are going to relate to other people, you need to be ready to accept differences.   You need great patience and tolerance in your contact with others; you cannot respond hastily, in the same way they may treat you.   If someone is provocative or offensive, you need to look to see what is behind it.

No one is perfect in everyone's eyes.   Therefore, we need to recognize the different stages of growth that other people are in and accept them the way they are now, if there is no great conflict in practical matters, especially emotionally.   First you should be open.   If the world does not accept you the way you are, then you are the one who must refine your personality.   It is not up to the world to change itself.   Different generations are built by different people. Each person has their own stage of life to cultivate and refine.

Student: Master Ni, how do I guard my life from the test of Satan?

Master Ni: I marvel to see your zeal in the pursuit of God. You define God as the creative energy of nature. It is right to describe the creative energy of nature as God; but by establishing God, at the same time you recognize the destructive force in nature too. You then use the terms Satan, or devil, to describe destructive energy or circumstances, as distinct from God. In the learning of Tao we observe that the world and all lives are the result of harmony between two forces. In the descriptive sphere, the learning of Tao is not conceptually so different from the thoughts of the ancient Jewish tradition, or popular Western beliefs of today. Surely it is not a problem to distinguish between godly creative energy and devilish, destructive energy. What matters very much, though, is that human beings utilize the concept of God to engage in destructive, devilish behavior, which brings about spiritual confusion.

The world is confused today because people can no longer distinguish between godly, creative energy and devilish, dominating, destructive energy. People, whether they do right or wrong, all think God is at their side and that on the other side is the devil. Godly belief and devilish behavior characterize modern powers. Because of egotistic establishments, people lose their sense of distinction and are confused about what is godly creative energy and devilish destructive energy. They do not know how to respect the creative or restrain the devilish energy. If they did, the world would become a paradise, a heavenly kingdom. This can only be achieved, however, by the harmony of two kinds of forces. Usually any creative activity generates difficulties. Those which cannot be overcome, people call "devilish," but they are only side-effects of hasty, rough movement in the creative flow.

One thing we can observe from nature is how to learn the complete lesson, not just one part. We need to see the creative, godly energy as the energy of integration and harmonization, which brings true peace and prosperity to humankind, which is the offspring of the true God.

The one true God is not named Jehovah or Allah or Brahma or Imperial Heaven. True God is not bothered by name or title.

Student: In reading your invocations in English, I understand that my mind is guided by following and comprehending the meaning of the words.   However, in your more recent books you have introduced some invocations in the original Chinese.   How is the response caused here?   Is it purely through the vibration of the sound?   If so, is it important to read them aloud rather than silently?   Is there any further guidance concerning the use of invocations to aid our spiritual cultivation?

Master Ni: The invocations are used for the purpose of channeling personal spiritual energy.   Some are to link your own spiritual energy to the spiritual energy of nature.   Most of them are for their meaning and can be translated into English.   Some are still in Chinese because of the vibration given, because sometimes in this active world you need to use certain vibrations to guide the mind away from wandering in thoughts which are of no benefit to you.   Both worded and sounded invocations can be used by the mind and read aloud according to the effectiveness expected by the practitioner.   Some invocations are spiritual messages and it may take long years of practice before you might be enlightened or receive the secret guidance.   It all depends on your consistent practice and on not giving up.

Student: I was with some people who were having a disagreement.   The energy was very disturbed, and I was influenced by it.   I felt somewhat depressed afterwards; the next morning my sleep was heavy and full of insignificant dreams. I was too heavy and sleepy to get up to meditate.

Also, if I have an emotional upset myself during a day, I wake up around 2:00 or 3:00 in the morning and cannot get back to sleep. This sometimes disturbs my energy and performance the following day.

Is there something people can do to clear themselves of disturbances before going to sleep?

Master Ni: By learning and doing the strong breathing system, exhaling the disturbing energy and inhaling the pure natural energy, you will be saved from mental disturbance. Quiet walking will also do.

Student: Master Ni, a reader of your books felt interested in going to the East to learn Tai Chi and spiritual art. He asked us to refer him to an oriental teacher. We did. He wrote back recently, telling us terrible things such as everybody there is proud and people do not respect him. So, he asked for guidance.

Master Ni: This is the problem of students in general. They are looking for a teacher, but they want to be accepted and respected as a teacher themselves in their new environment. Respect is something that needs to be earned. It cannot be readily expected like a cheap gift. He is there for learning and must focus on his purpose without looking to be treated as a special person. If he goes to a place as a teacher, instead of really wanting to be a student, it will never work. He should go back when he is truly ready to be a student. When someone approaches a teacher, he should be clear whether he is a customer or a student. Customers come to buy the merchandise and go; they are not students and do not accept discipline. By stating this beforehand, it would save trouble on both sides.

Student: What is the true standard of Taoist life? Some of your teaching is serious.

Master Ni: Right.   I am serious about giving an important spiritual message.   For a practitioner of Tao,
life is not stuffy or full of self-denial as with ordinary
religion.   The words "simple", "artful" and "artistic"
describe the life of a person of Tao.   He never becomes
dull and boring.   He lives the completeness of life if he
can.   He especially extends great appreciation to the
beauty of nature and what comes from high human
spiritual energy.

*Student: Master Ni, there is a book entitled "Taoist Sex" or
"Sex of Tao."   Some new books adopted the materials from
that book and promote it as the essential Taoist teaching.   Is
that book reliable?*

Master Ni: It is an ancient book concentrated on sexual subjects.   It may be that some teachers use it and
emphasize it as immortal practice.   Truthfully speaking,
however, it is not on that level.   It has some value, but
not absolute high value.   It would mislead people to
practice sex more than to adopt some of the useful
guidance.

*Student: Master Ni, I learned from someone in your tradi-
tion the method of enhancing the strength of sexual organs
in men and women.   Is this method valuable?*

Master Ni: There is a market for teaching these things.
However, if these methods are not properly practiced
with discipline, the detrimental side effect will be seen
rather than the benefit of learning them.   Study to
manage what your own truthful physical foundation
can enjoy.   It is more useful and safer than being motivated by sexual fantasy.   If you wish to become stronger, the strengthening of the entirety of your life being
should be the focus.

*Student: Master Ni, are the technique of orbit circling and
the small Kan Li and the Big Kan Li useful methods in
achieving Tao?*

Master Ni: No. Orbit circling is one internal energy exercise, a principle that has been used to explain the traditional practice. Kan means water. Li means fire. Big Kan Li means the intercourse of fire and water from the example of nature. The small Kan Li means the intercourse of fire and water in a human body. Both are nature. You do not need to do anything to bring about their intercourse. In the practice of sexual energy transformation, traditionally, the orbit circling practice is introduced. Other new programmed practices have no traditional background or any precedent evidence to show that anyone has ever achieved themselves spiritually by doing them.

Student: I have read many other Taoist books of other teachers and learned about sexual energy circulation. In your books you do not talk about it very much; do you teach or have any writings about it?

Master Ni: Doing this kind of practice at your age, mid thirties, would make you more conscious of sex and thus make it difficult for you to attain internal balance. In Taoist teaching, there is a skill and art of increasing or revitalizing sexual energy, but those things are taught to students of an advanced age. You see, when women or men reach their older years, their sexual gland starts to weaken. The purpose of that practice is to help them maintain that part of the body alive. Because sexual energy is the source of all general lives, the death of sexual capability is a sign that a person's vitality is gone. It is valuable to lengthen one's vitality by reawakening the sexual function for the preservation of health.

The purpose of doing it is not for fanciful fun or excessive enjoyment. These practices are for increasing the force of one's life, not to conquer another person out of crazy ambition. They are of no benefit for people of a young age, men before sixty or women before fifty, generally speaking.

To young spiritual people, sexual energy is annoying. It often tempts them to fulfill its need; then they might run into an improper partner or do it in an improper way. So why try to enhance one's sexual energy when there is already enough? Improper sexual activity or unnecessary sexual cultivation at a young age is totally against the teaching of Tao.

The ambition of men to look extra-ordinarily strong in sexual energy, to prove themselves with a conquering attitude, is spiritual undevelopment itself. It is as Lao Tzu says, something you learn that you think is of benefit may actually harm you by appealing to your desire. Thus, it is destructive to do such practices when your age and vital condition are improper for them. The improper practice turns to poison instead of doing good.

Orbit circulation is for people who have totally stopped sexual activity. Some people naturally have strong energy, and even when they are old have thoughts of sexual violence with women; such a person should not do any energy practice at all. There is similarly no benefit derived by the practice when you have a normal sexual life.

Student: Master Ni, we are told you do not teach the secret practice, but other teachers do. Yet the other teachers use your work to support their teaching.

Master Ni: My motivation is to help people's further spiritual evolution. Some people wish to use some small techniques, which are only good for having a fanciful purpose. It may help them to control their mind; however, another good lifetime of theirs is wasted. What is promoted by those teachers of small techniques is not what enriches one's life today; spiritual immortality is proven in each moment of a good natural life. This is living with a postponed, unrealizable fantasy of untruthful spiritual immortality in some time in the future. How much is this different from the psychological traps of general religions? Your questions are related to the teachings of other teachers. It is an important principle that each teacher take responsibility for his own teaching. Thus, no more questions should be answered by me.

Student: I have seen a few of your students in serious trouble, and it seems that you abandon them. What do you say about that?

Master Ni: In their spirit, there are very few who are truly dedicated students of Tao. Most people come to look without ever truly being students or are the victim of their own psychological condition. People who are overly extreme, overly serious or overly fervent in their personality or beliefs do not accept the learning of Tao. Thus, their difference of spiritual quality gives them a different path of life. Even a great teacher cannot make somebody learn. My humble offering is only to help as a friend, and give the big principle of learning the integral truth. As for how much they can achieve, this totally depends on their own effort, not on any force from any traditional way.

Student: You say one thing in your books, but I believe you feel differently in your heart. Is it true?

Master Ni: Books can take you just so far. We use a book such as *The Book of Changes and the Unchanging Truth* to find a harmonious way to respond to any circumstance. You yourself must find a harmonious way to respond to circumstances. In the end, we must leave the books behind and look at the situation.

There are a lot of examples of people of good heart who are misunderstood by people. One's harmonious and appropriate response to a given situation may not please other people. It may not be a popular solution. A protective mother who yanks a child away from a happy but very dangerous situation does not necessarily please the child, but her response is the correct one. Do not let your mind trick you into seeing a situation in a limited or one sided way.

I would like to relate this story as an illustration of how people see things differently from the way they really are. Someone told it to me.

When I was young, three of my father's cousins lived in one town. All were nearsighted, continually making fools of themselves. The first cousin could not see anything in the morning; the second cousin would have bumped right into an elephant at noon; and the third cousin was as blind as a bat at night.

When I was nine, the first cousin left to go to Nanding, outside the Yongding Gate, to attend the temple fair held from the first to the fifteenth of the fifth month. Halfway there he wanted to ask how much farther he had to go. He saw a man standing west of the road. Actually it was not a man, it was a stone statue in a graveyard - a stone man on a stone horse! First cousin asked this statue:

"Excuse me, sir, how far is it to Nanding?"

He repeated his question four times, but how can a statue talk? It just stood there.

"Hey! Are you deaf?"

A crow flapped away. First cousin chuckled, "Ha, you pig-headed fellow, refusing to tell me the way. Now your hat's blown off and I won't tell you either!"

See how his nearsightedness held him up. That was the first cousin.

The second cousin made a fool of himself too. One day in the street he met an old lady who had just bought a goose. It was the rule in Beijing that when you arranged a marriage for your son, after the engagement you must send a goose to the girl's family. The old lady had a big white goose under her arm. The second cousin saw how white it was, but could not make it out clearly.

"Not bad, that cotton wool! How much a pound?"

Cotton wool! The old lady thought he was talking to someone else who had bought cotton wool, so she paid no attention. The second cousin stepped forward to feel it, asking again, "How much a pound is this cotton wool, old lady?"

He stroked the goose's plumage, slick and slippery.

"Oh my mistake, it's lard."

He took it for lard!

"How much a pound is this lard?"

He reached down and caught hold of the goose's long neck.

"Why, here's a lotus root."

A lotus root! He tightened his grip. The goose honked and he let go.

"No, it's a horn!"

He got it wrong each time.

As for the third cousin, he was invited one evening to an opera. It was summer, and he started home after it had just rained. A patch of cinders had been washed clean, and a needle was sticking out of it, pointing upwards. Its glitter in the lamplight made his palm itch.

"A diamond, aha! This is worth money!"

He stepped over to pick it up, but pricked himself.

"Damm it, a scorpion!"

Under the street lamp he saw a sticky drop of blood on his finger.

"Why, this isn't a scorpion, it's a lizard. Lizard!" he said.

He rubbed it, and the blood stained his hand.

"Bah, bedbug!"

Wrong every time.

These three cousins lived separately in three different courtyards which opened onto two streets. The first and second cousins had houses on the front street, third cousin on the back street. In summer they would get together in first cousin's courtyard, brew tea and sit chatting in the shade. Somehow the conversation always came round to their eyesight. Why was that? A person with a physical defect always tries to cover it up, to show that he's as good as anybody else.

One day the first cousin laid back in his deck chair and said,

"Well, cousins two and three, my sight's improved so much recently that when a mosquito flies past I can see whether it's a male or a female."

The second cousin looked at him scornfully.

"Come off it.   The last time you went out, you bumped into a steamroller.   If you can't even see a steamroller, how can you see mosquitoes?   My sight, however, is better at night.   The later it is, the more clearly I can see."

The third cousin said, "Quit squabbling, one and two.   Stop boasting about your eyesight.   You know that the God of War's Temple is outside this alley. Tomorrow a tablet will be put up.   Let's go and have a look at the inscription and make a bet on it.   Whichever of us sees it most distinctly will be treated to a meal by the other two.   What do you say to that, brothers?"

The first and second cousins thought it was fine and agreed to go see the tablet the next day.

At about midnight a cool wind sprang up, and the second and third cousins went home to bed.

My first cousin lay on his bed but could not sleep. "This won't do. When we look at the tablet tomorrow, they'll see it more clearly than I can.   I don't mind treating them to a meal, but I don't want them to say my eyesight's no good."   Still, he had agreed to the bet, so what could he do?   At last he had an idea. "The monk in the God of War's Temple must know what's on the tablet, so I'll go and ask him.   I'll feel safer when I know the inscription!"   He got up, went to the temple and knocked on the gate.

"Monk, monk!"

The monk came out.   So promptly?   Well, at midnight he always got up to burn incense so, as soon as he heard knocking, he opened the gate.

"Who is it?"

He looked out.   "Oh, Master Chang, please come in."

"Thank you, I've come to trouble you...."

"What can I do for you?"

"I hear you're putting up a tablet for the God of War tomorrow."

"That's right. Donated by one of our patrons."

"Can you tell me the inscription on the tablet?"

The monk of course knew it. He said, "It's 'Loyalty Everlasting'."

"Ha, 'Loyalty Everlasting.' Good.... Many thanks."

Having found this out, off he went. The puzzled monk closed the gate and went back to bed.

Then the second cousin arrived. Like the first cousin, he was afraid he would not be able to make out the inscription but would have to treat his brothers, who would make fun of him. He left the alley just as the first cousin turned into it, but neither saw the other - that's how good their eyesight was! He knocked at the gate.

"Hey there, monk!"

The monk came out and saw it was Second Master Chang.

"Please come in and sit down," he said.

"No, thanks. You're putting up a tablet tomorrow?"

"That's right, to the God of War."

"What is the inscription?"

"Loyalty Everlasting."

The second cousin had more foresight than first cousin.

"What color is the tablet?"

"Blue with gold characters."

"So, blue with gold characters. Fine. See you tomorrow."

The second cousin left, and the monk went back to bed. But then along came the third cousin. He couldn't sleep either for worrying. He'd come by the back street.

"Monk, monk!"

The monk said, "No sleep for me tonight!"

He came out and saw Third Master Chang.

"Oh Third Master Chang, come on in."

"No thanks. Tomorrow ..."

"We're hanging up a tablet to the God of War. The inscription 'Loyalty Everlasting' is in gold characters on a blue ground."

The third cousin, being the youngest, was smarter than his brothers.

"Anything else written above or below?"

"Yes."

"What's written above?"

"The date in red.   Down below is 'respectfully presented by a true believer', 'presented' is in red, the rest in gold."

"I see.   Thank you very much."

He went off, and at last the monk could sleep.

The first cousin got up early the next morning.   He gargled and was brushing his teeth when his two brothers arrived.

"Elder brother!"

"Why two, three, come in, have a drink of water."

"Why drink water?   We can drink when we get back.   Let's go and see the tablet."

"You are right."

The toothbrush was put down, and the three of them set off.   As soon as they were out of the alley, the first cousin pointed at the temple gate.

"Stay put, don't go any closer.   If you go any closer, anybody can see it.   Ha!   Now we'll test our eyesight.   Look!"

In fact they were still some distance from the temple.

"A fine tablet, 'Loyalty Everlasting'.   'Loyalty Everlasting'."

The first cousin was illiterate, but now he tried to show off, "See how well the last character's written."

In fact he did not know the first thing about calligraphy.

The second cousin said, "Elder brother, your sight's certainly improved.   You can see 'Loyalty Everlasting' quite clearly.   But those big characters aren't hard to make out.   Can you see what color they are, the character and the tablet?"

That floored the first cousin.   He thought, "Confound it, I forgot to ask that last night."

The second cousin said, "Can't make it out, eh? The tablet's blue, the characters are gold.   Ha, I can see more clearly than you!"

The third cousin said, "Second brother's sight is better than elder brother's. But those big characters 'Loyalty Everlasting' are easy to see. And gold characters on a blue ground are so clear in the sunlight, you'd have to have very poor eyesight not to see them. Can you read what's written above and underneath?"

The second cousin was floored, since he hadn't asked. The third cousin said, "You can't eh, either of you? I'll read it aloud to you. Above is written the date in red. Below is 'respectfully presented by a true believer,' 'presented' in red, the other words in gold. Well, how about it? Not a word missing! My eyesight is better! Which of you is going to treat me?"

The first cousin said, "Well, three doesn't have to pay. But I was the first to see 'Loyalty Everlasting,' so I don't have to pay either. Two must be the one to treat."

The second cousin said, "That's not fair. I made out the color, which is more than you did. You must treat. Or suppose you pay four fifths, I pay one fifth, and three pays nothing."

"No, I'm not paying."

They were shouting now, about to come to blows. Then the monk came out.

"Ha, you gentlemen are up early."

"Oh good, here is the monk."

They tugged him over to where they were.

"Your tablet is to the God of War, right?"

"That's right."

The first cousin said, "'Loyalty Everlasting,' isn't that it?"

The monk said, "Right."

Second cousin asked, "Gold characters on blue, eh?"

The monk said, "Quite right."

Third cousin said, "And this is what's written above and underneath, right?"

The monk said, "You've got it all right."

"Good, we made a bet on this, and the losers are to treat the winner. You come and join us, monk. You say who's won and who's lost.   We'll take your word for it."

The monk laughed.

"I say you three brothers must treat me, because you all lost. I'm the only winner! You three will have to treat me to a meal."

"How can you be the winner?"

"You came too early, I haven't hung the tablet yet!"

CHAPTER ELEVEN

ON ORGANIZING YOUR LIFE

Discussion Between Master Ni and Students

Student: Master Ni, how do you recommend that a person organize their life? Could you give me some guidelines?

Master Ni: This is an important question. Some information is contained in my other books, but your question gives me a good opportunity to provide a more complete answer. I will give you a sketch about how a person of Tao might organize his or her life. There are many aspects of life, so let us take them one by one.

The first category is food. You should be flexible about what you eat according to the circumstance. It is best not to be too rigid about food. People of different ages and people with different jobs need to be supported by different types of diets. For example, the body of a person who does a lot of heavy physical work would probably require some meat. Young children need more rich food, while adults usually need a diet higher in carbohydrates. Older people usually require light nutritional food. Being a spiritual person, I eat primarily fresh vegetables and fresh fruit at home. When I go on a trip or to see somebody, I adapt myself to their situation or custom, even if it is different from what I do at home. If I accept an invitation, I am polite and eat as I am served. Sometimes, if I am a guest at somebody's house and they ask me, I tell them generally what kind of food I eat. On occasion, I will decline an invitation. When you are at a restaurant or potluck, you can choose from a variety of food and apply your knowledge to eat what is best for you. The kind of food is not hard to control by your body system.

If you pay attention to your body and how it responds to the foods you eat, you will learn to give it what is best for whatever stage of life you are in. Generally, I eat good nutritious food like corn and cornbread, tofu, a variety of vegetables that are steamed or pan boiled, nuts and nut butters, beans, rice, seaweed and other ingredients. One can use a combination of grains to make a porridge which, when served with dishes of vegetables or fruit, provides good support. I do not recommend using a lot of spices, salt or sugar. Taoists also enjoy gourmet food, but only under two conditions. The first is whether your health can take it or not. For example, can you eat a lot of shrimp or oysters and still be able to maintain the balance of your sexual energy in peace? The second is your pocketbook. Can you afford to purchase such food financially? If you manage your money and find you do not have enough income, do not let your appetite enslave you, pulling you down from your balanced life. Do not let your appetite become a burden on your personality.

The second category is clothing. Taoist clothing has one important feature. It does not matter if your clothes are old or a little worn, but it is important that they be clean and not dirty. Sometimes when you travel you cannot control this, but in your daily life it is wholesome to keep clean. Avoid totally synthetic materials which suffocate the breathing that takes place through the pores of your skin. Your skin is a breathing system. Breathing only through your lungs is not sufficient for the body; you must also breathe through your head and your skin. When you buy clothing, it is helpful and practical to purchase pieces of a more classic style that can fit different occasions, rather than buying new fashions that change regularly and require a lot of money. Generally, a plain color can help you manage your mind and benefit your health, which is more important than looking good on the outside. Have your clothes fit the situation rather than attract people's attention. Also it is better to keep a little cooler when you dress than become too warm. Plus your clothing is best if it is loose and comfortable. That is the principle of dressing, which is keeping neat, clean and fitting the situation.

The third category is living. One way to discover what geographical location is most fitting for your personal living is to consult an achieved astrologer to read your birth chart. Individuals all have different nerve structures and some people do better in certain environments than others. The Taoist knowledge of geomancy, which is the study of where to live, where to sleep and where to work, can help you to gather better natural energy from the environment for your benefit. That may be too specific for today's modern living, however. So basically, it is healthful to live in a quiet place with little disturbance. Try to live in a safe place that has clean air and a climate that is comfortable for you. Always have enough space for your emotion. By this I mean try to have a little place for yourself, which can help avoid emotional friction among people in a crowded house. There was a philosopher who once said that "People are like porcupines; when they are too far away, they feel cold, but when they are too close, they bump together and feel each other's stings." Either way is an unhappy situation. My suggestion is to maintain a little distance by not being too far away or too close; enough to feel the nearness of your friends, but not close enough to cause emotional friction, quarreling or inconvenience to one other.

The fourth category is transportation. Speed makes your mind wild. It seems in modern life that we are slaves to a time schedule, always being pushed or pressured. But it is wise to take a little longer on the road and be careful driving. It is better to start a journey a little earlier by planning a little extra time, rather than rushing dangerously en route. Avoid driving fast before you rest or sleep because that accelerates your circulation too much at night.

One very important thing in life is walking. Do not let modern life deprive you of your natural right to walk. Walk as often as you can. Even if in your work you already walk enough, that is different from what I am talking about. Outside of your job, you need to choose a good quiet time and place to walk, perhaps in a forest or countryside, without any disturbance. This is a special privilege for us in modern life. We must not let modern life take away the special light of enjoying a natural life.

The fifth category is education. Living in a modern society, most people are educated in school according to the demands of society. One does not have to be a scholar, but it is important to learn basic academic capabilities like writing, calculating and so forth. After your basic education in school, continue your education by participating in lectures, seminars, workshops or classes to awaken your innate capabilities in a direction toward which you would like to develop. Also, you might like to keep reading and studying widely before you specialize in something. One problem of our time is that many people become specialists very fast, but never learn how to manage their basic everyday life. Specially directed education makes each individual into a special tool for society; but not enough education in basic life will cause individuals to be ineffective in the handling of their own life. I suggest you keep a balance. Learn the arts and skills to help you manage your own personal life, then specialize yourself for earning a living. Both sides of life are of equal importance, so do not miss one. Sometimes it is more important to learn about life in general than about one specific thing.

The sixth category is recreation. After talking about such essentials as eating, wearing clothes, living, education and transportation, we must include recreation. Human life without recreation is missing something. Work can sometimes be enjoyable, but that depends on the type of task. For example, if a person does a lot of mental work, he will find doing a handcraft to be recreation in his leisure time. Simple housework, gardening, carpentry or machinery, etc., is all recreational activity and is better than sitting in front of the TV.

Watching TV is very passive and is not really a great enjoyment because it gives you no return benefit. If you do something with your hands, some energy is always returned to your brain, comes back to your life and makes you feel good. Such activity is healthy because it does not scatter your energy. When you watch TV, energy is scattered through your eyes, which remain looking at the television screen. It is better to do something with your hands, body or feet to make you happy. Recreation contains the benefit of self-balancing. Self-balancing can help you avoid becoming too serious or stiff in your life, which can cause you trouble. People are not robots, and some recreational life has many benefits.

The seventh category is physical treatment or the category of medicine. Learn to take care of your own small troubles before you need to rely on an expert to take care of you. This is part of the knowledge of living that is not taught in school. It was traditionally taught by older people, who learned survival in life, to the younger ones. This information needs to continue to be passed from older to younger people or gathered into books and shared before it is lost. It can be used by people before they are in a situation where self-help is impossible and they need to rely on a specially trained healer or doctor.

Basically, your life is your personal responsibility. Specialists only look at a specific problem and often neglect its connections to other parts of the body. Physical troubles do not only connect with the body; they also connect with one's emotions, psychological make-up, living habits, background, societal pressures and so forth. If there is a holistic approach available, first look to those healers, because their range of treatment is wider. Sometimes we need specialists too, but they do a secondary job. Mainly, you need to take care to keep yourself in good shape, fix any small problems that you can by yourself and, if necessary, obtain help through the holistic approach to healing. If you need to be treated by an expert, ask for your trained holistic healer to recommend one to you.

The eighth category is your faith or belief. Find a broad and direct teaching that is not too radical. In this special and very important category, this guides you to shape yourself spiritually. I recommend that people carefully study what is offered by the ancient naturally developed ones who lived before the domination of religion. Open yourself to sufficient discussion about the right way of faith and how it can benefit your personal spirituality.

Besides these eight specific categories, there are some principles about how to live a good life, a natural life, available from the teachings of the integral way. There is much information and guidance you can discover in the books I have offered. Now let me talk about standards or goals of development that can help you decide how to live. You need to decide those goals and standards for your personal development.

The first is virtue. Virtue is the greatest goal of your personal development. The material demands of life today are very strong. However, material possessions are not a goal, but a means to accomplish and develop a good life; and development of a good life does not rely on only making money. This is why we put virtue and your personal development, rather than money, as the first important goal of your life. You need to develop the quality of sympathy and learn to understand the human nature of your fellow people. Through this, you discover how important it is to develop your virtue. Otherwise, you are like one beast living among a group of beasts and the significance of human developed life is lost. What is called virtue is the balance you attain in your personality by not being an extreme, radical or violent person and maintaining your sensitivity to the world's troubles. In that way you can manage your life better. This is not a religious virtue; it is a virtue of life. This is the first goal of your personal development.

The second goal is wisdom. It must be distinguished from intellect or intelligence. Through the general education we receive in school, we develop our intelligence. Intelligence is a gift of nature, but it can be developed by education. Wisdom, though, cannot be taught through the intellectual system of general school education. Once one dedicates oneself to spiritual development, wisdom can be attained. Without wisdom, there is no flower or spiritual fruit in your life. Your life is empty when it is only occupied by different material attractions or social pulls which tear you in pieces. First accomplish your virtue; second obtain your wisdom in developing yourself.

The third goal is well-being or spiritual vitality. Spiritual vitality depends on your health and general well being. Health and well-being come when all the different levels of mind, emotion and intelligence, rational thinking or behavior and your body, are attended to and maintained. Well-being does not mean having big muscles or being named "Mr. World" in a contest. The real Mr. World is you, after you have attained the well-being of your developing self. From your physical energy, nurture a higher energy called chi or vital breath. From chi, nurture an even higher energy called shen, or spiritual energy. At this point you will demonstrate balanced well-being. That is the third goal of your life.

The fourth goal is harmonious relationship or co-existence and cooperation with people. In general, we do not need to teach you to become an individual because most people, through their life experience, learn to take care of themselves. However, many people become disappointed in their relationships with others and then narrow themselves. Their suffering causes that response, because they feel the others have taken something from them. This is a less-than-healthy way of having relationships, and we can have something better. This goal of something better is called living in cooperation and harmonious coexistence. People can live together happily in different relationships with proper attitudes toward each other. Modern education and conventional religions do not talk much about how to relate with people in your family, about different relationships with your parents, sisters, brothers, sons and daughters, or about interactions with friends, teachers and students. Here I can give a little insight about individual relationships. For example, a relationship with your father and mother is one you pass through. Your life passes through theirs. It does not mean you stay with their way. When you are a child, you do not know right from wrong, but once you become an adult, use your own development to understand your father or mother as another individual needing development. Give them sympathy, but do not extend your hospitality to them if they do wrong. All people pass through other people to come into this world, so if you can offer some help, please do it. If you cannot, then continue your individual development without coming back to them to bring up old conflicts or attack them. The same is true of brothers and sisters. Each individual may be at a different stage in their growth, and good communication may require a little understanding and effort. If you can be friends, surely you should do it. If not, I think you can maintain your love and your friendliness towards them, without being blind or affected by the closeness of your relationship.

Now we come to the relationship between husband and wife, or any long term relationship between man and woman. It is naturally different than the relationship between family members, because you do not choose your father, mother, sister or brother. A husband and wife relationship is usually formalized like that in a family system. There are productive, cooperative couples and negative and conflicting couples. There is a lot of trust in a couple who cooperate and are of mutual help to each other's growth. A conflicting relationship between two individuals indicates that growth is not sufficient either from both sides or from one side. If there is too much trouble in a relationship, I think each individual should consider looking for their own separate potential for growth rather than keep an unhealthy marriage. Follow the same principle among friends, parents and siblings too. The harmony or closeness existing between individuals is a matter of each one's growth, maturity and level of development. Trouble happens when there is not enough understanding or if each have goals that lead in different directions. If it is a question of lack of understanding, communication usually can be improved. If there is trouble, do not hurry into marriage or hurry to separate or divorce. The best solution is for each person to work on improving himself or herself, not trying to get the other to yield.

The issue of human sexual relationship is not a closed book. In this area, rather than following one person's advice, each individual must find what is appropriate to manage their own life. People have different sexual needs, just like they have different dietary needs. Stiff, structured systems of regulations do not work. However, each individual needs to practice maturity in this aspect of life, especially with concern for their children's well-being, the growing problems of sexually transmitted diseases, care for their sexual partner and the effect of any relationship on their own spiritual health.

Sexual fulfillment is also a means in life, not a goal. You need to learn some knowledge and techniques for managing and fulfilling your sexuality. If you do not choose to fulfill your sexual energy through physical relationship, you can transfer it to something higher.

The same is true of emotion. Emotion is only a side effect of life, although it so strongly influences you. Most people's behavior at any time is involved with emotion.

As with sexual energy, emotional energy can be used for a higher purpose rather than in unchecked expression. Emotion can be guided, controlled, channeled, improved and fulfilled by following the four goals of life discussed above: virtue, wisdom, well-being and harmonious relationships.

Another relationship to consider is one's relationship with the majority. The majority has its own psychology. It moves politically and in other ways, and usually its movement is managed by emotional force rather than rational strength, by blind action, rather than practical action. Without correct guidance, the movement of the mob is like a jellyfish floating on the surface of the water, waiting around for any shrimp to jump over it and lead it somewhere, anywhere, though it still goes nowhere. With the mob, anything can happen. Usually somebody comes along and stirs people up to create a reaction. This can bring about difficult situations in which people are neither able to participate in creative, positive action, nor walk away. The wise ones of our tradition, when dealing with this type of situation, do not respond negatively. We find another way to help, to do something positive. For example, China has been suffering from continual revolution for over two hundred years. Not for one day has the power struggle among leaders and people stopped. In the Taoist tradition, we do not directly fight one system, but instead look for a fundamental solution to help the people and the world through each individual's and society's spiritual development. That is our direction. I also recommend a similar direction to my friends and students when they become developed individuals. We do not participate in small wars. To fight a war is not a true solution. The solution is to let all of us make an effort to reach the goal of fundamental spiritual improvement for all people.

Another relationship is between teacher and student. Any student that comes to you is somewhat like a patient in a doctor's office. If you can offer help, you should always do so. You need to specifically understand the person and give guidelines for where you will stop. Do not let one student pull you down or make you work excessively for him or her, and do not be discouraged by the failure of one case. In fact, the failure is already decided by the degree of your understanding. This means your understanding of the person will usually tell you what the result of your effort will be. No person can be saved by another, unless he or she is strong enough and open enough to work out his or her own problems.   When a student comes to a teacher, the student should not hold a psychological attitude of "I come here because I do not like my parents or my husband or my life.   I will make you take care of my emotion.   I need the sweetness that comes from you."   Most students carry their psychological needs on a subconscious level when they approach you.   You can usually quickly tell what part the person is looking for in you.   It is important to make your student understand, "You can learn.   I'm not your father, mother, sister, brother or anyone else.   I am your friend.   In the process of your growing, I am at your side to watch and help you, but I cannot grow for you."   The student can decide if he wants to use your program to work on himself by accepting your discipline.   If the student does not accept discipline and only wants you to treat him sweetly, that usually indicates stumbling in the process of growth, for there is already an obstacle in him.

In ancient times, a wise teacher accepted only a few students who had good energy and were not a bother. Today we do not think that is a good system; it is too narrow and cannot help the world much, primarily because people with good energy do not need much help.   You only enjoy friendship with someone who is intelligent, wise, kind, considerate and has lots of sympathy and friendliness to offer.   A teacher should not be afraid to take the trouble of one individual without being defeated or pulled down.   A student must understand that the teacher will not wash away his wound.   The teacher has sympathy, but he will want you to wash away your own wound.   If you tell him you are full of sexual energy and do not know what to do about it, he will tell you to have patience and learn the cultivation to transfer this kind of heavy energy into spiritual energy to benefit your life.   But he cannot do it with you or for you.   Many troubled people are not truly looking for spiritual development, but just for someone else on whom to put the problem.   Fortunately, not all students are like that.   Usually a teacher, even at the beginning, can see clearly whether or not the student can understand.

Let there be a little distance between the teacher and student so the student can grow better; being in the teacher's shadow will block his growth.   A true relationship between a teacher and a spiritual student has a sweetness to it of mutual concern and consideration.   There is nothing more valuable or sweet than spiritual development.   Depending on the development of the student, you can see the true heaven, the true love, the true god.

Balance is the main essence of success in the four goals.   The practice of attaining virtue serves the balance between the internal and external.   The practice of attaining wisdom serves the balance between your poised mind and your poised spirit.   The practice of attaining well-being serves the balance between physical and spiritual energy.   The practice of attaining harmonious relationships serves the balance between yourself and others.   The principle of balance can be better understood by studying *The Book of Changes and the Unchanging Truth*, also known as the *I Ching*.

This is merely a sketch in answer to the question of how to organize your life: not an easy question to answer.

Student: You have given these guidelines to people for how to eat, how to dress, how to live, but what about a person who has no control over these things, such as somebody who is in prison, in the army, someone who cannot leave home because they are taking care of an invalid or living in a community?

Master Ni: Most of the guidelines I have given here are for people in general circumstances and not in a specific extremity.   There are people that correspond with us who live under these conditions and who read our books.   Under these conditions any type of special cultivation may be difficult.   They should accept whatever extremity they are in and work on themselves as best they can spiritually, because internal development can still help them to grow.

It is appropriate for someone living with people who have a different eating or dressing habit to adapt to the situation they are in. If later they have freedom, they can use their development to influence the more undeveloped people. As much as possible do not follow those who are undeveloped, or allow yourself to be influenced by their mood or their society in organizing your life. Do not follow the habits of the general population. If you do, you lose everything you have learned.

Student: If something has gone wrong in your life, generally speaking, how do you fix it?

Master Ni: In any life situation such as a job, marriage, children, addiction, health, etc., if there is something wrong with you, correct it. Immediately. If something is wrong with others, you cannot correct it. If possible, you can help them understand. But generally, people are stubborn, and if they refuse to understand, do not make trouble. We call this the path of self-cultivation because we do not like to interfere with other people's growth. Instead, in our own growth, we choose that which we understand is the right thing for us to do. We do not like to influence others negatively or accept negative influence from others. We call it spiritual self-discipline because we do not need to rely on a church, society or teacher to give us discipline. In our tradition the teacher instructs us in self-discipline, which is a kind of helping system. When you are ill, who has to drink the prescribed remedy of the bitter herb tea? It is still yourself, but we encourage you to take it because it will heal your eye, stomach or whatever part needs remedying.

Student: Master Ni, will you give me some instruction on how to organize my spiritual life?

Master Ni: This is a big subject.   I must not have done enough in my work recorded in all these fourteen books.   I would still like to give you an answer.

Of all good behavior, filial duty is the most important.   This is not because a person must carry his parents with him, but he should not disgrace them by foolish or radical behavior.   Being a person of upright behavior, he can achieve greatness by his outstanding characteristics.

Of all bad behavior, promiscuous sexual activity, using drugs and alcohol, and violent actions are the most self-destructive.   When a person does not respect his life and does things out of impulse and destruction, he ends up by refusing no evil.   This destroys his personal virtue, causing him to lose his life unnaturally.

Nothing in the universe is static and no force is everlasting.   No one can always depend on position, money or social connections.   No blessing can always be enjoyed to its fullness.   No poor person will be forever poor.   No rich person will be forever rich.   This is the subtle cycle that keeps turning around.   At some time you will be on the top of the cycle and at another time you will be at the lower part of the cycle.

When you behave nicely, even if a blessing is not received, you move far away from trouble.   When you behave badly, trouble may not be seen, but blessing moves further from you.   One of virtuous behavior, like grass in the springtime, grows daily, even though its advance is not seen.   One of evil behavior, like the mill stone, decreases daily, even though its erosion may not seen.   Thus, it is not wise to harm another in order to profit oneself.

Your intelligent quality is because your parents have lived a simple healthy life.   You can preserve this intelligent quality by living a simple and pure life of your own.   Thus you see the value of a simple and healthy life.

Your time on this earth is like an oil lamp.   Excitement is the flame and your life is the oil.   The more excitement, the faster the oil is exhausted.   Which would you prefer, to enjoy quickly or to enjoy longer?

The spiritual enjoyment of a person is like having the light with a connection to the great source. It shall never be exhausted.

If you have helped people, do not expect repayment. If somebody has wronged you, forgive them. In so doing, you give yourself freedom.

If you are faced with someone or something you cannot tolerate, by utilizing your strength, increase your tolerance. If you are faced with someone or something you cannot endure, with great strength, increase your patience. By doing this, you win the crown of triumph for yourself, and nothing can defeat you.

When people attack you maliciously, you may protect yourself; tolerate the person who causes you such trouble. When people humiliate you, you may defend yourself; you may also transform it into encouragement to do better. When an arrogant person is overbearing, again you would be wise to tolerate them. By facing these circumstances, your capacity for dignity is deepened.

Diligence is invaluable. Prudence is protection.

In an attempt to accomplish what has not yet been attained, sometimes it is better to be conservative and be content with what you already have. Repent and correct your mistakes of the past to prevent mistakes of the future.

Do not make friends with untrustworthy people. Take nothing unrighteously. Give forth no evil ideas, and speak nothing that is not upright.

Have no worry by being prudent. Have no humiliation by being tolerant. Have peace by being peaceful. Have happiness by self-contentment. Never be vexing by being greedy. One is happy who knows when he has enough, even if he is not well off. Similarly, one who is unhappy does not know when he has enough, even if he is well off. One who knows he has enough will suffer no humiliation or defeat. He stays in peace by knowing when to stop; thus, he is saved from disgrace.

In spiritual discipline, always look at someone who does better than you do, so you will motivate yourself to go forward. In day-to-day living, look at those who are not doing better than you, so you will have no resentment.

Those who pass by occasions to debase or humiliate others are bright. Those who forgive themselves are not foolish. The brilliance of the wise one is that he corrects himself and others. The wise one's kindness forgives himself and others.

It is better to be poor and peaceful than rich and worried. It is better to eat ordinary food and maintain one's health than to become sick and buy expensive medicine.

Student: Master Ni, I am a family man. I have two children. I do well in my profession of investments. You have mentioned that a parent should be a good example to his children. I myself lost my father at age eleven. My mother was a simple country woman who could not support all of us, so I grew up earning a living from gas stations and garages. I am vague about the example I should give my children.

Master Ni: You have achieved a great deal. I would like to give you instruction on the general discipline of a good family life. This is what I often heard from my elders and parents. They followed these simple rules for living a family life that were passed down from generation to generation:

A family is founded by a couple who decide to devote their life to each other. The man and woman are supportive of each other but have different capabilities. From this foundation, the man and the woman equally share responsibility in building a lovable family life. The authority over family matters is love, responsibility and good reason. Above all, mutual understanding is the best measurement for each side. Generally, the man is the leader of the physical well-being of the family, and the woman is the spiritual leader of the family. It can be vice versa, or one can do both, as long as there is sincere love and care. In daily family life, the man and woman take turns, each taking charge of matters that he or she is good at. Without the above formation and attitudes, family spirit is damaged. Thus, there is no second page of this book.

To be a good individual who lives a creative life, or a good disciplined family member, rise early, exercise and clean indoors and out. Go to bed early. Close the doors of the house and inspect them to be sure to make everything all right before going to sleep. Though some people are night owls, this is a healthy schedule. Do not waste food or any useful material; keep in mind that it is people's labor that brought it to you. Be prepared for all situations; do not wait until you are thirsty to dig a well. Be frugal; do not be overly luxurious in treating friends. Let your furniture and other tools be of good quality and keep them clean. It does not matter if they are expensive or not; practicality is the first consideration. Eat simple, healthy food. Cultivate enjoying the taste of vegetables rather than special gourmet food. Do not eat much meat of animals and birds. Drink no more than that which will maintain your sobriety. Neither a house of grandeur nor a kingdom of land is needed. Keep no company with immoral people. Mixing with undisciplined people will burden you. Keep no servants, thinking it is one of your blessings, but treat necessary helpers well. Do not encourage your daughters or wife to use cosmetics. Respect the universal divine nature. Support your children's education, even if they are not smart. Keep your self in good order. Train the young ones with moral discipline. Do not be greedy for a sudden fortune. Do not take advantage of small business people. Have sympathy with those who do poorly. You will not enjoy life long if you are cruel. Respect ethics among all people or you will be in trouble. Help your family or people. Establish discipline among all members of a family. It is not a wise habit to listen to one person only.

You do not set a good example by disrespecting your own parents. Do not use your daughter as your property. Do not make your son marry for money or position. It is humiliating to flatter the well-off. It is debasing to be proud over the poor. Avoid litigation with anyone; it is always troublesome. Do not be opinionated; there is fault in too much talking. Do not press the lonely and the weak. A self-righteous person has usually made many mistakes. One can accomplish nothing by being satisfied with disappointments. A cautious person is the most dependable one in an emergency.

Do not be sure somebody's words are reliable without examining them objectively. It may be necessary to think them over again before a response is made. When arguing, be open to the possibility of your own mistake. Think carefully and talk slowly. Do not hold the thought of having done a favor for someone, but remember when someone has helped you. Give people some room and do not force them too much. Do not be jealous of people who achieve. Do not rejoice when others have troubles. If you do something with the motive that others find out about it, it is not truly a good deed. If you do something which you must hide from others, it is truly evil, unless it is a noble deed. Chasing after beauty invites trouble in the long run. Secret revenge causes misfortune. Having peace in a family is greater happiness than wealth. Pay your taxes to make yourself feel free, even if you leave no money for yourself. Be very loyal to the people of your country when you are in public office. Be joyful within your means. To straighten your goal in life is the fulfillment of spiritual development. Be harmonious with the Tao and obey the heavenly law. Whoever behaves in this way is truly wise.

CHAPTER TWELVE

YOUR THOUGHT SPEAKS
LOUDER THAN THUNDER

In our everyday self-cultivation, we reassemble ourselves with fresh qualities of life in order to attain fitness of body, mind and spirit. Balance is impossible without maintaining our fitness. However, there is something that cannot be disassembled and reassembled. It is your spiritual unity; do not surrender to discouraging dramas of material and semi-material phenomena in life. Reincarnation in this world is still a life of partial experience; only a life that attains Tao is complete. The life that has attained Tao is a complete life with the complete experience of all lives and all times.

In our everyday spiritual self-cultivation, we reassemble ourselves freshly with respect to the quality of the spirit of life, in order to attain fitness of body, mind and spirit. This is how we attain a new quality or new element for strengthening our life being. We cannot afford to do harmful things because they become evident in our physical health. Take, for example, the development of a new bad habit, such as overeating, overdrinking or overdoing something; it might immediately cause you to experience physical suffering. When you suffer physically, your mind and your spirit suffer as well and this thing will have affected your entire life being. The same is true in talking about fitness of mind. Some people are too emotional and do not see that they need to maintain a good healthy mind to live a good healthy life. Hesitation, procrastination, skepticism, jealousy, aggressiveness, hatred and prejudice can all prevent your mind from being fit. If your mind is not fit, you undermine your life being by these unhealthy mental qualities.

Various mental qualities such as unfaithfulness, disloyalty, unrighteousness and immorality sometimes connect with the mental level and sometimes connect with the spiritual level. Then the fitness of your life in society or the environment may become weakened or wrecked and this might cause your life or your soul to be taken. Some people die physically before their soul leaves the body. Some people's soul is already taken before their death. Individuals suffer for different reasons, but mostly from their own actions.

The way any person is treated is usually consistent with the attitude with which they live in the world. An achieved person meets trouble, excitement or lack of interest just the same as anyone else. However uninteresting, exciting or ruthless the treatment you receive may be, it is totally the same as others receive. What makes the difference is your objective feeling about your life, which causes a response that demonstrates your mental, physical and spiritual quality in worldly life. For example, we go outside. For someone who is unprepared, if it suddenly rains, it could be a bad day. But for someone whose spirit is good, whose mind is fresh and whose body is strong, he does not care about the rain and it does not affect him. It is the same rain, but it might cause a person who is not in good physical or mental condition to complain; then they become gloomy and cloudy themselves. They suffer more than the person who has a healthy mind, body and spirit. This illustrates that the way the world treats you is not just a matter of the condition of the world, it is also a matter of your personal fitness. Without fitness, personal balance is impossible.

Yet above all, there is something that cannot be disassembled when your life is finished. So why should you resign yourself to the discouraging drama or scenes of any situation? Some people who are young and ignorant do many bad things. A long time ago, if caught they would be shot in public, and sometimes the offender would say, "It does not matter. In eighteen years, I will be born into a fleshly life again."

However, the truth is that it does not matter if you are born into the world again. What matters is whether or not you make an improvement in your life condition after you are born. Reincarnation is only a partial expression of life; mostly it is an opportunity to demonstrate your personal capability to master a situation.

Only a life that attains Tao is complete. A complete life is lived by one who can extend his spiritual power to experience universal life, the unlimited universal life, in our time. For example, every morning you get up, dress yourself and start your life activities. A day passes. In the evening, you undress yourself and go to bed; the day is finished. The question is not the day's activities under the sunshine. One question is, when you dress yourself, are you fit for the day's weather condition and the activities you are going to do? Do you forget the things you need for the day's work? The other question is, in the evening when you undress yourself, can you undress all your problems before you go to bed? When we come into fleshly life, we dress ourselves; worldly life is like clothing. Some people dress themselves with a healthy body, healthy mind and healthy spirit, which is called being completely equipped. Some people dress unfittingly, with a weak physical body, poor mind and low spirit.

Life is natural and has different cycles, some long and some short. Earthly life has day and night because of its rotation and sunshine; this can be a metaphor for your life and death. Your soul in daytime is active; you do many things. When it comes time to undress yourself, you go to sleep and rest. In the evening, active life must cease and rest; but if you have done anything wrong, your soul will suffer. When you undress your fleshly body, all the trouble you have made, especially from your bad mental, physical or spiritual qualities, will hang on your soul. How can your soul have peace? Life and death occur only to the body, which is a covering for the soul. In daytime, the soul enters the mind and is active. At night it goes to the lower body area, without 'good' or 'bad' activity.   Generally, people open their eyes only to look for something that benefits themselves without watching to see if they are doing something that is also fair to others.   Spiritual and mental damage occurs, whether it is a big bad thing or a small bad thing. The earnest quality of your mind is lost and the good quality and health of your soul is damaged by what you do, constantly, day after day, month after month. It is by accumulation that you damage your soul and put yourself in a stage where your soul needs repair; you are terribly sick and you are not, therefore, a healthy soul.   Then you are sent to a hospital for your soul, but you are not sure whether your soul can be repaired or not.

A healthy soul does all good things in a lifetime. Everyday, he or she accumulates good deeds, not in exchange for social honor or anything like that.   Good deeds bring brightness to your soul by increasing the quality of your mind and the healthy element of your life being, so the day you undress your fleshly life, your soul is light.   Your mind does not conflict with your soul.   You do not have an internal battle, so your life is light, and your life energy ascends.   It does not sink to a soul hospital for repair or to be recycled onto a different level.

Modern people are over-active mentally in their lives.   They do not have a chance to look for the spiritual reality of what they do.   They look nearsightedly for the benefit of the moment without knowing how it will cause them to suffer spiritually and mentally.   I use the term "spiritual evolution"; when we arrive into this life we have an opportunity to be creative, to learn new things, to improve our soul and our mind, which supports our soul.   We can also improve our health condition which supports our mind and emotions.

In positive and virtuous living every day, we may still suffer the same treatment as other people, but we earn a spiritual profit.   People are always looking for material profit; and indeed, we do need material gain to support our physical life, but a developed person looks at profit not only materially.   He also looks for mental and spiritual balance. Some day, or even now, you might make a lot of money. Consider whether or not it is healthy money that benefits your spirit, too. If the money helps your three levels so that you enjoy a healthy life-being, then surely pursue it. But if the material gain pulls your mind down and damages your soul, should you do it? I do not think a spiritual person would do it, because it is not a whole profit; it only benefits a partial level of life, while doing much harm to a more subtle and more important level. So it is best not done. For example, many people looking for power or political positions compete for leadership. It does not necessarily mean the position is enjoyable; it may just serve their emotional fantasy or swell their ego. In reality, it may damage their soul or hurt their mind, because in the process of gaining the position, they might do something unrighteous. If such a position comes to you, gain the position out of a moral sense, with the natural honor and natural glory of your life. Do not earn it by doing something that hurts your mind, pulls down your soul and damages your spirit. If you gain a position by evil struggling, doing things that damage others, or causing them to suffer for your personal gain, it is not worth it, because you damage yourself in the invisible sphere more than you gain in the visible sphere.

We come to worldly life for evolution. We should allow ourselves to maintain only positiveness every day, and not necessarily look for special performance in exhibiting our specially achieved morality or virtue. We remain our best selves everyday, continually adding to our health with physical, mental and, especially, spiritual fitness. If you can do this, your life and especially your soul will greatly benefit and suffer no death. If a person is well balanced in these three spheres, in a lifetime he might not be as famous, rich or powerful as someone in a social position, but he will already be enjoying the fruit of his own wisdom. He is already heaven. A person who is very rich or in a high or famous position might lose his balance for external gain, and in reality, suffer greatly for the imbalance he creates.

This is important for modern people who have busy lives and who have not taken the time to look deeply into the other more hidden spheres beyond the physical, which can be seen.   Mentally, they do things to undermine themselves or their health, and consequently they suffer.

Student: There are people whose behavior, for the most part, is good and appropriate.   They do not try to undermine other people, but yet seem to have a lot of trouble in their own life and cannot attain the stability, clarity and well-being they are looking for.

Master Ni: These people are superficially nice and superficially accommodate the conditions of their lives without attaining the important positive qualities that support mental and spiritual fitness.   Physically they seem healthy and capable and receive pay that is equal to other people whose lives have better qualities. They live a general, standard life, no more or less than others, but they do not enjoy life, because of a lack of mental fitness.   That is what is missing from their behavior.   It connects with self-cultivation.   Everything comes back to being spiritually responsible.   We need spiritual cultivation to enable us to continue our positive spiritual evolution and make positive spiritual progress.   In this way there is spiritual leadership, and mind and body follow.   We then can live as heavenly beings with a natural organic being as the standard of our lives.

Student: Since it is so important, would you speak about how a person attains mental fitness?

Master Ni: You always need to check things out. For example, sometimes you may feel poorly; immediately you need to check out why this is so. There are many reasons for feeling badly (and we are just talking about the feeling level; we would like to separate it from the emotional level). Maybe you feel badly because somebody said something to you that was not polite or proper. Then you establish an attitude of resistance, or you take what someone said seriously without checking to see if it was your fault. If the fault is yours, you might write it down and remember that what was said was appropriate, and you should accept it. If the fault is yours, you should correct it. Once you correct the situation, you do not allow yourself to act in the same way again. Do not allow your pride to get in the way of apologizing to another person, so your mental fitness is not disturbed. If you are selfish and only follow your emotional indulgence by taking the direction you habitually like, without consideration for others, in the long run it will make your emotions too strong. You will become aggressive and not care what people say. Over time, you become spiritually and mentally weakened and then you become unfit.

Physical health is apparent and easy to see. Mental and spiritual health are just like physical health: you attain them by establishing a good routine for your everyday life, including discipline and exercise, and by not doing anything disordered. Mental unfitness makes you suffer from small things. Your mind may be happy if you check it out and say, "I didn't do anything wrong." People say that habitually out of their spiritual undevelopment or ignorance after becoming aggressive because of jealousy or other emotion. I do not take responsibility for anyone else; only for myself! So my mind is not damaged by that; my spirit is not damaged. If someone is healthy and physically aggressive, he does many things wrong, when he grows old he will become sick; for his spiritual condition has become weakened. In that time, he will be visited by all the ghosts of bad memories of when he made people suffer. Before, it was what he enjoyed; now these scenes return again, like a punishment, like a spiritual accusation. When a dying person remains in his bed for many days, each few seconds brings back another scene of bad treatment. At the moment he finishes seeing all these bad scenes, he knows one thing: at his death he will go to hell. It is a sad death. Naturally people become old before death. Some show sickness, but some do not; for some the memory system is just the opposite, showing them scenes of the good things they have done, one by one, to remind them of the gratitude and appreciation of their good record in the spiritual world. They will smile, knowing there is no problem with their soul, that it will ascend to heaven. They do not need any priest to come. Generally, people do not pay attention about whether they are doing anything good or bad, if they are being overly strong or hurting other people. But by accumulation, your mental health and spiritual health are affected. All things are recorded in your own brain. The natural equipment within you, when you come into life, records your good and bad doings. Then, at your death, it is all shown over again, and you will know where you are to go. When you see the good things, you become happy because, for instance, you did not perform any extreme or outrageous action toward a person who once hurt you. You proved you are spiritually strong. This is the evidence which proves you will ascend. How beautiful it is that even though in your life you may have suffered unfair treatment by your family, your friends, the world or whomever, that you gained the strength of your soul. Each good deed adds to the strength of your spiritual wings so that you can ascend.

The problem is that we are all confused when external religious teaching collapses. In reality, the truth is in our life, not in external teaching. We could be equipped with a poor mind, or a poor physical condition, but that is not what is important relative to your soul. We could be born into a troublesome, turbulent world environment, but if we are equipped with a good soul, we learn how to pass over the troubles. Make each moment of your life a new dose of tonic to strengthen your soul. It is not a pity to be a good person and suffer; it is a pity to be a bad person and enjoy, because you relinquish the opportunity to revise or rewrite the script of your soul's destiny.   In the learning of Tao, we know our life is a small model of the universe.   It is a given potential, like a rich father who gives $500 or $1000 to each of his sons to see how wisely they spend the money.   Some go out and use the money for a profitable return.   Some use the money for unhealthy enjoyment and then suffer for it; they come back.   Some give away all their money to help somebody else.   Which is right and which is wrong? It is evident that they enjoy or suffer because of what they do, but not just because they have come back to the old father to be judged; a person is already rewarded or suffers in each moment depending upon how he spends the life energy provided by nature when he is a life being.

In trying to attain mental fitness to nurture the soul, one may feel rather like a person on a raft lost in the middle of an ocean, trying to reach land.   You may not remember what land is like, or perhaps you have never even seen it before.   One feels as though there is no map or no directions to find the way out to land, so one keeps drifting in circles, without a sense of purpose.   There is no shore which you have full knowledge of.   The true "land" is how you live each moment.   You will find it by what you do that is positive and of service to yourself and others.   Each moment of positively virtuous life is the inner direction and support which is available to a drifting raft in the rushing, narrow current of a ravine or on the endless ocean.

Student: Where does the soul live in the body?

Master Ni: I have previously described that through a very scientific manner of practice, you can be led to arrive at a stage of development that enables you to know the spiritual agent of your body and the spiritual agent of your mind.   Psychologists call it the "higher self."   That which is able to know is the main soul. The soul is associated with mental elements, spiritual entities and physical spiritual entities. It is the captain of the life boat. But aside from one's individual life-being, there exist two possibilities of living with other souls. A healthy individual life may be supported by the developed souls of ancestors, especially developed teachers or good natural spiritual beings; or it is possible that another bad person's soul can live within one's brain or body. This morning, I met a young American girl around eighteen years old who had previously attempted suicide. Her father was an East Indian who died from alcoholism, having suffered from emotion or disappointment in his life. Now his grown daughter is naturally visited by the ghost of the father, who wished to help her, but because of her intense emotional problems and because her energy was not refined yet, she could not receive the message correctly. She responded in a confused manner to his help, attempting to kill herself instead of growing healthily. This was the cause of the internal spiritual conflict within the young daughter.

Another similar event happened when I was a young spiritual teacher. Spiritually and philosophically, I was well-educated by my mother, father and teachers. Although I had heard many ghost stories and had seen some people do channeling, I did not have the spiritual power to see them, nor had I searched out any ghosts, so I did not think there was any truth or value in these stories until this personal experience occurred.

One year I met a man, who was around forty years old, who had come to Taiwan at the age of sixteen and later was a soldier in the army. He used to go to a small village store run by a woman who had adopted a daughter. The woman's father had been a religious Taoist, performing rituals for peoples' births and deaths to earn his living. (This is not the type of Taoist that I am.) The woman, who had no son, showed much affection for the young man. She made him leave the army and marry her daughter. Shortly after that, she died. The young man slowly became friends with a member of a gang. Gangs usually have their fun in groups of people. Being without money, they find ways to obtain it from business people and use it for gambling, wine or women. They frequently compete and participate in fights, using knives to kill people. This young man made friends with this type of person and participated in the gang.

At this time, his spiritual mother-in-law and grandfather-in-law, both of whom had already passed on, became nervous. The old man's inheritance had gone to the young man, who expressed himself generously among his friends in the dark society. He earned respect by his bravery in doing bad things. However, after several years this young man started to become sick. It was interesting to see that this sickness manifested itself in no special physical problem, but his nervous system began to break down. He went to see all kinds of doctors and spent lots of money. He no longer had time to be a gangster, but only to see doctors; he spent the rest of his inherited money on them. Generally, people who are physically strong have a nervous system that is also strong and they cannot communicate with spiritual beings, especially ghosts. It took about twelve years of not sleeping at night for him to suffer such weakness. When he stood up, he became dizzy, and he also suffered some deafness and spells of vomiting. At the end of the twelve years, he felt a ghost-being push him to rise early to do some Chinese martial arts. He was guided to do this, and because he heard my name from some of my students, who were schoolteachers in the village, he came to me and asked to be a student.

He was about forty when he came to me. I became alert because of my spiritual energy and the knowledge that he was from the black society. He came to me because he suffered from a ghost problem which he did not understand. Spiritual teachers usually have great sympathy, and, especially since I was a young teacher with more guts than wisdom, I halfway accepted. Usually I only accept people who are educated as my students, although there are also people who are spiritually strong among those who are not intellectual.

People who are more intellectual are more connected to me because sometimes I offer profound spiritual teachings which cannot be handled by someone not having any additional education. In my practice of Chinese medicine, my attitudes are different from the doctor in the West. My door is open only by special recommendation to those who beg me to treat them. If the treatment is not successful, they need to be treated by an ordinary doctor.

So my door was closed, but he knocked and I accepted him in. I had just finished meditation when he came in and sat down. He somewhat troubled me and I thought about why he had come since there was no one who had recommended him. I needed to make him reveal what spirit was inside him and, because I had learned some special practices, I went ahead with them. He suddenly changed into another person and started crying. I asked him, "Who or what are you? Why are you crying?" The ghost then told me, "I am the mother-in-law of this young man. Because I do not have a son of my own, I adopted him and took him into my house, treating him well. It could be that I spoiled him. If he asked me for money, I gave it to him. If he did anything bad, I never said anything. He grew careless and became a gangster. After that, I saw what I had done and suffered for it. My soul has never received peace." She went on to say, "I invited my ghost friend to attack his brain every night so that he could not sleep. It took twelve years to weaken his nervous system, so he could feel the ghost at his side making him get up to do the movements. The purpose of doing that was not to make trouble for him. I wished to help him out of my love and pain to awaken him from his wrongdoing. He is strong, tall and speaks well, but someone with these good qualities should not serve as the leader of a gang. These capabilities should be used for something better in life."

She was concerned, so this is why she constantly made trouble. The purpose of her causing trouble was to save him from his bad actions. She told me the truth, and she also told me that her father was Taoist.

She was interested in what kind of a Taoist he was, so I gave her a few minutes to invite him over for a talk. The woman's spirit went out and, after a few minutes, the man's ghost came in to talk. Surely because I helped him he gave me many blessings.

At that moment, I knew a mind can be affected by ghosts. Your health can also be affected. However, I am still not totally open to accept students who are halfway in the world of bright and halfway in the world of dark. Even though he told me about his past, I was still cautious about his old habits. Because of his past moral condition, I did not totally accept him, so as a young teacher, I established a kind of preference. I appreciated the young students who came from college and did not pay too much attention to the one from bad society. This was felt by him, and he once had the opportunity to create a subtle riot among my students. At that time I was young and thought perhaps it was my emotional treatment of the student that was not fair and caused the trouble. One interesting thing happened. He had already stopped collecting money from the gambling house, but one day, for no reason other than habit, he went to that place. A policeman there and some other gangsters gave him a bad beating, and he was jailed for a day. I understood that this was brought about by his spiritual guardians in order to discipline him. So it has been my experience that spirits actually can cause considerable trouble for human people.

In our daily life, most people do not really do anything too bad. However, our knowledge is limited. We think perhaps people do not know about the things we do, but in the spiritual world your thoughts are louder than thunder. The spiritual world knows totally. You have the guts to do wrong things only because you think nobody knows what you are doing, but all the tiny spirits are watching you. Whether you are a good person or bad person is already marked on your forehead. It starts from your thoughts. By your thoughts you might attract evil spirits; you can also attract good spirits.   Never think you are doing something that nobody knows, such as going into the kitchen to eat something your mother does not allow you to eat.   Do not think your mother does not know.   Your body already knows the bad things you do to yourself.

People dare to do bad things because they believe that nobody knows.   If they were spiritually sensitive enough to know that even their small thoughts are loud as thunderclaps, they would not dare do anything bad.   Unfortunately, the spiritually developed person becomes too good or too nice and stands away from the world.   Most people without spiritual sensitivity do whatever they think will not get them caught by a policeman, or be seen by their neighbors or leave no evidence.   If they grow their spiritual sensitivity just a little bit more, they will know that they are watched all the time.   In the worldly legal system you are only punished for the result of actual behavior, but on the spiritual level you are punished by gathering bad energy as a result of your motivations and small thoughts. That is very important.   I have a thousand stories giving proof that I could tell you, but I am not a good storyteller.   I like to teach people to be spiritually responsible and develop to attain their natural spiritual health and be aware of the natural environment, especially the spiritual environment, where you are watched all the time.   Spiritual cultivation will help you; when your thoughts are negative, it is a spiritual sign. Whether you can still be helped or saved can be seen. So if there is a thing you should do, do a good thing although you may not see the reward today.   If you do a bad thing or think a bad thought, you may not be punished this moment; but you should direct your footsteps in a different direction.

People who move on the path of life, both forward and backward, go nowhere and do not attain spiritual progress because they are not totally aware of the progress that can be attained by reaching positively and virtuously for the light.   Many people make a little step forward but retreat three steps back.   This is one of the reasons why the world's spiritual condition is moving so slowly. Fortunately, in the range of living, most things are not involved with the internal sense of being moral or immoral, good or bad, but mostly affect yourself. So, in terms of health, this is more significant than real punishment and reward, but be aware that reward and punishment are seen in your own spiritual life-being. This is why I like to give this knowledge to my most beloved trustworthy friends and students. I like to see them make spiritual progress and not struggle in the pitfalls of emotion, ignorance and spiritual darkness. Once a person is benefitted by the truthful facts I give, I will say it is the accomplishment of my personal spiritual nature.

II

Student: You say the most important thing is to have a good soul. How can I tell if I have a good or a bad soul?

Master Ni: Everybody has a good soul. It can be made bad, which becomes observable in a person's eyes: whether the pupil is centered with gentleness or deceptiveness. It does not depend upon the kind of family into which a child is born but upon the growth of the child: one has good discipline, the other does not. The children who do not take drugs or alcohol, sleep late or do bad things, all have very clear and lucid eyes. The others all have murky and unclear eyes. One knows whether water from a well is good or not by how clear it is. If it is clear, then we use it. If the water is murky, we do not drink it, nor do smart birds.

So the eye gives away the secret of whether someone's soul is good or bad, healthy or sick. People with good souls do sometimes have problems of a physical nature associated with their eyes, so do not judge anyone or yourself wrongly by it; that is merely a physical problem. A thief may have vision as sharp as an eagle, but he does not necessarily have a good soul. Also, when your mind is shaken or shifted too much, the instability of your eyes will express your lack of spiritual peace.   One's physical condition is usually expressed in the eyes; by looking in the eyes, one can know whether one has a healthy body or not.   It is much easier to look into the eyes to determine whether one has a good or bad soul because the eyes do not lie.

Do not go around judging other people's souls, unless you are selecting a marriage partner, a business partner or a good friend.   It is easy to tell whether someone has a good or bad soul from their behavior, habits, words and expressions.   Even though a soul is enveloped by a fleshly body, it still gives out the secret of a person's personality characteristics and whether they do good deeds or are aggressive and untrustworthy.   It is important to be a person of spiritual cultivation because your everyday handling of life takes care of your personal soul.   You learn unconsciously and your spiritual energy grows so you can then know about the soul of another person.   In early China, the skills of face reading, body reading, voice reading and feeling the head bone were developed as special forms of knowledge for assessing the potential of a person, which was associated mainly with the person's energy.

There are three ways in which a soul takes a fleshly body.   The first way is the concordance of the soul and the form: a good soul takes a form with a good appearance and a bad soul takes a form with a bad appearance.   The second is the dissonance of the soul and the form, where a good soul takes a form with a poor physical shape or incomplete unfoldment in order to develop the goodness and trueness of the soul.   The third is an evil scheme from an evil source, wherein a bad soul wears a healthy body and a good physical appearance.

A good spirit cannot be judged by appearance.   A person may look unattractive but still have a good spirit.   If a person is homely or suffers from physical stress, one can read his aura to see if it is harmonious and good and thus decide if that person has good spiritual health.   Personal spirit is the result of a soul developed in a good or bad way.

Spiritual cultivation enhances the goodness of your soul.   It is like cultivating good soil in agriculture. You take good soil and then, through your living experiences and life circumstances, your life-tree can grow fruitfully.   When a good soul comes into the world, that person's life is generally pretty well balanced and there is some potential for ascending further in their personal spiritual evolution.

You may wonder why some people have a very good material life even though they may use an evil approach to obtain some things to feed their psychological emptiness.   Those people enjoy a temporary excitement.   A thief who occupies a big castle is excited and enjoys everything, but that is only temporary glory unworthy of admiration, because the thief is not a real master.   A real lord needs long cultivation to gain people's trust and faith, then he builds on this trust to form a community or society.   Military success cannot be trusted as true spiritual success; it takes a totally different direction.   People who do not learn spiritual truth look for shortcuts to become successful.   People who learn spiritual truth do not take shortcuts.   For example, let's say you find a briefcase full of money and gold.   While you might be tempted to take the briefcase full of money or gold for your enjoyment, you know spiritual truth and thus you do not take the money.   You do not take shortcuts to becoming rich. You wait for the owners to return for it or take it to the proper authorities.

Student: I think I know somebody who has a bad soul. When you look into his eyes, something does not feel right.

Master Ni: Over ten years ago, I taught an evening tai chi class in the square of a town with beautiful trees and a quiet setting. Many students came to learn. I taught there about six months. One day, a local government leader brought his son to learn tai chi from me. Tai chi classes are open to whomever signs up for them. He was a handsome young boy about sixteen years old and had nothing wrong with his face or body, but he would not look at me directly. I tried talking to him many times, but he always averted his eyes from mine. I was very busy teaching and he did not give me much time to study him, nor did he continue the classes. Not long after, I read in the newspaper that he was arrested for raping a middle-aged woman, and many other women, many times, and now he was finally caught. When people do bad things, their minds say they are doing well or being smart, but their souls are against it. A soul, unless it has been morally weakened, does not normally avoid facing righteous energy from another's eyes. Generally, the mind of such a morally weak person will refuse or evade help from spiritual teaching. Then the soul is further hurt or damaged by what the mind does. The conflict is, thus, steadily worsened in such an individual's life being.

Student: If my soul is all right, more than just thinking about going to heaven or hell when I die, I am interested in attaining Tao while I am still alive.

Master Ni: While you are still alive, you have a brain, a mind. You can learn something that can reorganize your soul. Once you die, your soul is without the support of the fleshly body and loses the potential to be creative and learn in order to improve and correct itself. Obtaining a good fruit depends upon the tree from which it originates. Even among several different trees of the same variety in a garden, some do better by gathering more sunshine and more moisture and so they grow better than others. Among different apples on the same tree, some will do better than others, too.

Your life is like a tree, a kind of tree that during your whole lifetime will grow only one fruit. Your life being is the tree. What happens depends first on whether it is a good tree or a bad tree. The tree of your being is different than an ordinary tree, because yours can move. An ordinary tree is rooted on the bottom while a human tree has its root at the head.

The root of your life tree is in heaven and not on earth, so you can move around everywhere. The nutrition for an ordinary tree is moisture, the earth's chemicals, good sunshine, soft breezes and sufficient rain; then the tree will give you good fruit. For the good growth of human life, trees which can move, the nutrition is both in what they do and what they ingest, especially the subtle intaking through the life tree's nervous system, which develops into an absorbing organ on both a knowable and an unknowable level. This system of your life being can be controlled by following correct spiritual guidance. In general, on the knowable level of a life being, the most important thing is what they do and how they form themselves by their mind and their sub-conscious mind. One may think that there is no significance in what one gathers, but everything becomes a fact that affects the growth of the soul.

So in your question you tell me that when you die, you have no worry; that is because you are a good soul and you have not done anything bad. Objectively speaking, the soul is like the fruit of the human life tree. When you die, it is cut off from the tree. The human tree, in its whole life, only grows one fruit. Once you separate the fruit from the tree, the soul from the body, the body is also finished. The fruit develops from your real life experience. The person who moves and does things has a mind. The mind nurses the soul. If the mind is twisted or bad, then the soul suffers. The same is true on an emotional level; if a person has bad emotions, he mistreats his physical body with them. Later, his physical body releases the poison that these emotions have brewed inside, perhaps in the form of cancer. Spiritually, one is more affected by the mental than the emotional, and what your mind projects goes back to the soul. Everything from your body and mind comes back to your soul internally, such as hating or cursing or killing people; what you do always affects your fruit. Your life naturally endows you with the opportunity to grow a good soul, but when the soul is separated from the body, there is no further growth. The fruit is picked, cut off from the root. Therefore, while you are alive, you should do your best to cause no regret for your conscience.

You come with a pure soul, and you can increase the spiritual power of your main soul before you leave. The potency of the energy you have developed through your life experience increases the freedom of your soul. This is why spiritual cultivation is important. Spiritual cultivation is sometimes narrowly interpreted, but it means that if you really follow spiritual law, what you say and do is your spiritual cultivation. If you do not watch yourself, if you follow your emotions, appetites or desires, ambition and so forth, then you are only supporting your emotional life and not following spiritual law or practicing spiritual cultivation. You are the tool of your emotions or you are the tool of your desires or you are the tool of fashion. It is important for you to attain more spiritual energy so you can see where the thoughts and ideas come from that determine what you are doing. Ask yourself, why do you need to do something? The only purpose of a spiritual person's life is to grow a good soul. If you have a good soul when you came to this life, cultivate it and increase the potency, freedom and happiness of your soul. Let none of your behavior create any regret for the future.

Student: On the matter of good and bad, it seems to me that many decisions are not clear cut cases of good and bad. Sometimes things that I believe to be good have a "bad" effect on others. This was the case when I was small; if I did something good for my mother, my father got upset and vice versa. Is it that things are either good or bad, which seems simplistic, or that each action has both good and bad parts to it and one must learn to maximize the good and responsibly take care of the bad? For example, by paying attention to timing, or trying to understand the effects your decision will have on all concerned.

Master Ni: I understand the difficulty of your childhood.   Your behavior always needed to be looked at.
Do I please my mother, do I please my father?   If you
please your father, you must upset your mother and
vice versa.   This gave you a very hard time. I think
that this stage should be over for you.   Do not let that
dependency continue, because at that time you were
young and did not have good judgment.   You relied
on pleasing your mom or dad to decide which behavior was good.   You trusted their decisions, but their
decisions did not necessarily stem from deep thought.
Their judgment did not necessarily come from their
spiritual development.   They lived on an emotional
level, wishing to grasp your love, and each of them
tried to pull you away from the other.   So it was hard
for you to live with two adults who never really attained any psychological or spiritual growth, nor even
reached maturity.

Now you need to change.   Now you are in your
early thirties and are starting spiritual cultivation.   You
do not need to rely on your mom or dad to say, "Yes,
that's nice."   You must establish your own personal
judgment in order to know what is good or not good.
If you really know that something is good, do not care
about pleasing or upsetting somebody else; you do not
need to worry about it.   In my family, with my two
sons, I only give an overview direction of what they
should and should not do.   When they were teenagers,
they experimented just the same as ordinary children.
Normally I did not force things on them but let them
discover for themselves what was right.   I only inter-
vened when they overly extended their precious young
energy in a wrong direction.   Fortunately, they are
good boys.   When they were young, in primary school,
I let their mother be the boss and I did not interfere.
If she had trouble disciplining them, she would tell me,
and I would discipline them.   I did not like the role of
being the bad guy to the boys, but because it was for
the right reason, I did not refuse.   When they were in
junior high they started not listening to their mother

any more, but they did not come to me either.   I watched to discover what they were doing by their school record and so forth, and when I discovered something wrong, I corrected them.   I warned them once, twice, three times.   After three times, one does not need to be soft.   What needs to be punished needs to be punished, that's all.   I did not make things difficult, but neither do I think I am an excellent example of a father, because I was devoted to my spiritual work and did not have much time to be with them.   Fortunately, they learned things naturally from the family environment.

However, I encourage you not to let your old childhood ghosts haunt you.   You need to think deeply about this, because you never can get over the problem if you hold your father in the same estimation as you did when you were a child, relying on his authority to tell you what to do.   How much have they studied? You can still keep loving and respecting them, but correctly estimate how much they know about life.   It is not right for you to sit here and complain that you have trouble because you did not have good parents. Many people say that.   I also had a hard time with my mother because I was a restless boy, but I appreciated the strong discipline she gave me, which was the only fortune I inherited from her.   My appreciation is not because my mother was angry or strict; but because she did the right thing.   I was a restless boy.   I was disciplined when I was young and at home.   When I was thirteen or fourteen, I began, step by step, to become independent.   Do not mind giving strong discipline to your youngsters; you need to do the right thing.   Fundamentally, everybody is affected by their parents.   Some are lucky, some are not; but lucky or not, after age thirty, you have to be yourself and not mom or dad.

Student: When I do a dumb thing, I try to examine it and see why, so I will not do it again.   I look to see what is wrong and why I keep doing it over and over again.   How can I train my mind to creatively solve this?

Master Ni: I know that you have formed a theory about your mind.   It comes from your psychology, instead of spirituality.   Your spiritual energy is affected through the system of belief you have formed; you are then rightly or wrongly channeled.   It is, however, true that people's old psychological programs are hard to modify;   they are like an imprint on the plate of your mind.   It is sad to let your mind be kept in such a trap.   The reality of life is very simple and allows you to move in a different direction.   When you get a fleshly body, you get a fresh mind.   All good changes are possible.   If I make you sit in a room listening to some annoying music all day long, you can go away, because it is you who ultimately chooses to be there. It is hard for somebody else to suggest a change or to stop you.   Your life habits are a reactions mostly to the programs of your own mind.   It is as though you have listened to stimulating music all day long.   At night when you go to sleep, you still jump with the music all through the night because of the physical tension. However, it is a different matter once your soul is out of your body; it is clear.   Maybe there had been some sad experiences for the soul, nevertheless, the misfortune of physical life is not connected any more.

Earlier, I mentioned that the strength and fortification of the soul starts with a good tree.   Now that you are starting to be a spiritual student, you need always to relate to the life environment.   Are my emotional relationships the truth of my spiritual life or are they only an emotional connection?   If they are an emotional connection, you should not give them too much value.

Student: Do you mean that one's psychological part is mostly emotional?

Master Ni: One's psychological part is a condition. For example, in Russia, a psychologist established an interesting fact. Every time he fed an experimental group of dogs, he rang a bell just before he gave them the food.   The stimulation of the food created the condition of causing the dogs to salivate.   Then, after some time, he stopped giving them food and just rang the bell.   The dogs physically reacted with the same physical response of salivation.   Your mind can be conditioned like that.

A student who grew up in South China had a similar experience.   Every time he went on a short trip, it rained.   He did not notice anything at first, but after a while he made a connection and began to feel bad about it.   Why does it always rain when I go out?   He established a condition in his mind: if I go out, it will rain.   So he became afraid to go out!   He thought he had bad fortune because every time he went out to have a good time, it rained.   He began to believe that he was not naturally supported as a person and could not achieve anything. It seemed to him to be proven. When this person became my student, he discovered that his mind had become conditioned by the weather. The weather can condition the mind.   On some days when he went out there was no rain, but he ignored that.   The rain intensified his memory that every time he went out, it would rain.   In Che-kiang in South China, the rain in spring is like a drizzle.   In summer it pours.   In autumn it floods and in winter it hails. There are all kinds of water conditions in the sky, but our minds will create a story associated with something that happens again and again.

Here is an example of similar psychological conditioning from when I was young.   There was a square in front of a temple where people customarily sold medicine, gave martial arts shows or performed magic. I was usually in the audience in the afternoon, right around the time I should have gone home.   When I was on my way home late, I heard a crow making a lot of noise.   The country people told me that a crow cawing means that something bad will happen to you. I was conditioned by those thoughts and decided my mother was going to scold me for coming back after sunset, because she did not want me back that late. But there was a different reason for the cawing.   I was to find out that every night around sunset birds go to their nests, even from the fields, and the chickens and ducks come back after spending the day at the canal. Sometimes, if they do not come back right away, their owner has to make bird noises to call them so they will come home. So of course at that time the birds were coming back and cawed; and since it was after sunset when I arrived home, of course my mother would scold me. But I could not stop watching the magic show! I was too young! It was the only great entertainment available in town.

Nonetheless, each time I heard the crow caw, I knew I must go home and be punished. This is conditioning. Even when I was older, if I heard that sound, my mind was stirred with fear because of the psychological conditioning.

It is told in my home town that if at midnight you hear an owl hooting, in the village an old person is dying. So occasionally, if we were awake at midnight, we heard an owl and thought that somebody was dying. When you are young, you truly believe a bird is spiritual or there is a connection between the cawing of a crow and receiving punishment from your mom. You connect everything until you learn Tao. I observed my nervous reaction to the crow and gave myself a special study of the birds. Everything is natural; you cannot stop a crow from cawing. You also cannot stop owls from hooting, because they have a natural life and have no connection to your activity. You are also a natural life, and, generally speaking, there is nothing that has any supernatural powers over you or you over them. If crows caw at midnight or owls hoot at midday, things are not natural, there might be something wrong, but I observed that in a normal situation there is no connection. It is just that people are psychologically conditioned by thoughts, customs and superstitions.

Life itself is a natural being. We live a short span in the world. Longevity is 120 years or 150 years, or longer, but generally people cannot live that long.

Even if you do live that long, it is still just like a short second.   But do not be bothered about how long you live; you need to enjoy your spiritual attainment in this very moment.   Take responsibility for your own life without fear of the scolding of mom or dad or god. You cannot be bothered by this and that all the time. If you check out whether you have a good soul and do things right, if you need to do anything to mend your bad behavior, you will do it.   If you say you do not have anything to mend, then you should be calm and lead a joyful, natural life.

I would like to tell you a story that happened about fifteen years ago or so in the city of Kao Shiang, in the south of Taiwan.   The island of Taiwan is in the Pacific Ocean and is shaped like a leaf from a tree.   In the north end is the city of Taipei and in the south is Kao Shiang, where I lived at the time.   Kao Shiang is bigger than Santa Monica, maybe as big as Long Beach, but it is much more populated and has a beautiful harbor.   There something happened that was published in the local newspaper, the "Taiwan News." This is the story.

Two good friends were successful businessmen. One of them became well known because he had run for the position of city assemblyman.   His friend visited him regularly for many years.   He would always sit in the same chair, enjoy the same kind of tea and discuss different subjects with him.   One day something happened to his friend.   He fell ill but did not know what the internal problem was, so he went to Taipei to consult a doctor.   After being examined, it was discovered that the friend had cancer and needed an operation, but while the surgery was being performed, he died.   One morning, the assemblyman saw a bird sitting in the chair where his old friend sat and thought it was unusual, because birds do not usually come into people's homes. Later that day, he received a phone call from his friend's family telling him that his friend had died two days ago.   So he made an association that the bird was possessed by the man's soul.   He treated the bird very well, as he had treated his friend. The bird just sat there for a number of days, then flew away. Then the bird came to the home of the man who had died and sat in his office chair, behind his desk. The friend's family had heard that their father's spirit possessed the bird and had gone to the assemblyman's house, so they knew that this bird was their father, the head of the house, the boss of the business. Everyone was very friendly to it, even offering it good food to eat, but the bird did not take anything. It was very sad and stayed there several days, and afterwards the bird flew away. This story was printed in a big part of the newspaper, and in the beginning I cut it out to save as an example to teach that people have a soul. But since in Taiwan everybody gets the paper, I had no reason to keep it. I am sure that this article could be found at the local newspaper company even now.

Whether you are a happy or unhappy soul, the most important thing is your achievement, including not being attached to the good or bad experiences of life. The development of a soul not only benefits you after your death, but also during the time when you are with your fleshly body. The spiritual cultivation that I began, similar to you, prepares the good soil in which to grow your good soul, your good life, your spiritual life. That is your true attainment. In the world, people are busy looking for external gain. Yes, we all have pressure for material support, and some people do better, while some are poor. But wealthy or poor, when you compare material support to the preciousness of the soul, it does not mean too much. If you can support your life to a certain extent, that is all that is really necessary. The most important thing is to nurture the soul and nurture the potency of your spiritual energy while you undertake the tasks of everyday life. That is the real achievement. That is the true flower, the true fruit of your life being.

When you do good, when you do not do any bad thing to damage your soul in your lifetime, your fruit is complete and good and, naturally, your spirit beings are divine beings. If your soul does poorly, even if you are a rich person with all kinds of luxuries and expensive things, you will truly not have much for yourself if you have an impoverished soul. Someone may be very aggressive and their personal expansion may look great, but it is all hollow and harsh, like an empty shell. Let us cultivate what is true. Let us pay attention to that which supports the truthfulness of life, without overexpanding or doing something irrelevant with the everlasting soul. Your body lasts a short time; your enjoyment and influence are also short. However, in your lifetime, you can correct all the mistakes and attain a higher spiritual benefit. Your soul can live much longer than practical physical living. It can continue to enjoy or continue suffering according to what the physical living has brought about. It all depends on how you live when you have a fleshly life, which is the tree that brings about good or bad fruit.

III

Around twenty-five years ago, I opened my first clinic in a city. There was a young western-trained doctor who also worked with me. This young doctor had spent most of his time in school and did not have as much general life experience as I did because I was older than he. However, he impressed me and aroused my curiosity because he was very religious, which is unusual for doctors with modern education and no exposure to spiritual traditions.

One day, after working hard, we had tea together. He told me about an experience he had when he was an intern that changed his life. He graduated from army medical school, and was interning in an important hospital that served army, air force and navy personnel. It was summer in the tropical island, and during one afternoon of beautiful weather he was interning in surgery. It was a big operation. A sergeant about age thirty had cholangitis, which is an inflamed bile duct in the gall bladder, and surgery was required to save his life. Several doctors were working together, with the interns assisting. The chief surgeon was giving instructions during the tedious operation, as they looked for the duct. They searched repeatedly for it but could not find it. After looking unsuccessfully for the tube for three to four hours, the chief surgeon finally asked to know the patient's rank. The man was a sergeant of low rank, and since he was not a very important person, the chief decided to give up the search and instructed the team to sew him up. As soon as he gave the instruction, all the lights turned off. Believing it to be an electric company problem, they turned on their emergency generator, but the lights went off again. A moment later, the lights began to flicker, swing and sway. There were lights all over the room and it did not just happen to one or two of them. Nobody in the room had any spiritual experience at all, but it was obvious that what was happening was not physical but had a spiritual cause. Those present began to feel dizzy due to the lights swinging and almost fainted; some of them began to go into a trance. The chief surgeon began to pray, "Please, if we did something wrong, guide us. We could not find the trouble." Slowly, things came back to normal. They reopened the man's abdomen and very easily found the problem because surprisingly, a yellow liquid flowed out that guided the doctors to the sick duct. They took care of it and sewed the man back together again.

A couple of weeks later, the patient was much recovered and the doctors went to visit him. They were modern people and had never experienced anything like that and wanted to know if the man had caused it. But he was just an ordinary person. Sometimes such things occur because people have a strong spiritual background, or because the spiritual world needed to enlighten the group of young doctors there. After that, that group of physicians turned into strong religious followers and began to develop themselves. They paid strict attention to the care of patients, and my co-worker became an award winning doctor of surgery.

After I heard his story, I accepted his reasons for becoming religious. The phenomenon of the lights did not last for only one or two minutes, but kept the doctors there for around twenty minutes. In a half trance they accomplished their work.

From my spiritual knowledge, it is not God that punishes or rewards people. It is people, and how they develop their souls, that punishes or rewards themselves. People, whether with good or bad souls, still need to come back to enjoy or to suffer. Some people come back, or reincarnate, with spiritual defects and they suffer a lot. Some people come back with complete development and enjoy more. Even with a good material foundation in life, your spiritual condition makes your life experience different.

When we go out to play, sometimes we have rain. Young kids are excited and happy in the rain. The adults are unhappy and complain. One with a strong spiritual condition enjoys life in any event. It does not matter whether you are born into a good family or have good financial support, the naturally equipped spiritual quality comes from your personal accumulation of actions. Like doing sculpture, one chisel after another shapes a beautiful statue. By your words, behavior and thoughts, you keep or shape the spiritual life of your main soul.

Now I would like to conclude this chapter with an important spiritual message given by a divine being. This valuable guidance for all of us is called, "The Message from the Most Righteous God."

The Divine One said, "A person who lives in the world should fulfill all good spiritual virtues, such as loyalty, filial duty, righteousness, temperance and other positive virtues. By doing so, he will be free from disgrace to stand straight between the sky and earth.

"If a person does not fulfill the good virtues mentioned, though he still lives in the world, his soul withers and he is robbed of his future years. Because one's conscience is the light of God in a person, God is therefore the conscience of your soul. If you disgrace your conscience, you disgrace God. If you do not disgrace your conscience, you do not disgrace God. Therefore a virtuous person nurtures his awe toward the Heavenly law, the righteousness of history and the teaching of the sages. He always examines his behavior with four witnesses: Heaven, Earth, people and his own conscience. He is cautious when he does something alone, knowing better than to think he can behave differently in a dark room. He does not exchange his righteousness because of suffering poverty. Each movement and each retreat is supervised by God, as clearly as though all eyes were watching you and all fingers were pointing at you. All conduct creates correspondent feed-back; retribution is inescapable, it does not leave you even the distance of a hair.

Among all bad behavior, debauchery is the worst; it damages your soul energy. Among all good conduct, filial duty is the first, when someone who lives close to you needs help.

Do not do something for profit which is against your conscience.

Do not refuse to do something because you think there is no profit, if it is in accordance with your conscience.

If any people are against such principles, their souls must wither and be destroyed.

Therefore, the following advice is given in order to help the development of your soul:

Respect the natural being of the sky and the earth. Worship spiritual unity and clarity. Preserve the spiritual merit of all human ancestors. Fulfill filial duty in accordance with the laws. Respect your teacher, love your brother and trust your friends. Be happy with your family and be harmonious with neighbors and fellow people of the world. Be a dutiful husband or wife. Teach your children. Be helpful in all circumstances. Accumulate good deeds that are unknown to others. Help the one who is in trouble and the one who has an emergency. Have pity on the lonely and the helpless. Build temples and print spiritual books which break away the prejudice of all human people. Supply herbs for the poor during a publicly spread epidemic. Provide tea or pure water on the roadside where there are busy pedestrians. Stop killing and release captured wild animals. Build bridges and roads for people. Pity the unsupported widowed and relieve the entrapped who suffer from difficulties. Do not waste grains or food and never squander your blessings. Help dissolve misunderstandings and unravel emotional intricacies. Donate to help create beautiful accomplishments. Provide good guidance for the lost. Make peace with enemies. Do not cheat people by false measurement. Be close to the virtuous. Give no assistance to troublemakers. Do not talk about people's evils but exalt whatever good they do. Be kind to all and help all people. Turn your heart away from profit hunting to the spiritually rewarding great path, Tao. Renew your life by correcting all your problems. Fill your heart completely with kindness and leave no evil idea. Follow all good and balanced teachings.

"By doing so, people may not notice, but God knows and your blessing is increased. Your years will be lengthened and your descendants will be benefitted too. Trouble will disappear and diseases will be lightened. Big trouble will not attack you. Your peace and happiness shall be shined on by auspicious spiritual energy.

"Do not be evil-minded, do any bad things, rape people or break the harmony among a family. Do not damage a person's good name, envy their capability, scheme to obtain their fortune, instigate dispute between people or harm them in order to profit. Do not fatten your own pocket to decorate yourself, complain to other people about the weather or the environment. Do not spread scandalous rumors about a sage, destroy the good name of the virtuous, destroy spiritual images or statues used for educational purposes or rebel against good spiritual teaching. Do not kill the animals you do not raise, disrespect good books or rely on the force of your position, money, or social connections to mistreat the kind and the weak. Do not cause fighting among people's relatives, disbelieve right teaching, or lead the unrighteous to take pleasure in deception.

"Do not devalue diligence and frugality or squander grain. Do not fail to repay kind help or neglect your own conscience. Do not use false measurements in business dealings. Do not establish prejudicial teachings to attract fools by the lie of ascending to Heaven. Do not take things from people, take advantage of others or use scheming and cheating in setting a lasso to trap them. Do not curse others and make trouble behind people's backs. Do not seek retribution. Do not seduce people to do bad. Never do even one small bad thing, but always do good ones. The people who do these things do not respect the Heavenly Law or human nature. They shall struggle with all kinds of trouble, arguments and legal problems. They will suffer from water and fire, robbery and poisonous diseases. They will bring forth foolish and corrupt descendants: their sons will become thieves, their daughters, prostitutes. Their life will be destroyed and their fortune smashed. Immediate retribution will happen to them, and future retribution to their descendants. The god of righteousness and clarity watches all people and is never confused by the distinction between good and bad, which is as clear as the disastrous and the blessed. One of virtuous deeds is rewarded with blessings. One of evil behavior invites trouble. This is the explanation of the Heavenly Law. This is the advice from the divine realm. I wish people would wake up and follow it. My words are simple and they benefit your soul. Whoever disrespects these words will have his soul taken.

"Whoever heeds my words in his mind and in his behavior will become free of trouble. Celebrations of all kinds will take place. He will have good descendants, a long and happy life, and there will be a fragrance to his character. Success will come to him. All that he lacks will be supplied by correspondence from the spiritual realm to bring him a harvest of happiness and achievement.   All he asks for will be granted; all his wishes will be fulfilled.   All his trouble will be gone like melting snow, as around him, auspicious lights will gather like clouds.   All these blessings can be attained by correct beliefs and behavior.   I have no selfish interest, but my desire is to protect good people.   Those who learn good things will not easily lose their discipline.   Their good comes from their development."

Some of my beloved readers perhaps would become upset by reading this chapter if you would like to make spiritual progress, but you may be convinced that you are going to "hell."   Although you have a great desire to do better, you have made some mistakes. They may not have been really bad things, but you now understand they were not helpful to your development or to the world.   Is it possible that you can atone for the errors in thought, word and deed so that you can further refine yourself and move to deeper levels of spirituality in this life?

Beloved friends, life is giving new great opportunity for learning and upward moving.   All people make mistakes in their lives, but what is important is to keep on refining and renewing their life and not become stuck in the dead alleys which I have described.   Running into small mistakes is not a serious shame, but being defeated by mistakes is.   The worst is that your soul is chained and controlled by old habits that are dead ends.   Thus, I suggest that you move out of the tar pit with the help of the life rope of your own spiritual awakening and start your life anew, right in this second.   It is still hopeful and bright.

CHAPTER THIRTEEN

THE RESPONSIBILITY
OF SPIRITUAL TEACHERS

Discussion between Master Ni and Students

Student: Master Ni, someday I would like to be a spiritual teacher. I have been attracted to spiritual study for many years, and my learning is giving me confidence for teaching. I would like to have your instruction on my spiritual goal. If I am going to be a teacher, must I be a teacher who is completely knowledgeable in all spiritual matters and have complete understanding of all traditions before I teach? Also, I would like to know what motivates you to constantly write books and continue teaching people.

Master Ni: The blessing I look for is the enjoyment of witnessing a person's spiritual progress, whether as a leader in the world or as a person who puts his spirituality into practice each day. It is my spiritual ambition to see spiritual progress for the whole of human society, so that all people will awaken to know that religions, when functioning positively, provide different programs for psychological education.

The classification of different religions depends on their function and how their programs were originally organized. Some religions produce the effect of emotional and psychological support for a race, community or society. Some deeper religions, through the teaching of their programs, can help one reach maturity of mind. However, when any program is overused, a person's mind becomes habituated to its terms, language and expressions; since the mind is attached to rote it becomes controlled, which then limits his growth. Instead of the program working for him, the person ends up working for the program. All religious creations cause people to become separated from the

Great Path of One Truth.   The individual, as well as human society as a whole, has been pulled down by these creations and has become incapable of attaining higher spiritual development.

It is right that the mind receives education or support, but trouble can be caused by the methods one follows.   Let us understand this by an illustration.

Picture a well on the top of a high mountain containing the spring of wisdom.   In an attempt to reach the spring, some leaders or organizers of certain religious programs do what amounts to making themselves like a piece of stone tied to the end of a rope. They lower the stone into the well, dip it into the water and then pull it up.   They explain to you that here is the nourishing water of wisdom which everybody should enjoy.   The people who trust them use their tongue to lick the water from the surface of the stone.

In contrast, truly knowledgeable teachers approach the water by teaching you to have an empty mind, like a container with nothing inside, like a bucket.   Why empty?   Because if the inside of a container is stuffed with something solid, not much water can be put into it, and a person cannot get much out of it.   But once an empty container is dropped down into the water, the bucket can be filled and you can drink fully.   Then you might like to share some with whomever needs it.

You see, the other spiritual paths can only quench your thirst temporarily or make you thirstier by causing you to rely on licking the surface of a stone, thus never allowing you to drink fully from the sweet water of wisdom.

As described, all religions are educational programs which support people on some level.   If you stand on the point of a high mountain peak, you can see their conceptual differences and know what service they give.   Then you can pick whatever service you need for specific occasions, like using an umbrella on a rainy day.   However, you need to choose support that will not cause you problems or become an obstruction for your own spiritual achievement, or strain the harmony between different societies. In other words, do not accept any religious program as a school from which you can never graduate, unless the school is not a school, yet at the same time is of all schools, like the learning of Tao. For example, yoga in Hinduism has been practiced for several thousand years and has many branches and schools. People go into any one of those organized practices but few people come out because the practices are self-limiting. This means that few yogis achieve more than the practices were programmed for. The problem of such spiritual learning is that you cannot rise above it; you are limited by its organized formulas which eliminate the benefit of having the learner continue stepping forward. Nobody, through these limited programs or training, can reach the point of full maturity; only partial maturity can be expressed by using a program's terms and organization in teaching. The learner cannot get the true benefit of a program for himself or others because he is unable to break the frame of organization. The program is used for training, yet its very structure inhibits the interchange with spiritual essence, which is limitless. The formality of the spiritual training program limits the student and the practitioners.

Student: Master Ni, would you kindly give some practical examples of this? It is rather difficult for us to understand when you speak in an abstract way.

Master Ni: Let us review the knowledge and experience some of you have attained. Esoteric Buddhism is widely practiced and cultivated, especially in the region of Tibet, Japan and China. Tibetan esoteric Buddhism has at least nine hundred years of cultivation and development of different sects: red, white, flowery and yellow. Red was the first one. Some masters or lamas, after having learned and mastered several different programs, reach maturity of mind within the organized puzzles. But few teachers can simplify the tremendously complicated rituals and make them useful and serviceable for their own people and for the world. To teach new students, they still must depend on organized programs which are spiritually out-of-date. If they give up the old programs, they cannot teach any more. This cannot totally be considered a pity or a waste of energy, because those religious programs were prepared by people who conquered themselves and began teaching other people to do the same. It is correct to discipline oneself, unlike other programs which support people to become more impulsive and more aggressive. Good people conquer their own unnatural ambition, but undeveloped people expect to conquer others, neglecting the true rulership of their own being within. Thus it is important to have the right teachers in the world who can develop better programs to teach new people and purify the effects of the existing backward programs.

Chinese culture can be traced back 8,000 years. However, its maturity, once reached, could not be continued by the new generations. For example, the work of Lao Tzu and Chuang Tzu was produced around 2,300 or more years ago. At that time, the correct direction in which to go was made clear, but unfortunately only a very small minority of people appreciated and took it.

The troubles of society have worsened, especially in the last two hundred years. It is right that a society stays open to new things, but it is not right to reshape one's feet by surgery in order to fit the newest fashionable shoe. The new leaders of China, for example, have caused millions of people to suffer an unnatural death just to make their society fit a new fashion. How can the people of China have become so foolish? It is because the new generations have lost their connection with their original root and development.

It is true that spiritual development cannot be done by one person for another; each must do it for himself. Here is a small illustration of this. One of my spiritual friends developed his own spirit in a natural way. But his younger wife, who had just graduated from college, did not believe in any religion or in spirituality. She thought it was nothing but superstition, so she preached her modern beliefs to all the people in her surroundings. After some time, she became a Christian out of emotional need; she was young and Christianity suited her young ego. She pushed her new religion on her surroundings as the new expression of her life. Later, her parents died and her marriage was shaken up because of her strong temperament to be a savior, which was patterned after the image of Moses or Jesus as the savior. She could not see her confusion and became overly aggressive. Some years later, she became softer and became a believer in Buddhist occultism, which again she pushed on her sons, daughter--in-law and everyone else. Surely, she has not yet reached maturity, but everyone in her surroundings suffered for her growth. It is right that everyone should have sympathy and tolerance toward the growth of another, but nobody should push others to accept all of his or her beliefs, no matter what stage they are in.

Although Buddhism in India or China cannot serve all aspects of human life, it has expressed the stage of maturity of mind within its own walls of paper. However, this maturity was also lost; the scripts were written at least one thousand years ago, and all programs were based on those writings. No new maturity can develop by learning the old shells of worship. Today, in the spheres of spirit and human conception, new leaders who have studied the various types of old programs and who are not influenced by these programs must find a new essence. All the different paths need to meet, bringing about a new integration and a new light to the world, unobstructed by the terminologies and structural ideologies of old spiritual or religious programs. Then finally the great truth can be reached and be serviceable to all people, which is the real purpose of being spiritualized. The spiritual self has no color, no name, no form; all specifics depend on the one who creates the teaching program and how wisely and how well he presents it. Yet, all those creations are still secondary to the essence behind them. If the true unnameable spiritual essence is not taught by the spiritual teacher to advanced students, there will be no real benefit; conversely, a side effect of being controlled by special spiritual or religious programs will be the leading of their students into conflict.

It would be helpful for all people to know that spiritual or religious languages are metaphors, such as, for instance, the description in Genesis. They are meant to express something deeper than what the words describe. Some of these metaphorical expressions are more complete than others, but they are still all a metaphorical language that tells the story of nature and the life of mankind itself. No single religious terminology, language or conceptual image is the real thing itself. All wise students should respect what is behind the totality of human spiritual language and not insist on the wording or semantics. Also, it should be clearly known that no single spiritual language is enough to give an accurate description of the spiritual sphere of the universe.

Student: Master Ni, how about the modern psychological programs?   Even though they have no religious basis or structure, they are designed to help people.

Master Ni: Modern psychologists create many psychological programs which further their business. None of these programs is greater or more effective than the thousand-year-old religious programs or spiritual practices.   One would help oneself most by respecting the ancient creations and using them to help one's growth. Know that even these should be renewed and unified by the wise leaders of different cultural and professional backgrounds in order to be effective for today's life.   There is an abundance of creations and inventions from the old days that need to be objectively studied and renewed.   By utilizing the practices of timeless wisdom, a student can in fact build and develop his or her own spirit.   True achievement is one's own,   not the language presenting it.   For example, a person who is weak goes to learn martial arts.   After three years of training he becomes much stronger; but the real benefit of his practice is the health he has developed.   He does not need to get even with anyone or die or fight for the school he attended.   His purpose in life is not to live for that school.   The same thing is true of the special instruction of meditation or religious practice: calmness, management of your mind and the spiritual energy you develop is what you gain; do not turn back to support the separated ego-identification that the teaching would cause.   If you do so, you become controlled or sacrifice yourself just for a spiritual program.

Modern medicine sometimes uses drugs that have a side effect which may be worse than the patient's original small illness.   Similarly, religious or spiritual programs can also have a side effect and not benefit you at all.   A wise person makes sure that the program he chooses is an unobstructed path or that he is able to keep it from limiting him.   Once you are finished with a program, you should not stay attached to its special way, terminology or construction.   As has been mentioned, we positively expect new integration and new serviceable programs that can produce unification in understanding.   This is what the teaching of Tao offers: the highest, and at the same time, most fundamental unified understanding about all worldly religions and religious training, and the awareness that practices differ according to the stage and life condition of an individual.

It is a fact that understanding has levels, which are accessed by the depth of one's spiritual vision.   However, education and the correct broad direction in life combine to make a great unified goal for the development of an individual.

In the interest of awakening your own individual spiritual energy and achieving maturity and in the interest of helping develop human society, you must learn how to evaluate all conventional spiritual religious programs.   Different spiritual, religious or intellectual educational programs produce different students.   Once you learn to evaluate these programs, you know what is needed for today's modern society and what is not.   Some are mixed with politics; they are not pure.   Spiritual matters should be pure and not confused with politics.   Some programmed religions are aggressive and interfering, trying to push themselves on other people.   That is not what people need; it serves only to disrupt the political stability of different nations.   Some religions devitalize people's lives and make them like vegetables, ready to be conquered or slaughtered by a strong enemy which cannot, in any event, bring forth the growth of the world.

On the other hand, too much self-denial is not correct either.   All good spiritual qualities, such as virtue, should be learned and developed, but some should not be developed or promoted too far without teaching the accompanying principle of integrity and balance.   If a true leader wishes to benefit the future of all humans, he must know which cultural elements need to be promoted and which should be allowed to die away.

The world can be saved by both internal and external changes, though the internal changes are more important than the external ones.   External change must first receive strength from internal change.   Therefore, this is the goal toward which this timeless tradition works: to awaken your internal spiritual nature.

Student: Master Ni, what is the reason that older nations with spiritual traditions reaching far back suffer more trouble than the modern nations?

Master Ni: The trouble is global when human society comes to a new stage.   As for the reason that conventional practices cannot help, but instead create new problems, let us look at the Asian countries.

In the tradition of Tao, there are 3,600 different so-called spiritual practices.   The popular Chi Kuan (Qi Gong) energy transformation practices cannot save China from trouble without also encompassing the goal of attaining Tao, the integral truth of universal life.

Chi Gong is now being used as a political slogan for the principles of politics and economics that should be serving the people. In India, the leaders would do well to learn that Hinduism, Islam or Sikhism (the religion of the people who dress in white robes and turbans) are meant to serve the Indian people and not make them vehicles for their ideological differences. All religions factually serve the same purpose and motivation of attaining the same spiritual reality, but their terms or colors are superficially different. In India, there are hundreds of different practices of yoga; in Tibet, there are also many schisms or replicated programs of esoteric Buddhism. In the totality of human religious creation, many new programs of practice were developed and taught to groups of students according to the students' spiritual condition and the purpose of the practice. Some programs are designed to improve a person's spiritual quality in order to promote spiritual development; some offer emotional support; others serve to develop a specific spiritual function of each individual; and some have a positive effect on people's healthy states of mind. Those benefits, though under different terminologies, still depend on a few truly achieved ones who have the ability to sort out the ancient existing programs to see if there are any that should be used and taught to the students of the new world. It all depends on the achievement of the teacher.

Today is a time for positive change; a time to be opened up. Some materials and programs have weakened people's motivation for material improvement in life, especially in areas of Asia, such as China, India and Tibet. These are conventional societies whose progress is very slow, like some other undeveloped regions of the world. However, all people need to open themselves to look for the best things that will improve their spiritual, mental or healthful conditions, that will promote the balance of their lives and which will develop them further. Responsible teachers should come back to society to reprogram and create new programs that teach the great path that lies above the petty paths.   Some teachings were so complicated that they served only a few special, mentally complicated individuals who were capable of understanding them. These teachings need to be simplified to benefit the public. People's backgrounds are very different.   Many different programs were created to guide different types of people, step by step, to reach the integral truth of one universal spiritual nature.

Student: Master Ni, could you describe the relationship between spiritual teachers and their students?

Master Ni: In ancient times, a student earned the trust of the teacher over a period of years. Then the teacher would instruct him.   Teachers worry about your sincerity and intentions, so many have created approaches to teach you something without immediately teaching you the key method or key practice that they learned from their own teachers.   But this profusion of new small approaches and techniques only created more confusion.

Whose problem is it?   The responsibility for creating more confusion belongs to both students and teachers.   Some teachers developed something only to establish a novel attraction, while others devised methods that served as the teachers' own means of protection from the evil minds of undeveloped students. But how can students become attained if the teachers do not teach the real achievement?   There are few practices with a foundation of truth available to educate the younger generation.

An individual's development can be taken much further if correct spiritual education is added to intellectual education. The purpose and principle of doing these important practices is expressed in the *Tao Teh Ching* and the work of other achieved ones.   One cannot say that among all the many different human religious creations there is no repetition, no unimportant practices or no meaningless junk.   It is important to choose carefully what one learns.   How does a student choose to learn what can truly help his development? Sometimes it depends on personal choice. If you are not interested in learning the small practices from teachers of different backgrounds, you can learn from the great path directly. You can learn the principles and the practices from a responsible book which is also available to you without a teacher. If you have a teacher, usually it is helpful for your growth if the teacher does not control you and make you an everlasting customer to buy his service.

Student: Master Ni, how can we become good spiritual students?

Master Ni: In the process of learning spiritual truth, one must know that understanding is intellectual; the mind is but the interpreter. Sometimes the interpreter can make a mistake. Through some of the five senses, the eyes and the ears for example, we gather external information for the mind. The mind then makes a judgement on the significance of the information gathered; the judgement must also be judged. The following story illustrates this.

There was a farmer who had a good plow, which he used every day in his work. He also had an extra plow, and he took turns using the two. One day, he could not find his good plow. After thinking about it, he decided that his young neighbor must have stolen it, because he believed, or perhaps it was a fact, that his young neighbor was mischievous. So he went to visit his young neighbor. From his neighbor's smile, greeting and posture, he concluded that his neighbor was guilty of having stolen the plow. So his mind decided the young neighbor was a thief, but he had no proof to bring up the matter openly. He anxiously wished to find something to support his taking action to recover his plow. The next day he discovered that he himself had misplaced the plow in the field under some grass where he had last worked. He looked again at his young neighbor's smile, his gestures and greetings, and today none of them told him the youth was the thief. This is a famous psychological example given by the ancient wise ones.

The knowledge of the mind must be supported by reason. A suspecting mind may pick up a rationale or idea based on wrong knowledge. This happens in everyday life when we listen to the intellectual mind only. The knowledge of spirit is straight feeling. It cannot give you any reason. It avoids your reasoning mind. But it is powerful and truthful. Once a friend of mine was driving on his way to go shopping. His mind thought of going to a shopping center which contained a bookstore where he usually picked up a book or a foreign magazine. However, his feeling expressed resistance. Nevertheless, he thought it reasonable to continue his routine, so he turned in anyway. That very moment, a police car stopped him, and he was given a ticket for making an illegal turn, the same turn he had made many times before and seen many other people make. The insistence upon reason is sometimes unreasonable.

Another example is of a general who was fleeing the arresting force of his political enemy, who held a high position in the government. A poster bearing his picture was hung everywhere describing the big reward that would be received for helping to catch him. On his way to a rural village, he met a friend of his father's. The father's friend knew nothing about his situation, but was happy to see his old friend's son. He greeted him warmly and took him home, where his family began to prepare a feast for him. The fugitive, in the room where guests were received, became very nervous. The old man said, "We have everything for the meal, except some good wine. I will go to the neighboring town and buy some wine so we can enjoy ourselves," and he left. The fugitive was still worried. He heard somebody sharpening a knife, which aroused his suspicion. He thought that the old man had actually gone to the government to report him to the soldiers, who would then come to arrest him. Out of his great fear, he took out his sword and went inside the house, where he killed every member of the family. It was only when he went into the kitchen that he discovered they had been preparing to kill a cow for the meal. The sharpened knife lay on the table and the cow was bound there. He was shocked at his mistake, but of course, it was beyond remedy. Hurriedly, he mounted his horse to run away. As he started out, he met the old man. "Where are you going?" asked the surprised old man. "Now I have the wine. Let's go back and enjoy it with my family." The fugitive felt trapped in this terrible situation, so he tricked the old man into looking away. When the old man turned his head to look, he took his sword out and killed him also. In the end, his distorted sense of reasoning caused the loss of thirty lives.

It is similar with what has gone on with the misguided teachings of man-made religions. While some ancient spiritual leaders created them, certainly not with any intent to be hurtful, many people were ultimately killed by their mind's misinterpretation of their "salvation." Sometimes you make big mistakes in your life, your investments or your relationships; mostly they are problems caused by the misinterpretation of your mind. You cannot trust your intellectual mind only. You need to let your mind learn more, develop more, achieve more and be more open, so that it will follow your spirit instead of your shallow intellectual worries.

Therefore, it is necessary for you to develop your spiritual understanding, to go beyond your intellectual understanding. If there is something you do not understand, it is because your spirit is blocked and you do not know. Once you become developed, you know. Knowing is partial if both aspects do not work together: intellectual and spiritual. Some spiritual practices can restore the pleasure of natural life, the pleasure of the integral person. All spiritual teachers and spiritual students should stay open to looking for higher truth and never be satisfied with limited intellectual knowledge. When you make a mistake, it is because you overly trust the interpretation of the mind as the truth itself. People fight for their interpretations and even die for them, but the truth does not ask people to die for it. Undeveloped people are either laughing stocks or dangerous fools.

For instance, you go to a Chinese restaurant. On the menu, you see a dish called "red lion's head" or "ants on the trees." You feel nervous about it, yet you could be mislead by the term. The so-called lion's head is a meatball, and the ants on trees are, in reality, mincemeat on rice noodles. Also in some Cantonese restaurants there is a dish called the "great meeting of the three: dragon, phoenix and tiger." That is a really disagreeable dish, it is the meat of snake, cat and chicken.

People go to learn matters of the spirit. Unfortunately, what they learn are games of names and terminology. Spiritual reality cannot be described by any terms that, of necessity, limit it. You cannot see the true thing; it holds nothing which one can fight over. On a certain higher level, you agree to say that all religious practices and all spiritual paths are equal. Even that level is incomplete in showing the complete, which is far beyond limiting words.

Some spiritual practices are an art as compared to a rigid belief. These arts can attract your appreciation because so much fun can be gotten from them and they take you away from paying attention to worldly troubles. Unlike worldly fun, which brings both good and bad return, spiritual fun can produce pure joy. It can also be costly; it may consume your time and numb your sensitivity towards the realities of the world. Yet from these practices may come the management of your emotion and mind. These practices are not approved by the Zahn (Zen) masters who continue the teaching of Chuang Tzu, yet a few continue to view the worldly creations with the sense of humor of Chuang Tzu. I believe that other great spiritual teachers maintain a high sense of humor and flexibility more than the rigidity seen in general religious practice, teaching and personal contact. It is a great opportunity to study different works by great masters of true achievement. They teach us what they gathered through their lifetime of achievement, by simplifying and giving us the essence they attained through their own cultivation, study and practices. They omit teaching us the small practices. Therefore, I have reproduced in simple form, fourteen books that cover the highest achievement of all spiritual effort made by the greatest achieved ones who have ever lived on the earth.

For example, *The Book of Changes and the Unchanging Truth* offers great guidance for learning to be objective, adaptable and balanced. It is not like a rigid religious practice that makes a person too subjective and stubbornly sure God is on his side in conceptual or theological disputes. True spiritual achievement is derived from shifting the subjective to the objective, shifting the heavy to the light, the stiff to the relaxed. It would be a great waste for an individual to spend several decades of a precious life to learn one side of a stubborn, subjective argument. Most people's problem is too much subjectivity. A conceptualized faith in God only aggravates the habit of stubbornness in the face of a conflict, be it a small problem with a few individuals or a big one in the international community. So it is important to learn to achieve a mind that can be flexible, balanced and objective, one that can also see what the opposite side sees. Seeing the balanced truth produces the highest guidance in the personal sphere of human life. The books of Lao Tzu and Chuang Tzu are the conclusion and essence of a far greater accumulation of human growth that evolved through a very long time of darkness and came to see light. However, it was unavoidable that later generations of people lost this enlightened vision and became confused among so many cultural and religious conceptual creations. This confusion misguided them into all kinds of separation and conflict. My books, *The Uncharted Voyage Toward the Subtle Light* (previously titled *The Great Path of Awakening All People*) and *The Footsteps of the Mystical Child* (previously titled, *The Path of Spiritual Evolution*) express the essence of spiritual awakening of the great human masters.

All the other works I present to the people of the modern world are the conjoint effort and distilled essence from those of the highest achievement of universal mind.

Student: Master Ni, you are my last teacher in my spiritual studying journey. I am more sincere than ever to learn from you only.

Master Ni: Better not.   Spiritually, there is no last teacher.   You can have many teachers, even of one good direction only, because an individual's levels change from low to high like children change grades in a school system.   The learning I can pass on to you can be discussed briefly as the following:

If an individual has the ambition of learning all different systems of yoga, different programs of esoteric Buddhism and different techniques developed in other traditions, you might think this person would become very admirable and very knowledgeable. I think he merely entertains himself from all the learning; he is amused and enjoys seeing a thousand moons on the surfaces of lakes, streams, rivers and seas.   But he cannot see the one moon which is high above in the sky.   The wise one is the person who can utilize the essence that others have already gathered, which enables him to use this foundation positively for his life direction and to go further to higher levels of achievement.   So knowing about all kinds of religious beliefs and techniques is like a husband who calls his wife "honey," "sugar," "sweetheart" and other such names, but forgets her real name.   Is her real name not nature?   I wish that you may extract the true essence of spiritual truth from the different obstructing terminologies, conceptual layouts and ideological confusion.

It is better to use Zahn (Zen) Buddhism in discussion because Zahn (Zen) Buddhism is more open than other religions; this is especially so of the masters who truly understand it and make it a continuation of the

parables of Chuang Tzu. For them, things are discuss-
able. Somebody may have spent a lifetime learning
Zahn Buddhism and can stand on the Buddha head,
while another may also have spent a lifetime and learned only general Buddhism. The Buddha still stands on
his head and nothing ever changes.

The different programs you learn are for the purpose of achieving yourself. Different scripts have been
written and passed down for people needing new ex-
planations. These different scripts are specially valued,
and from them a sect of practice is established. It
amounts to illusory effort; the achievement is wasted
because the achievement is to explain the chosen scripts
by using attractive language. Finally, the explanation is
worn out and a new one is needed by different generations. People rely on language to explain and translate
another, ancient language in written form, called holy
scriptures. People forget the long, trustworthy company of the sun, moon, stars and sky. Are these
things not nature? Is your life not nature? Since the
truth also must be nature, then everything is nature.
So all religious teaching suggests something of a waste.
However, most oriental people, like other humans, need
to pass time in their life. They do not know how to
guide their energy in a positive, creative way, and they
meet trouble if they have too much energy and too
much time. Therefore, people do many different
strange things. Religious creation is one of the strange
things, though it aims to help people maintain themselves in a correct way of life. Thus, this creation is
more of a positive contribution, than, let's say, joining
in a political riot or mob movement or personal sexual
or emotional indulgence. For this reason, the achieved
ones give their support to a good religious path and
channel for people who do not know how to guide
their energy creatively and positively to contribute to
human life. They simplify what they have learned and
offer it to other people to help meet the need for true
individual spiritual growth.

Student: Master Ni, what is the responsibility of a spiritual teacher of the new age?

Master Ni: As it has been pointed out, all different religions and spiritual programs need to be learned, studied, researched, investigated and filtered.   Does anyone have enough time, energy and financial resources to do that?   I do not think everybody can do that, but the leaders of different traditions can objectively offer the essence of what they have learned through the years for the use of the majority.   The best work in the world is accumulated for this purpose, to supervise all human spiritual contributions.   It is the learning of Tao, the Integral Truth.   Tao, in later generations, presents the totality of human spiritual achievement.   Once you learn Tao, you learn a totality encompassing spiritual, mental and physical aspects.   You do not learn one thing and neglect another, because Tao is the integral subtle essence.   While the manifest universe is divided into three spheres - mind, spirit and physics - Tao heads and is above all three.   So anyone who learns the essence of all spiritual achievement can be above all spiritual expressions and practices.

It is the principle of people who learn Tao to re-integrate the essence as the ancients did as expressed in the ancient spiritual books of Tao.   The work of Lao Tzu is the essence of all achievement of different spiritual practices before written history, from those who originated, through natural inspiration,   a genuine spiritual expression for all people.   A person who learns Tao, the Integral Way, can assimilate all teaching.   If a person learns a particular religion or particular spiritual practice, he learns one thing.   He will become partial or prejudicial if he is limited by one specific religion or practice.   There is still lots more for him.   It is important for all people to learn Tao and not be misguided by the learning of partial paths.   A person goes through many lifetimes for his further evolution, which in reality is to break away from partial studies and prejudice before reaching the great path of Integral Truth, Tao.   To learn Tao, you do not need to be against anything you have already learned. What you have learned, you digest and absorb. Do not keep it as undigested food. In learning a partial religion or specific spiritual practice, you might establish antagonism towards other practices. In an open society, it is recommended that each community have a specific religious library with all kinds of spiritual books equally displayed so people can study them to enhance their emotional and spiritual activity, and their further development. In that way, a person can safely reach the maturity of their spiritual development and attain spiritual growth without being controlled by specific churches and temples. At the same time, one might produce something better to promote the benefit and welfare of the entire human population, not just a single race or society. As has been pointed out, the world's problem is one of spiritual blindness which is caused by a conceptual cataract in its vision.

Student: Master Ni, teaching faith to the masses is simply teaching all people what you can see, is it not?

Master Ni: People need correct faith to live with the world. At the same time, they need a spiritual awareness higher than faith to supervise this faith. Therefore, spiritual development and faith form a metaphor that appeals to personal preference. This can work for an individual to support one's life in times of difficulty, and is compatible with true spiritual achievement if it does not also cause conflict with the genuine integral spiritual achievement of all people.

We have seen that through experiencing difficulty, people make economic and political progress. Each step leads toward a higher, better achievement in their life. But it is also expected that broad spiritual freedom can cause or bring improvement and develop the new light of society.

When people experience the difficulty of wars and hostility among societies internationally, and struggle materially and emotionally in their individual lives, the only way out is to have all people cooperate to reach the great goal of harmony and prosperity, to respect all the differences of custom.   It is harmony that brings about spiritual achievement.   It is peace that improves the spiritual energy of a society.   From harmony, Tao is expressed.   From disturbance and difficulties, disparate religions, specific kinds of faith and spiritual practices are produced.   As the wise one says, pressure from the outside unites disputing family members. Similarly, pressure from other nations unite the conflicting leaders of a nation.   The same thing will happen to the whole human world when great pressure comes from another part of the universe.   This is an objective observation, not spiritual achievement.   The united strength of spiritual achievement can keep people from feeling outside pressure.   Achieving spiritual strength and the power of spirit over any pressure will subdue further pressure; then a better life can be brought about.   The forefathers of a society, through their hard work, built a great nation; but the hard work and material achievement which gave their descendants a foundation of wealth and a time of prosperity has become infected by looseness and corruption, which without spiritual development,   invites a dangerous future.   History has shown us that unless spiritual achievement is cultivated, the result of this progress will be negative.

Student: Then, Master Ni, what can be done in order to help ourselves?

Master Ni: It is Tao, the Integral Truth.   Tao includes all aspects of an individual life and the prosperity of human society conjoined with universal spiritual integration into a great harmony as oneness.   Oneness is the trend of nature.   Splitting is the trend of the small human mind.   Tao does not possess you.   Tao does not own you.   Tao is above god.   Tao is the spiritual essence of the entire universe.   As a path, you can utilize it and make it serve you.   Whether it serves you, however, depends on your awareness and determination to reach it and break through all your partitions and separations from it.   Therefore, I hope you can identify the great universal subtle truth in your life.

CHAPTER FOURTEEN

THE PURSUIT OF SPIRITUAL UNITY

Discussion between Master Ni and Students

Student: Master Ni, I sincerely wish to learn more about true spiritual knowledge. What is the most important guidance in life, and what is the final achievement?

Master Ni: Let us review Lao Tzu's teaching. It is concentrated in one small book, yet it is very valuable because it expresses thousands of years of human spiritual achievement. His guidance is mostly for your internal spiritual life in contrast to your external worldly life. This invaluable teaching says, make your mind embrace your body and your body embrace your spirits. Have all large and small elements cooperate and embrace each other closely in enjoyment of the concordance of oneness. Oneness brings life. Concordance brings endurance. Spiritual endurance brings immortality. Lao Tzu also uses the external human world as an illustration of the internal spiritual gathering or society. He does not suggest a great expansion into a big society, because it would bring disorder and confusion. He offers you the secret of your own life being so that it can function as a harmonious, unified society. In other places, he also uses the illustration of governing a society and people, without stimulating people or filling them with desire and ambition, which would cause them to have a difficult time maintaining their peace. His spiritual guidance is to rarefy desire, ambition and intellectualization so that you can live a simple and peaceful life that is naturally joyful and full of organic interests that are consonant with universal nature.

Life energy has three levels: physical, mental and spiritual. The way you form yourself and the way you use your life energy becomes the way people view you. If your physical energy is overextended, you will be aggressive sexually and materially, and people will see you as rude, insensitive and greedy. If you overextend your mental energy, you will have too much desire for good positions and so forth, and you will scheme and plot to get things. People will see you as crafty or tricky, and they will not trust you. But when you use your spiritual energy, you will be helpful to other people; not falsely helpful but genuinely helpful. People will see you as someone reliable that they can trust, and you will become a leader. Therefore Lao Tzu recommends making spirit the center of individual life, and does not advocate the overextension of the other two aspects. Combining the three energies to work in harmony creates a complete, balanced life; it is the great unity of life. The person who attains the great unity of life is a god who experiences heaven on earth. He does not need to look at other people's response to him to prove this to himself, because he understands that people on different levels view things differently; people set up different standards. Not all of them are wise or accurate. The most balanced person is not always recognized for what he is; when you look at him, you will not see anything outstanding about him. There are two kinds of people like that; one is really a useless person, but the other is a highly achieved person. Sometimes the one of high achievement seems to be crazy! But the balanced one does have something different about him, which some people can intuitively sense. The highest secret of spiritual learning is this simple guidance from Lao Tzu; the purpose is to attain oneness.

If you have the chance and take the time to learn, you can come to recognize, by yourself, your own different faculties. Spiritual functions can independently govern your life harmoniously without need of any special restraint given to the spirits. (For other information on this topic, read relevant material from my other work, regarding any questions about spirit, such as *The Book of Changes and the Unchanging Truth* and *The Gentle Path of Spiritual Progress*). Through development of certain spiritual functions, miraculous or wonderful things will happen in your life and in the lives of those around you when you wish to serve in this way. You might think that it is great.

The teacher from whom you are learning will determine whether you are earnest, worthy, virtuous and never do a bad thing, which proves you are a living god or living heaven, and if you have learned a special spiritual practice of independent missions. A special spiritual practice will help you establish your spiritual faculty to carry out various kinds of independent missions, or work in specific ways for you. The body spirits usually know what you need, even if you do not give them a special assignment such as waking you up in the morning. This is establishing the faculty of your own spiritual energy to carry out an independent mission. At first, when you attain this achievement, it brings you happiness because you think you do not need to worry about anything since you have somebody taking care of you safely. Later, however, you will find there is not one second when you can give up your centeredness, prudence and your wholehearted practice of awareness towards each situation developing in front of you. You are the one who is responsible for your entire being and the carrying on of life. I personally do not think there is anything better than being awakened by the regular tides of your natural energy, nowadays called the biological clock within you, which are really the spirits. Once activated by your cultivation, your energy, itself, wakes you up by ascending to your head. When your spiritual energy descends down to your abdomen, it means you will fall asleep easily. So the unity is shown.

To the truly achieved one, the highest accomplishment is to be united with Tao, the universal, natural spiritual unification at all times, and not to overly individualize oneself. To attain Tao is to attain natural spiritual unification with universal nature. When that happens, at your physical death, the souls that compose your essence will not scatter but will form a continuing function of universal nature that will operate with deathless eternity. Even though your physical bones and flesh scatter like old and worn out clothes, your essence will remain as strong and unified as a new spiritual baby born within the natural world. This is not just a theoretical or conceptual layout. You can prove it by doing it. You can prove it each day by knowing your achieved soul, staying centered and experiencing the expansion and contraction of its light.

In the primary practice, when you are in your meditation and cultivation, you come to know that there is another element beside the existence of your body and mind. It is your breathing. Unify your breathing with your own being in your meditation and in your exercise. Re-gather your scattered vitality, and the very least that will happen is that it will encourage your health, physically, emotionally and mentally. You will not do strange things that endanger your life. Also you will not look for strange things as a reward for your life. You will find that circumstances in your life change and improve. Old, unhealthy or destructive habits will drop away with little or no effort. Areas in your life that were trouble to you before will clear up. And you will feel better. The development of the earnest teaching did not come in one day, but through thousands of years of spiritual development and testing. All kinds of adventures and misadventures produced the simple teaching of Lao Tzu.

Lao Tzu continued the spiritual vision of the truth of life that came from the developed ones before him through the long period of time before recorded human history. Chuang Tzu was a great student of Lao Tzu about one hundred years later. Because the world had changed for the worse, as Chuang Tzu predicted, Hui Neng then echoed Chuang Tzu and made his teachings and those of Lao Tzu understandable to the world of his time. We can see that the function of each of the three masters is different. Lao Tzu, the ageless one, simply wrote about spiritual development. Chuang

Tzu related that great teaching to the practical life of the world. Hui Neng further elucidated the great spiritual teachings.

The teaching of Tao is very simple. Why do we need so many books to talk about the simple truth? Because the mind of later generations has become so complicated, the simple truth must be fully explained for people to utilize its guidance, understand its value and receive its benefit. I consider my work to be an echo of the ancient sages and an understandable voice to the people of this time. Simply, the teaching of Tao is instruction for how an individual can return to a natural, normal life. The principle of the teaching is not to recommend any special belief or conceptual idea; it shows the principle of how you can put yourself together again. If you work to put yourself back together, the world can also be put together in right harmonious order. The problem is that individuals do not understand the wonder and the joy of the process of returning to wholeness. The experience of life in the world has torn or cut them apart into many pieces. Therefore, they hold onto their sickness. Learning the way of Tao serves each individual deeply; it is not a superficial social program. If each individual put themselves together first, it would be a great help to society. You see, social leaders respond to the problems of their times. Most of them stand up and fight, but unfortunately, few of them have ever put themselves together first. Such an ununified person might be successful for a short time, but his service or contribution will not aid the order of the harmonized world. It will be short-lived.

So the fundamental solution is for each individual to take responsibility for himself, whether he is a social leader or not. If he is not a leader now, he may become one later. Cumulatively, this would create a responsible society as well as a responsible government. The problems of the world will not be solved by extending the ununified ruling power of the governments. We have already experienced many strong leaders who have attempted to change the world by these means, and all of them have failed. Some had a basically good motivation and principle, while many have been tyrannical, thinking the power of the police can set society at peace. All manner of beliefs and actions have been tested and failed.

Tao is neither a belief nor an action; it is a path itself. It guides us to cultivate ourselves in a practical way; to develop ourselves. It is really not hard to prove or understand the existence of Tao, but in general, people are only looking for something to distract their attention from their lives instead of making positive improvements for themselves. This could be a new political idea or a religious belief, but they do not see the truth of each individual's development as it is made possible by self-cultivation. They are psychologically or emotionally attracted to new political ideas or religious beliefs because they do not understand they could develop themselves by self-cultivation. Each must cultivate himself.

Physically, people want to be sexually fulfilled and have a nice place to live. Emotionally, they would like to be loved, needed, wanted, respected, supported and have all kinds of fun and enjoyment. Intellectually, they would like to know things which may be useful to them, or things that just stimulate their intellectual process. Spiritually, they would like to have peace and natural growth without being pulled away by attractive but foolish or risky situations. The above mentioned are just the different internal demands of one person. One usually also has pressures from the external world: from society, family and friends in all sorts of connections and contacts. A person has to face all aspects of life. The different faculties of your life each has a different function in relationship to the internal and external world. Your mind is the manager and it is also the coordinator of your company. Can it respond to all the demands in all the situations of your day correctly and skillfully? The mind needs to be educated and developed. Where is there a school or teacher who can excellently train a person to manage and bring about the beautiful performance of a successful life? I'm not talking about career training; I'm talking about your life! - the wonderful performance that brings forth satisfaction in all departments of your life. I am not talking about having sexual fulfillment and then being spiritually pulled down. I do not mean being intellectually wrecked or over-developed. Where your internal elements show some basic conflict, you need to develop your mind to help manage your life and to attain unity inside and out. The management which can bring great satisfaction to all departments of your life manifests as success, prosperity, happiness and personal glory. In my words, it is living an effective and balanced life. Obviously, there is no single school or teacher which can do such an excellent a job as to bring you this type of satisfaction. Nor can you employ someone to manage your life for you who can guarantee satisfaction for all of your demands. It is far simpler than that: all you need is to reasonably organize yourself first. With regard to their own lives, most people are emotionally looking for some strength or force, some person to help them manage; they wish to shift the responsibility for their own life onto someone else and escape to the side. No one can do that!

For a long time people have been struggling emotionally, making all kinds of tests or experiments to see what is right and wrong in life, and they are becoming tired of it. Their results have not been either good or apparent. Therefore, most of them settle on a conceptual remedy. They accept somebody else's idea of a God who runs their life for them, and they just settle back and do nothing about themselves. Or, they decide there is no God and they rush around like fools, doing things that are unnecessary and irrelevant to their lives and well-being. Do you think this is a realistic or effective solution? To the people who accept this way of life, it is an emotional solution. But as a solution, it is more than merely emotional; it is a real, factually unhelpful solution. The idea helps your emotion, but not your life; this kind of life has no life to it. And to most people, this is the meaning of

"God." This is what happens when you do not learn how to live your own life. You become one among many cattle, driven by cowboys, or subject to the terror of thieves or wolves. Emotionally giving up and living passively is not the answer.

The way of self-cultivation is the only way of life worth living, practically, factually and truthfully. It is ultimately not helpful to live your personal life passively, then move aggressively in the world, collecting or destroying people according to the incomplete knowledge you have gathered. This has been done before. It has ruined other people and destroyed many things, but one thing it has not done is save the world. All knowledge, intellectual or moral, is subject to continued completion and development by human life. We have been troubled by the strong assertive leaders of the world who act like they are playing with building blocks, as demonstrated by their destructive nature. Children with a destructive nature like to put building blocks together, but their excitement does not come from the new combination they have made; it comes the moment when they are finished and they destroy their creation. For some children, building blocks help them develop their creative mind. But these other children have only learned that enjoyment comes from destruction. This kind of undevelopment among adults, especially among influential people or world leaders, can cause large scale suffering.

The learning of Tao is a gradual process, because it promotes each individual's development. Children who are impatient are still impatient inside after they grow up, but now they have become world leaders. Each generation desires to establish a new social order, and puts a lot of energy into it. However, it is usually not only a new social order that the leaders wish to establish; it is often also externalized personal ambition and desire. The negative nature of the people who make up the world in different generations has not progressed much in morality nor in wisdom. By observing human society through different generations, we know that we have been guided by different social leaders who have brought about experiences of great disaster. That hope of a great organic human world is gone and it cannot be brought into existence through temporary remedies.   We have not been given any true, good solutions by any of these leaders.   This confirms that the only hope of a workable solution is as the ancient achieved ones recommend, to live on the path of spiritual development.

But we are small people, some of you may be thinking, we are not people in positions of great influence.   Although you are not in an important position, your own personal influence is no less than that of someone who has a big name, because each person holds the key of safety, not only for himself but also for his society, surroundings and environment.   Whatever a person is doing, it is important to be alert, aware and helpful, because although a person may not be great in position or society, he may have a great effect.   We know that one small spark can start a fire that burns the entire forest.   Similarly, it only takes one person to put out a spark to save the entire forest.   An ordinary person, who is neither famous nor great, still has the potential to kill many important lives when he drives on the freeway.   Even the person working at a job that pays only a few dollars an hour, working in a control room, pushing the buttons on a machine, is important.   The timing of his actions is important.   No one can afford to be negligent, which would prove harmful to himself if he loses his job but could cause much damage or destruction in the world.   Each individual's spiritual cultivation is more important than how much pay they receive.   Each individual takes care of the world.   The one who regularly takes care of himself is the one who takes care of the world.   Nobody can afford to think that he is not important. People who think they are unimportant, do not care about what they do, which leads to ruin.   A person who thinks he is unimportant may lose his self-cultivation or self-discipline, which is as important as making a great spiritual achievement or great progress for the world.   One's own spiritual progress and achievement is important, because everybody affects everybody else's life. There is no escaping this fact.

What spiritual progress do we make? Do not misunderstand and think that spiritual progress is for the purpose of earning the attention of the high god, who may some day choose to seat you at the left side of his throne.   It is not looking for worldly reward or achievement or attention or respect, or to be given flowers by somebody. The spiritual progress of society has nothing to do with man-made concepts. We discovered long ago that the conceptual tool, belief in God, is unfit. It serves only to make leaders, special sects or societies of believers become assertive, and they only concentrate on their personal conceptual structures of being and do not naturally extend proper care to the life of the entire world. This causes further damage in today's world, which is already confused by a great deal of prejudice which people have taken for the truth.

At the beginning, prejudice was only a conceptual tool to support one's emotions. Fortunately or unfortunately, human intellectual capacity has improved. Now the intellectual mind holds improper beliefs, improper fervency and narrow dogmas, all of which are very destructive. These are much worse than being an unintellectual person who leads a natural life without any conceptual spiritual beliefs. Power in a person with prejudicial beliefs can turn become a weapon or a destructive tool to be used against people who believe and live differently. We would rather such a person become balanced and give up his narrow established beliefs - practical, political, economic and religious - because those beliefs bring trouble.

Today, many people still think that putting all the people of the world under one belief or one faith will help the world. We obviously do not need to develop the argument. The fact of conflict is already seen; it has one face. Are Christians unified? Is there unification between Christianity and Islam? Both religions

have a similar aggressive nature.   True belief or true
faith, together with an unprogrammed mind free from
narrow or prejudiced motivations, enjoys more peace
because it does not contain any confused, undeveloped
religious creations.   At this stage, human intellectual
capability can create or release destructive power
against all people in a few seconds.   We can see that
in this way people are now very developed, but have
they equally developed their spiritual wisdom to handle the power of that possible destruction without
letting it happen?   What, then, is the strength of the
teaching of any of the religious leaders?   When intellectual leaders view religion, they do not see it from
the viewpoint of a balanced mind.   Neither do religious
leaders view the world from a balanced mind.   They
see things from a particular perspective at a certain
stage, even if they have natural kindness, a natural
great heart and the intent to manage today's destructive power.

We can appreciate and admire the achievement of
modern people who created a power that can destroy
the entire world in a few seconds.   We need, however,
to improve and refresh our spiritual sense, the deepest
spiritual knowledge, which is above the destructive
power.   Misfortune or fortune, tragedy or happiness
arise out of the issue of balance; and now the imbalance is seen.   We also need to change old conceptions, such as the rigidly-held belief in God, which
was a conceptual tool or emotional support meant to
restore the dignity of a believing race.   It is time for
spiritually developed people to know that God is at
once all parts of a life being and all life beings existing
in harmonious unity.   Could we make that our ambition?   It is a necessity in our time.   In our everyday,
personal life, when we are in good shape, it means that
the harmony of all spiritual and non-spiritual faculties
of our life being supports us.   You are God.   You do
not need to look for any extra God beside you, because
your energy is complete and full.   When you feel some
difficulty, even one you do not actively notice, it means
your own spiritual world in your physical body

contains some conflict. You have not put yourself together completely. So you must be doing something that is not in accordance with universal law; consequently, your actions will not be right. In this situation, you had better not go out of your house until you first put yourself together! On such a day, do not try to extend your intellectual or emotional power to save the world, because at that moment you are not a god. You are only god when you are supported by the attainment of the harmony of all departments of your life being: emotional, spiritual, physical and rational. This includes the details of the many different aspects of your life, such as your social environment and how you provide for your material needs. Nothing can be neglected. Do not make one emotional thing your god; nor one physical thing; nor anything that is unbalanced. Only when all things are harmonized and come together is it God.

In the past, individuals believed in the name of God, but they unfortunately projected one element, such as emotion, finance or ambition, as God. This belief caused disturbance in their life being and society and did nothing to improve the world's condition.

All people are special, not only some people. For example, some people do not think they are special, so they do something bad to become special or attract attention. A special person, by his small, modest efforts, supports himself, his society and the world, quietly. He does not need to do anything special to make people think he is special. He may not even notice that his discipline and patience have already greatly supported the world. One with such value does not need to shoot the president or do something destructive to attract attention and so become proud of himself. Living a stable emotional life is sufficient cause for someone to be proud of themselves. That is a spiritual achievement. Do not think that anybody is unimportant. Do not think that you can become important by doing something strange or something that is different from what others do. Your importance stems from your constancy and the strength of your normalcy in the expression of your daily simple life. People do not comprehend how respectful that is.   It is equal to God!   God is the highest thing in daily life; ordinariness.   You are special already because you are already uncommon.   You are extraordinary because you have the strength to live.   You may think your life is difficult, but you are supporting peace and the development of other people, while at the same time working on yourself.

I have already mentioned that Tao is very simple. Many people who are interested in my teaching come to me and say, previously we only trusted a system of belief because we found nothing higher.   Our belief was dogmatic and produced prejudice.   Now I would like to improve myself and find something else beside prejudice and an imbalanced life.

To these people, to all people, I offer the simplicity of the highest Truth.   It is the oneness, within and without, of Tao.

CHAPTER FIFTEEN

ARE YOU TOO TIGHT
OR AM I TOO CRUEL?

Master Ni Discusses Some Questions with Visitors

Visitors: Master Ni, we are looking for the teaching of your tradition. We have visited mainland China and met some old Taoist Masters and Chi Kuan teachers. Some of them mentioned you and recommended you to us. We also visited Taiwan, where you published a number of important Taoist books in Chinese. These books mostly connected the skills, method and practice of spiritual cultivation. They are not similar in content to the books in English that you have published here in the United States. We also contacted some of your Chinese students in Taiwan. It seems the training you give to them is different.

Master Ni: I do not have any personal communication with the mainland except through some old connections. It is true that my books and teachings are somewhat different for my Chinese students; this is because my Chinese students have the inherent cultural background. Although the reality of China's new lifestyle is now different, I can still simply teach them the direct and essential discipline and practice from my tradition. Here in the West, however, the precedent of teaching a natural and healthy life through integral principles from an ancient culture is missing. It is soon going to be lost in its motherland by those who are overly enthusiastic in the pursuit of materialism. Therefore, I dedicate myself to preserving the essence of the high spiritual achievement of the forefathers of the human race and making it available to modern people, whether Chinese or Western.

Modern people have as features of their life, in contrast to their ancestors, that they earn much more money and also have much less time for themselves.

Their life span is lengthened as is the average age of the majority. However, their time is shortened by too much distraction. Thus, they do not have enough time to do everything they would like to do, nor do they have time for themselves. Even when they have some unstructured time, they are hardly happy to be with themselves. They are artless in being with their own person.

In my personal case, it has taken me long years to learn Tao, the natural integral wisdom. It has also taken me an equal length of time to learn the modern way of living. I am clear from my learning that my destiny is to serve modern people and not just to enjoy myself with the ancient art of life. Thus, I have been following a strenuous schedule to teach and write, on top of conducting a busy practice of ancient integral medicine, which is how I support my life.

After understanding the characteristics of modern living, I appreciate the original teaching of Tao even more. It is very simple. The small book of Lao Tzu, *The Tao Teh Ching*, shows the simplest essence of the great path of Integral Truth. It is derived from the profound observation and vast exploration of universal nature made by the great minds of the authors of *The Book of Changes and the Unchanging Truth*. It provides sufficient guidance for living a good life in any era. Chuang Tzu, Hui Neng and other masters whose teachings I have adopted, have provided great elucidations of the understanding of Lao Tzu and further developed the useful and serviceable application of *The Tao Teh Ching*. Having all those valuable teachings come to my hands, I have faithfully presented them with their correct meaning to all of you in the new languages of English and Chinese, though some important writing of mine is still in ancient Chinese. I dedicate all my work to the people of the new great epoch of spiritual awakening. The cultural essence belongs to whomever makes good use of it in their personal lives and to those who offer to continue the teaching.

Visitor: Master Ni, I wish to learn directly from you. Would you accept me as your student?

Master Ni: I recommend that you learn directly the important principles in my books. They will serve you better and more clearly.

Visitor: We enjoy reading your books. They are good books and very helpful. We know that you are a very busy person; how do you write them?

Master Ni: I do not start out with any book in my mind; it is only when I come into contact with people and modern society that my spiritual energy flows to respond. I do some part of the writing. I do better with written material, because I can see it and correct it immediately. As for my talking, while it is important too, my spoken English capability is not high. My heavily-accented English has caused a lot of jokes! When I listen to the tapes made from my own lectures, and I see the   poor condition of the transcriptions of my recorded talks, my face feels flushed most of the time. Fortunately, my writing helpers can accurately understand what I mean, and then I also take the opportunity to correct and improve it. It is very hard work for me. Each time I endow my energy and vision to correct my own speech, it is like an old man of over a hundred years rolling a huge stone up a mountain. In other more pleasurable circumstances, I never admit I am old like that. This is the exception.

Visitor: But your books are very good. You must feel proud of your achievement. Nowadays, it is hard to find a true master like yourself. We feel greatly honored to interview you.

Master Ni: I feel it is my moral obligation. When I finish each book, I wish it to be the last piece of stone. As I am working on this one, I wish it is truly the last piece of stone I roll up to the top of the mountain. I do not mean I feel spiritual exhaustion. I believe that my spiritual vitality has not been born yet. It is the physical strenuousness, because by doing the books, I miss a lot of sunshine, ocean breezes and the sweet smell of the pine trees. In the tradition of Tao, no one true master writes or talks as much as I do. It is not so admirable that I do it while the other masters do not. It is a problem if I must do it against the joyful peace of natural life, which is full of life energy or if my speeches are needless for my work. However, the sum of my writing serves only as a blackboard on which to sketch the attainment of all those truly achieved masters. It is not what I have achieved, it is my sacrifice. I have been making 'big noise' since my youth; by this I mean that teaching is not my innate tendency. Thus, because of the inadequacy of embracing the serenity of universal nature, I would like to give up the title as a master in Tao, but I do not disqualify myself as a student of Tao. I love people, and I cannot forget the troubled world or refuse to work for it. So if anybody approaches me in the future and addresses me as Master Ni, I shall still courteously respond to it, though I have come back to be just a student like all my friends.

Visitors: You are still a great master. We appreciate all your work.

Master Ni: From listening to the tapes of my speaking, I know I cannot correct people who hear me in person right away. But I feel it is safe for all of you to read my books. Not a particular line, but all lines; not a particular book, but all books. I feel stronger in taking responsibility for my writing, because giving a correct spiritual message is the most serious thing in the world. It is, at least, a very serious matter to me. I do not wish to be misunderstood or to have something partial taken as the whole teaching of Tao.

Visitor: Master Ni, I would like you to personally teach me, if possible. I know you are travelling a lot now. I would like to tell you my background. Our parents strictly follow the Orthodox Jewish faith. We have never gotten along well with our parents and there have always been a lot of problems. Now they are older and retired. They visit about every other year. They think the Wailing Wall is very inspiring. But it is not inspiring to us. They are very unhappy with the spiritual direction we have taken. They think we are all wrong. It is a troublesome that we can't convince them to look for new spiritual inspiration as we do.

Master Ni: Culture and religion are like personalities. Some are tight. Some are loose. It is not good to be too tight. It is also not good to be too loose. It is appropriate to be balanced, neither too tight nor too loose.

No religions are bad; however, judgments can be made as to their spiritual quality. A religion which builds people too tight spiritually is harmful to the people who believe in it and to those in their environment. If a religion causes people to produce a spiritual quality that is too loose, it would be consumed by the people who follow the too-tight religions. Why? Because they are afraid if they do not conquer, they will be conquered themselves. Even if two believers from two different tight religions were promoting their faiths, if their belief in their own way was rooted deeply enough, they would fight until death. Neither can truly live, however, until both see the light that the truth of individual survival is a balanced spiritual quality: neither too tight nor too loose in life. It is the same truth for the co-existence of two races or two nations. Jewish people are smart, but like the Japanese, they are too tight. They have a magnificent capacity to produce some great creations, but they also have the great capability to bring about suffering through their tightness. Chinese people were too loose for many centuries, but recently they have adopted a system which makes them tight. Of course, they have tasted the bitter fruit produced by it and suffered from the tightness of their new institutions.

The problem of the world is the problem of the world's culture. This is why my work is to promote a global cultural and spiritual renaissance to reform all existent religious beliefs and restart from the natural normalcy of organic being. By doing this, I have also become tight, which is another reason for me to step down from traditional mastership in Tao. I have lost the good quality by pushing myself very hard to work and talk too seriously at a time when all people have already become too serious.

By being overly serious, some people are driven to kill themselves when disappointed in love. People kill themselves if they lose money in stocks. A great many people die for somebody else's lie by taking it as the highest truth. People kill many other people by imposing an immature political system on them. People can start destructive wars for all kinds of false beliefs and prejudices. You are even nervous when the neighbor's kids play in the tree in your front yard because your insurance might have to pay if they fall. You get nervous when you drive in a busy town, or park your car somewhere, because you might get a citation or penalty. On the highway you hear yelling and honking between two drivers, each calling the other a jerk, even though there may be no real damage. In a family, between father and mother, husband and wife, sister and brother, or youngsters and adults, small emotional frictions turn into fights. In all of these cases, is there any matter of right or wrong? It is mostly caused by one side who takes something that is not serious to be a very serious matter. In conflicts among schoolmates in a classroom, colleagues in an office, people on the street, in different churches and in different countries, usually nothing is involved that is moral or immoral, people are just emotionally too tight. Their spiritual education is too serious and it has spoiled their nature. In some countries now, you need a coupon to buy meat. Someday you will need to buy a coupon for laughing. In some country, maybe America, someday anybody who laughs will be taxed.

To be an adept of Tao, you cannot be as serious as all that, even in the moment of natural transformation between life and death of someone, or yourself. It is a laughing matter when it is a fine day. It is also a laughing matter when it is not a fine day. However, I have become very serious in telling people how to distinguish the false from the true. I am too serious in giving spiritual messages. In a different generation, the adepts of Tao never bothered to do the teaching of truth. Even the achieved Zahn masters could jest and fool around with the things they rejected. I dare not joke when I give serious spiritual messages, because I think it must be done properly and carefully. It is the teaching work that prevents me from joking; then I become limited. This makes me unable to attain spiritual unlimitedness. Even if I cannot attain anything, I still cannot be too serious. It is a dangerous tendency when a person becomes too serious. It is an even greater dangerous tendency when the people of the world become too serious. Those who are emotionally too tight must soon suffer nervousness. When the people of the world become too tight emotionally, wars happen. People do not pay enough attention to themselves to know in good time when they have become too serious and are going to be sick mentally. Who should take responsibility for making people too serious? It was the fault of the religious leaders and the religions, who made people serious in order to organize them. The spiritual awakening of all people from mischievous religious customs can prevent them and their children from suffering the same destiny!

About your great interest to learn the techniques of cultivation, my sons Daoshing and Maoshing and other students consistently give classes that you can take. I will continue to occasionally give spiritual seminars to teach special techniques and methods of cultivation from different achieved masters in our tradition. Notice will be given to centers in different places about when and what I am going to teach. Studentship can also be established by correspondence for those who live far away from a center.

You are accepted as a student of Tao. You may join one of the centers and work with any of the mentors to help your learning. I hope your learning will be fruitful.

Last, I would like to tell you a story about the great Chuang Tzu, an earlier master in Tao. It is similar to a Chinese opera entitled "The Butterfly's Dream."

Chuang Tzu married a very serious woman. Her name is un-recorded. I give her the temporary name of Maria, but surely she was Chinese and not Western. First I need to make that understood.

The Chinese Maria had been brought up according to the ideals of leading a serious life, which included spiritual obligations to religion and following strict rules of behavior. She was a very religious person, constantly instructing her husband on the merits of the dogma, unable to understand that his natural wisdom was far greater. Chuang Tzu always told his wife not to be too serious.

One of the spiritual doctrines she frequently argued about with him was the notion of eternal love between a husband and a wife. Spiritual custom held that upon a husband's death, a wife was obligated to live out her days alone, thus maintaining her love for her husband, and she was never to remarry.

One day after one such discussion with her, Chuang Tzu left the house and went for a walk. He happened to go by a place where a grave had been recently dug. A woman was sitting next to the grave, fanning it. Curious about her behavior, Chuang Tzu went over and asked her what she was doing. "Before he died," she replied, "my husband told me not to remarry, unless the dirt on his grave dried."

When Chuang Tzu returned home, he related what he had seen to his wife. He thought the woman should remarry without having to fulfill the unusual request of her deceased husband. Maria thought that it was shameful that the woman should even think of remarrying, and went on and on about the merits of guarding eternal love between husband and wife, to the dismay of Chuang Tzu.

Shortly after, Chuang Tzu went out in the rain and caught a cold, then died of a heart attack. Maria was very sorrowful and followed all the proper procedures for the funeral and burial. She prepared herself for spending the rest of her life alone, with only a maid to keep her company.

A few days later, there was a knock on the door. It was a distinguished-looking man, obviously a traveler. "I have just arrived from Lu," he said, "and there is no inn within twenty li of here. It is nightfall, and I am in need of rest. I respectfully request a night's lodging and offer payment for it." The maid was about to refuse his request, but seeing that he was well-dressed, finely mannered and obviously not an ordinary person, went in to ask Maria.

"Since he has no other recourse," she reluctantly replied, "let him stay. We have an empty room." A meal was prepared; the man was well-bred and was delightful company. In the course of the evening's conversation, he remarked that he had come to the village to consult a certain doctor, seeking a cure for a disease from which he had suffered since childhood.

He left in the morning, thanking them for their great hospitality.

That evening, just before nightfall, there was again a knock on the door. It was the gentleman, who said, "I have come to ask your generosity again in obtaining one more night's lodging. The doctor has given me a prescription and although I have spent the entire day searching for the ingredients, I have failed to find all of them. If I spend one more night, I can continue my search in the morning for the things that are difficult to obtain."

As he had been such pleasant company, Maria agreed. The gentleman entered the house and the two of them dined together happily as they did the previous evening. "What ingredients do you need?" she asked. "Perhaps we can help you locate them."

"I have all but one," he said, "and it seems hopelessly impossible. I do not know how much longer I can live if I do not find it. It is some unspoiled matter from a human brain." And then he bid her good night and retired to his room.

Maria stayed awake a long time, thinking. The gentleman's visit had eased her loneliness and she had enjoyed his good company. It could not be her imagination that he also had appreciated her presence and care in the same way. Perhaps a life of being alone was not what she really wanted.

She finally decided to help him. The next day, she arose before dawn to accomplish the task. It had only been seven days since Chuang Tzu had died, and she went out to the grave.

An axe of that time was rather heavy for a lady to use, but she persisted and after some time, managed to open up the coffin. Chuang Tzu sat up. "You're still alive!" she gasped.

"Yes indeed," he laughed and said. "Thank you. I am well now. The box has made me sweat a lot and the warmth saved me from the cold." He climbed out and went with her back into the house. There was no trace whatsoever of the gentleman visitor.

However, Maria could not learn anything from the joke. Some years later, she died of being overly serious in her life. At the funeral, Chuang Tzu used a stick to beat on an earthen basin like a drum, as he sang to mourn her:

"Oh Maria, my love, did I not tell you
Physical life cannot be too serious!
It is not supported by all the riches!
It is not even supported by all the happiness!
Yet, it is supported by being not too serious!
Because you are too serious,
The seriousness grows cysts in your breasts.
Because you are too serious,
The seriousness grows tumors in your uterus.
I have given you a good life
You were away from meat and wine

and any stimulation.
Alas, you are not satisfied with such a great fate.
You do not take it as a great protection.
You complained.
You have given your life to your silly beliefs.
You pray everyday
But you have never known,
God cannot help you because you live too tight.
My warning given to you was wasted.
You were beautiful, you were a good woman.
But you have never learned to enjoy your life."

At that moment, Hui Tzu, Chuang Tzu's best friend, hurried over. Seeing Chuang Tzu singing, he became angry and said, "Are you not overly cruel? It is enough that you are not weeping, but how can you sing?"
With a sigh, Chuang Tzu continued to sing:

"I have met the king of devils,
His name is Serious.
He has swallowed one of my loves.
This one, a great friend of mine, will soon be as
Food in his mouth too."

Hui Tzu was a very talented and serious scholar. Unfortunately, as Chuang Tzu prophesied, it was not too long after that he was also eaten by the Demon King, Serious.
Neither Maria nor Hui Tzu, close ones of Chuang Tzu, had ever learned the martial art from Chuang Tzu that beats all troubles.

CHAPTER SIXTEEN

THE NEW GLOBAL SPIRITUAL DIRECTION

Discussion between Master Ni and Students

Student: Master Ni, many of us feel the culture and civilization of human society need a new direction.   Conventional religions and spiritual teachings are not good enough to face the global problem of internal and external human conflict.   Though there are all kinds of religions, we do not know or have enough knowledge of the spirits of different planets and galaxies.

Master Ni: Human religious worship started by imagination; this is not spiritually achieved wisdom.   We need to remove all such obstacles on the road of human spiritual progress.   We need true spiritual knowledge and achievement to cope with the change of human intelligence.   We also need the expansion of a healthy political influence to reach all individuals.   With these in mind, as I see it, the most important thing is to open up the minds of all humans.   Spiritual responsibility entails a change from the imposition of religious control to the promotion of the natural development of all individuals.

A person of natural development is not narrow minded.   He is open to all important scriptures, religions and spiritual experiences, but he does not lose his own unique nature through exposure to books, rituals or religious programs.   A person who is spiritually achieved can also enjoy the spiritual fruit of different cultural achievements from various traditions.   He enjoys spiritual limitlessness, which Chuang Tzu describes as riding on a ship and traveling freely around the world of his life.   The cruise, however, must always bring one back to oneself.   He does not take a cruise on the Titanic and sink in the ocean; he returns home, to his own life-nature.   Once a person comes back to nature, he can appreciate that other things can reflect his own nature.   People can meet easily when they enjoy all kinds of achievements - mental and spiritual - different philosophies, conceptual creations, ideas, ideologies, different religions and spiritual practices.

The new spiritual direction should be universal spiritual integration.   The path of universal spiritual integration is not a program established by someone; it is the nurturing of the natural evolution of a person, internally and externally.   There can be spiritual devolution too, which results from incorrect development.

All human spiritual teaching can be classified as one of two types.   One is the sun type which is to be and to do; it expresses one direction of the creative human spirit.   Another is the moon type which is to think and review; it represents the reflecting mind. Those two types are exemplified by the characteristics of the original religions, which surely have their defects.   The sun type can be illustrated by Judaism, Hinduism, Christianity, Islam and the ancient Chinese religious faith in Heaven, from which their knowledge originated; the moon type by Buddhism and the mental training of Taoism.   However, the learning of Tao as the path of universal subtle integration is symbolized by the Tai Chi diagram, which illustrates the integration of the energies of the sun and the moon.

We need faith and confidence and, most importantly, creative energy to live in the world.   You cannot expect to be creative and smooth every day, particularly general people who have a different experience and who are in need of an awakened mind with which to reflect upon the problems of life.   If you rely only on the sun of faith, you may become too strong or pushy and use it as an excuse for your ambition.   It must be balanced by the moon, your mind, which reflects on whether the interpretation of your faith is fitting and proper.   To unify both is to have a complete spirit and a good human life.

All life is nature; it is active and moving, not stagnant.   Nature is a continual proceeding; we need to proceed to brightness.   Spiritual goals, political goals and economic goals should not conflict with each other. They should be united, assisting each other just as the mind can assist the impetus of life and the stimulus of life can assist the mind.   They work together as life nature.   The nature of life is to keep moving, to keep progressing.   No dead religion or inflexible doctrine should be adopted if it controls or restrains your natural growth.   Follow only nature itself and make all the stars your brothers; make the entire sky the fatherly, motherly, sisterly and brotherly energy to support your human growth.

Let us look at the former leader of communism in China, Mao Tse Tung, as an example of personal ambition.   He created the greatest tragedy that has happened in human history.   An enormous number of people were destroyed by one person's evil ambition to make himself the center of the world in conformity to his dream of the old type of empire.   All young ambitious people, men and women, exemplify this too.   It is not refined nature; it is stagnation.

We can also see that as external religious functions became weaker than in ancient times, modern society became more affected by mass communication and recreational tools such as radio and TV.   All kinds of criminal stories become a sort of new religion, the content of a new culture that pushes people to a lower level.   Today, people need to guide their own natures, their families and their children away from extinction with the best education that can be obtained from the external world.   How?   Develop yourself.   You set the example; work with all the members of your family and your friends, following the naturally developed, balanced suggestions and advice that have been given us by the ancient achieved ones to further our spiritual development.   Every day, if you find something new and right, do not forget to correct what has come before.

If it is helpful, people may certainly keep using the tools they have learned from religious education, such as prayer, beads, mantras or anything else that can keep the mind channeled in the pursuit of enlightenment and the reaching of the subtle light. The final assessment of a tool is this: can it still be useful once you know how to follow and join the new concourse of all spiritual currents in the great ocean of life? No good tool should be forsaken. All good tools should be sharpened and kept useful in daily life because tools can help you and can carry you toward the destination you seek. But narrow thoughts or narrow conceptualized learning limit you and are not beneficial because they express negativity. A wise one always utilizes good, useful and healthy things. Therefore, we respect any good conceptual tools and practices we have learned that still support new growth as part of our learning on the path of universal spiritual integration.

All religions are means, not ends. If correctly applied, they can be helpful in your personal and social life. But the understanding derived from following a religious program may limit the intellectual scope of your spiritual attainment, unless you are naturally centered and spiritually within yourself. Then we can be happy about our own spiritual achievement and also respect the spiritual achievement of the ancient leaders, taking into consideration the background of their societies, the times they lived in and their limitations. They did their best to assist people and help society pass through one stage of growth. Now it should be you who continues on your way to develop into a great leader to bring about a new epoch of human life.

Earlier, different points were discussed in order to understand and demonstrate that Tao itself is a high truth, a high principle that can be utilized in specific circumstances. We can decide whether a circumstance follows the normalcy of the universe or goes against universal nature. It is always good to integrate the teaching of Tao with the lower sphere of facts and circumstances.

We have pointed out that the teachers of Tao integrated the high use of Tao with the teaching of Buddhism in China to produce Zahn (Zen) Buddhism. It is not necessarily restricted to Zahn, because Tao itself can be applied to any religion to guide a follower, step by step, to reach the subtle level of truth, the high truth. Tao itself is not the circumstance but it is inexpressible apart from a circumstance; it cannot independently be told or explained. Therefore, it is right to use Tao to integrate and give life to all religions in order to find the real spiritual significance in the religious education. Also, if we were to do away with general religious practice or teaching, Tao could not be shown and the high truth could not be taught. Therefore, integration and cooperation is necessary. You cannot see existence without high truth. The high truth still needs to be expressed in a generally correct, or even superficially manifested, organized teaching system. In that way, the truth can be easily shown through a terminology, rhetoric and conceptual layout, eventually reaching the point where it no longer needs to be conveyed by words, pictures or other concrete means.

The person who learns the subtle truth has something which cannot be taken away from him. You cannot stay fixed with the high subtle truth; you must realize it at the fundamental, basic level of life, in your thoughts and conceptual activities; then you can find the subtle truth everywhere. If you are alive to the subtle truth, everything is full of meaning. If you lose the subtle truth, then everything loses real significance. This confirms the fundamental nature of Tao, which can be integrated with existing, reprogrammed, refined or purified new systems of teaching that can help the world through its emotional problems by introducing the spiritual level into general human life.

The ancient developed ones always taught that fish cannot live without water. This means that the subtle truth itself cannot be truth without being implemented in general circumstances, activities or levels of life. We must not make the subtle truth a separate thing aside from our physical, mental or spiritual activities; the truth itself must simultaneously be manifested in our activities.

Because Tao is the subtle truth, it cannot be shown directly, just as the root of most trees cannot be exposed above ground. As people's bones and tendons and internal organs are all wrapped up and protected by muscle and skin, similarly, Tao can live within many different conceptual vessels. Tao can hardly be discerned in times and circumstances of balance and normalcy; it is like snow in a bowl of white jade. Tao is the normalcy of nature and of life. This is important knowledge about how we learn Tao and how, over a long period of time, we attain spiritual achievement and make this achievement useful in general life and all circumstances.

Once the minds of all humans reach the natural truth, the methods and practices of the tradition of Tao, which teaches the association with all spiritual levels of nature, become available. This spiritual development can be attained by many.

Thank you for asking me about the new global spiritual direction. What I offer in answer is very old, from the time before the artificial creations of the human mind became dominant.

CHAPTER SEVENTEEN

GROUP SPIRITUAL PRACTICE

1
Spiritual Study by a Group

Humans learn from each other, imitate each other and influence each other in good as well as bad ways. Spiritual group study can be a good vehicle to help one another's growth if the negative or destructive trends are watched and restrained. A natural spiritual group studying the Universal Integral Spiritual Truth can be family members, friends, schools, classes, parties, clubs or any other association, large or small or any group that opens itself up to the true light of universal spiritual nature. There are two types of study groups; public, which are open to any person with interest, and private, which are a small group of family or friends. Mentors are teachers and helpers who aspire to help themselves and others and offer themselves for organizing group study. They may become ordained if they wish to obtain recognition from this time-honored tradition. However, if their motivation and means are right, they may also assume such virtuous work with recognition of the high spiritual realm. Those who obtain ordination make a vow that they will work as an expression of the universal spiritual nature.

For most people who wish to develop themselves spiritually, participating in a study group can be of great benefit. It is unfortunate that spiritual groups have lost their prestige in modern times due to many misguided groups having failed to be of real value in helping people change their accumulated, habitual secondary natures for the better. However, when established in a correct way, group spiritual study and learning has a positive value. The advantage of group study is clearly seen when a healthy direction is maintained. Our tradition welcomes and encourages responsible people who want to offer their help and positive influence to society by organizing spiritual study groups. If enough people did this, the world would move in a healthier direction.

The ancient monastery or church type of spiritual study may be one way of spiritual life, yet it has lost its appropriateness for the new generations because it clearly has been unable to uplift the world from its troubles. Let us avoid the negative repetition of these old types of spiritual group learning. Let us reform spiritual group learning by creating a more natural way to learn that does not create dependency or operate by manipulation.

However, some churches, although still using the conventional shell, have started to teach the positive attitudes, the open and healthy life, instead of a sacrificial and extremely dogmatic practice. I appreciate their work and contribution to promote healthy human minds. Correct faith always invites the light to people's dark mind. God is a positive and virtuous life; this is the essence of all religions. Some interpretations deviate from that direction; however, only the developed individuals who are dedicated to the spiritual improvement of the entire world can significantly correct that mistake.

Some interested people have established centers or study groups to teach the Integral Way in the United States. Such centers functioning in a healthy way are a good example and supplement the limits of written work. My written work gives the high spiritual essence and wisdom of realized people for 8,000 years, but cannot replace fundamental training and basic discipline. This is where group study is valuable. Here is an illustration of the importance of learning the basics: when you wish to teach the horse you are riding to dance, you first must learn how to ride the horse well yourself. You begin with learning a simple thing and then you learn the higher skills. The high wisdom from my written work is like teaching someone how to make a horse dance, but in general, people do not understand its use or value, or know how to put these achievements into practice. Other regions of the world, in ancient times, had received the basic discipline, but without being given the teaching of the high spiritual essence, they become insulated in a religious environment, unable to attain either the breadth or the high essence of true spiritual achievement. If one has only high wisdom or only basic discipline, one is incomplete. True realization comes from first maintaining basic discipline in your life and then learning the higher level of wisdom. In that way, we can have hope for the next generation and a better world.

In an organic, self-directed group study center, nurturing the spiritual organics of all, a mentor is a teacher, an adviser and a friend. He or she is the coordinator of the group. He or she can choose assistants from the students to help his or her work and teaching. Basically, all students teach and learn the most important basic disciplines; a less experienced one can request a more experienced one to be his or her sponsor in learning. By employing the system of helping each other, the study of the natural wisdom of generations infuses in the new blood a truly constructive way to build human beings so that their deep spirit can be reflected in an orderly, peaceful and healthy world. This is the wisdom that has been written about and examined in my books.

All mentors are students of Tao. In a local center, there can be a directing mentor who has a co-mentor working with him or her, or there can be two co-mentors working together. Mentors can recommend candidates to become mentors. Through service, one can improve and attain high respectable spiritual qualities.

When a new student has a question which his or her sponsor cannot answer sufficiently well, the sponsor can seek the help or advice of the mentor. If the mentor does not have the complete answer, or if the question is of a different nature than that answered in my book or has not been previously asked, the mentor can talk to Daoshing or Maoshing Ni, who will answer the question or seek my advice when I check in with them from my spiritual retreat for work and cultivation, or from my travels.

It is a stable educational process. A little is given at a time, and not all at once. One does not feed a horse with his entire month's feed in only one meal. It would be ineffective to read over these books and see all the spiritual attainment without following an orderly educational process. The study group can help this. However, the purpose of publishing and teaching the gems of this spiritual tradition is to preserve them lest they be lost. Group study can compliment the individual work with my books.

Spiritual attainment should not be held by only a few special, achieved individuals. It is not hard for us to find individuals who have set a good example in human history; however, the human world as a whole has been moving farther away from the truth of life. The more achieved human beings should be put to use in order to influence society; because this has not happened, the world has become worse. The highest achievements were the enjoyment of a few developed ones; however, it is terribly wrong not to realize these achievements in general society. So with all my might and the good help of others in my writing and publishing these books, I wish to extend this wisdom so that each individual life as well as the larger society may gain from it. We encourage people to form study groups for their own learning and that of others.

2
Things to be Avoided by a Study Group

We promote group study with the purpose of cultivating a higher level of awareness among all people. During the past few years, I have been advised to take the more formal Western approach of giving certificates to ministers, mentors and teachers. However, it has not helped greatly. A spiritually developed individual fulfills his duty in helping and teaching people and is naturally recognized and given respect by people. The certificates are not for achieving that purpose, but are a means of conferring my personal recognition of achievement and appreciation for giving help to me. All mentors should make their own real effort of fulfilling the duty of their position by earning the respect and recognition from the people they work with, as well as from myself. Those who have been ordained and would like to have a certificate to show the connection of their spiritual source with the Union of Tao and Man and the Great Path of the Integral Truth may request one.

Now it is important to warn you about the disadvantages of group spiritual study or learning. In any group, one exposes oneself to the temptations of money, sex and power; these form the true trinity of universal worship for most people. In the practical world, power is god the father, money is god the son and sex is the holy spirit. The order of the father and son is sometimes interchangeable. To most people, money is god. They wish to take it by doing evil, immoral, mischievous, deceitful, detrimental or harmful actions with no consideration for others; all these things are done just for money. However, even if one can ignore god the father and god the son, they can never ignore the holy spirit, which means, people indulge in sex. It is people's minds that abuse spiritual energy by sexual indulgence. Being afraid of this trap, the most ancient religions tried to avoid its temptations or enticements through a formalized monastic type of spiritual education that separated people from everyday life. It was, however, a very unrealistic and unhealthy spiritual educational approach; it is like having once experienced being choked by food and thereafter deciding to stop eating altogether. The truth has not been learned. It is important to develop your wisdom so that you eat healthy good food, of course. True achievement comes from living in a normal society and not by caged discipline. Therefore, all new students are encouraged to join the group learning of the great spiritual path of the integral truth, and expose themselves to the temptation of the above-mentioned, most powerful trinity to learn how to correctly fulfill their desires.

It takes honest delving and learning for one to achieve oneself as a true whole person and not remain as a follower of an artificial religious standard. A true person cannot be manipulated or molded. If a person becomes a nun or a monk, hiding from power and sex or anything else during their whole lifetime, he or she is not being true; he or she is being artificial, because such a life is artificial. True spiritual strength can be built through group spiritual support and study, not by escaping all enticements. I bless your success in the fulfillment of all three areas, but all three must be practiced in a healthy way to attain true upliftment. If a person can achieve that by either way, then he has built a strong personality. This is the goal of the Great Path of Broad Practice. Then we shall see healthy, strong people building the world, people supported by spiritual group study who have learned to manage themselves when exposed to temptation. One cannot really manage a situation without learning to manage oneself. It is not only a matter of temptation. It is also important to develop your wisdom to see that only temporary success can be reached by shortcuts, but can never build great, true enjoyment or even earn respect from people.

All the great ones lived their lives with patience and endurance. The young people who are strengthened by a true organic spiritual group practice will similarly be of strong character, with patience and endurance, but will also have power, and thus be a serviceable personality in the world. Good sexual behavior or proper celibacy are the basic spiritual disciplines of the great path. One develops oneself to know the natural cycle of individual life and the correct and healthy way to fulfill or restrain it. Knowledge of these matters has been described in my books.

There are many spiritual by-paths; especially with regard to sexual practice. The teachings in my books should not be mixed with any teachings from other, different teachers who are less achieved or of lower character. Students of this path should take the pure nutrition and pure nourishment from the natural wisdom of the ancient great achieved ones as I am offering it. A mixed practice would become the source of trouble. I encourage all my friends to join me in undertaking the task of both our own reformation and that of our human race, and with me, to refuse to make a connection with morally or socially inferior behavior, even while acknowledging that people can change and grow. People need always to learn and cultivate the basic discipline as the foundation of their training, then reach for the wisdom and higher techniques I offer in my books.

3
To Female Spiritual Students

The following instruction is specifically for my female students, girls and women of all different ages. Usually my teaching is broad enough to include both men and women. Spiritually and socially, modern people consider that there should not be any delineation of gender, especially in spiritual teaching; however, physiologically women are different. Many women wish to change their nature by fighting or competing for their survival or emotional freedom, because of the new social phase we are in. However, the instruction given here does not relate to the highest sphere of spiritual principles, where there is no discrimination of gender, but relates to the basics of female human life. We have only respect for women who can be spiritually contacted; for the teachers, students and others who use this information for their own help.

This instruction was inspired by the trouble and problems of today's women. In contrast to their ancestors, the education of women today is concentrated in learning to keep jobs. Modern women do not learn how to be daughters, mothers, sisters or wives; they have only gathered intellectual knowledge in the same way as men. So, simply, they have never learned to be women, and they have lots of problems being daughters, sisters, wives and mothers; they do not know how to do it. There are lots of problems, as is the similar case with men. The modern time focuses on commerce, which creates jobs to find a better living, but the spiritual quality of one's naturalness, which is basic to the family and society, is ignored. People are very focused on how to sell their skill, time and energy to bring money back to help themselves. Concurrently, in all different aspects of being a female, there are more problems than at any other time; today a young woman's development is focused on commerce and not on living a natural human life.

In my eleven years in the West, the prototypical modern society, I have been called upon to respond to all kinds of problems. Thus I have offered books of my teaching, and most of them talk about larger principles. There are some sections that are very specific to women students. I do not think I have done enough for my women students because I still see them in trouble. The purpose of my work has been to preserve the spiritual attainment of the developed ones. I have not given enough basic spiritual discipline about how to be a daughter, a wife, a mother or a friend, although my work in the West has been supported and helped by many female students. However, because they have lacked basic training, they remain intellectuals. They come and learn some information and leave, never going deeply enough. Then, new helpers come to do the same thing. The spirit of my work does not come from a desire to find fame, power, money or sexual satisfaction, but out of my own self-awakening. I feel a responsibility to warn modern people about the important part of their lives which has been ignored and neglected. They must find themselves unable to have a complete life. The basic training of both men and women, in different aspects or different positions, cannot be included in this short discussion. We can shed, however, some new light.

First, I feel that most younger women, in general, like to have fun. They regard it as an important goal of their life. To them, sexual fun is more important than self-respect and they have had sexual experiences very early in life. By overdoing it, doing it improperly or having an inappropriate partner, their healthy energy is diminished and they are emotionally harmed. So, in their twenties or later, most of them have already lived a life of regret. Further, there is not much left that's new or fresh for them. Because they have already tasted the good things and become bored, they allow the long period left of their lives to become boring or they become embittered. At the end, they live with the past problems of the early life experience. Human life generally lasts close to one hundred years, but for people of this type, most of their life is spent living with a very damaging psychology. They do not even know what is wrong with them. After gathering negative experiences to themselves they repent or are sorrowful for those experiences for the rest of their still young lives. It was caused when they were young when they did not consider - because they never learned - what was best for their own self protection; especially that which comes from respecting the wholeness of their spirit, mind and body. It is not helpful for women to have sexual contact so early due to their being misinformed or encouraged to have sexual fun.

After beginning menstruation, with increased physiological pressure, the sense of femininity is intensified. It is incorrect to make sex the center of their young lives. If they do, they grow up shaping themselves only as sexual beings. A sexual being is not a complete human being. A complete human life being is a spiritual, mental, moral, good working and family being. Only one small part is sexual. If they are miseducated and misdirected culturally into assuming that their sexual being is the center of life for a woman, then naturally, after beginning menstruation, their thoughts will be full of imagined sexual satisfaction or dwell on a special man who could come into their lives and satisfy them sexually. The goal of life becomes limited to that level.

On the other hand, today women in the business world are very competitive, the same as men, until they go home and into the privacy of their rooms. Even in that moment, I am not sure that they stop thinking about business, making money or their profession. Do they ever stop to nurture their being as a woman? Perhaps in the moment of physical sexual contact, they become a real woman for a few seconds; sometimes even before they are finished in bed, they turn back into being no more than their job or business, thinking their habitual, professional thoughts.

Just as women today are not complete, neither are men. It is not that I am here scolding my women friends; I am only pointing out for my beloved women students that they need to find a way to complete or restore the good qualities that a women can enjoy in herself. The root of life is spirit. Spiritual cultivation is important for everyone, man or woman.

My first point is that a woman should not engage in sexual activity because of physiological pressure, especially before she is mentally mature and can be responsible for what she does. Generally speaking, women achieve psychological development and maturity earlier than men. However, as I see it, there is no benefit for women in being obsessed with sex. Some women utilize all occasions to look for dating and mating. They lose their energy by having too much sex, having abortions and using unnatural birth control methods. I suggest not rushing into early, possibly regretful, sexual relationships; wait until the growth of your mind equals the growth of your body.

Second, women have physical cycles of menstruation and ovulation which are much more apparent than the emotional cycles of a man. Because of these cycles, they are more emotional than men; this is normal and there is nothing wrong with it. Because your body energy should be well maintained, I do not recommend the use of tampons, because the insertion absorbs not only the blood but also the healthy female energy. Many young girls, even without their sexual organs being touched by men, have had their energy sucked away by tampons. The holy medicine is thrown away. Like a fruit, nourishing energy can be taken away by early picking; overcooking a good vegetable can lessen its nutrition. Today's women do not have sufficient feminine energy to offer men in order to make them soft and gentle in their behavior; they destroy this potentially balancing energy through the use of tampons and overwork. The easy part is to use pads instead of tampons. The hard part is that you need to learn the effective management of your own life, as my teaching always insists.

During menstruation, it is better for a woman to be less active. Much of today's activity, however, does not allow a woman to live in a restful environment. With tampons they can be as active as men, but eventually they are harmed by using them. This points out how to maintain strong feminine energy for a complete and fulfilling feminine life. Do not destroy it by doing something improper in everyday life. Although emotionally you may wish to be active at all times, it is important to have the knowledge to slow yourself down during menstruation or ovulation. For example, do not do much physical activity or exercise when you are menstruating. You have different cycles and need to watch them so that you may adjust your activity to the periodicity of your body. In one month you have two different cycles, which work together like a big gear and a small gear, one catching the other. It is better to live more naturally, and whenever possible do not be mechanically pushed by the speedy flow of modern life.

Before, society considered a woman as an inner or indoor human being and a man was considered as an outdoor human being. Rigid practice of this is not proper. However, women need a home; women need a room or a tent. They are different than men; a rough life may be all right for the men, especially the young ones, but not for a woman.

Third, the communication media of television and novels serve to influence and make all the young girls overly sexy.   Homosexuality, which is considered mixed up sex, oral sex and the use of artificial devices is harmful.   After engaging in these, they cannot enjoy a more natural human life any more. It changes their psychology and their attitudes.   Anyone who wishes to pursue spiritual attainment should immediately stop any unnatural behaviors.   Though I have not positively suggested how to solve sexual problems, I will talk more about this later.   But in this moment, I do not support or approve of the use of vibrators or rubber penises or any kind of masturbation.   All of these are unnatural forms of sexual release.

It is also not natural to use pictures or books to stimulate your sexual energy.   This is relying on an external thing to stimulate you, rather than having sex because you have a sexual need.   Thus, it is not real sex, it is not a real need, it is just mental stimulation that affects your body.   In this matter you should let your body be the master to have good mating.

Some men who are in special positions, like psychologists, healers, religious leaders or teachers, have the opportunity to be around many women.   Sometimes such a man is tempted and would seduce women who are his patients, clients or students.   Why do such things happen?   One reason trouble of this sort occurs is that a woman does not really take responsibility for her own goodness and her own life, so she trusts someone else to take care of her.   Those in the helping professions are flesh-made people, not robots, and they have desires.   Thus, they are sometimes tempted to be involved in sexual activity with a group or a number of women, without a rational agreement.   A woman should be alert to such behavior and not become sexually involved.   There is poison in the sugar.   However, given such an opportunity, some women rush into sexual release.

Generally, sexuality occurs on a one-to-one basis. Sometimes there is an emotional disturbance involved, as when a woman cannot be with her man all the time because of the nature of his work. Or if the sexuality is not part of a committed relationship, be it husband and wife, or any stable situation, then the woman becomes depressed. Depression changes to anger, which after a long time can become psychologically damaging.

So in the case where someone in a special position has taken advantage of a woman, the woman or women will decide that the responsibility belongs to the teacher, psychologist or healer. In reality, spiritually, who should take responsibility for it? There are two ways to look at this. Firstly, because the people in the helping professions are human, you cannot trust them to be robots who do not need sex. A good professional person should never be involved sexually with their client unless they entitle themselves as a sexual therapist, which is not a very respectful profession, but it is a phenomenon in our society. Because the work serves women, surely a woman can legally charge a person who sexually damages her, but as far as her own self-awakening, she should take most of the responsibility and not let the same thing happen over and over again.

In one case that became known to me, a woman came to a specialist who wished to treat her in this way. The sexual involvement occurred repeatedly for six or seven years. Then several female clients of the same doctor discovered that they were all receiving similar treatments. They became dissatisfied and wanted to sue him for doing this, saying that it was damaging. Surely it is not helpful. Sex is like going to a restaurant and eating; you still need to eat later. Then they became angry, thinking that the psychological therapist was irresponsible, and they planned to sue him. The hidden psychology is not that he did it with them, it is that he did not do enough with them or satisfy them all. Then, who should be punished? Who should enjoy seeing the pain of the punishing? He can be punished by being unfair, but how about the women who were involved in this unfair revenge? Clearly speaking, if it was the man who misled those women to have sex with him, he is responsible for his behavior. If the women made him into a momentary solace, and later when they expected more from him were unable to attain it and so wished to punish him, then they are responsible for the behavior. I would like to advise the ladies, if you wish to be responsibly related with someone, firstly be responsible for yourself. If both sides were acting out of immaturity, both of them should use the damaging event as an educational process. (The above refers to a particular matter which occurred some time ago.)

This is mainly advice for my women students to be more responsible, to respect themselves and their bodies. Do not allow sexual abuse to happen and charge the other with responsibility for it. A sexual relationship can be ideally a one-to-one, close friend relationship or with a person who is not involved with many people. Sometimes, it can be different from that. Sincerity provides one with spiritual or emotional support. In the traditional practice of Tao, in the moment of sexual relationships, there must be love or emotion involved, or at least it is done in a healthy way, even if it is a short-lived relationship. If there is nothing emotional, at a certain level there is a close one-to-one base. At other times, it is not rigid to meet external standards. However, my wish is that people have relations in a way that is healthy emotionally, physically and spiritually; but there is no one single way that can be held out to all people. This is an achieved knowledge, more than a formality. The simple advice from me is that it be accomplished beneficially and harmoniously on each side. Also, there should be no possibility of bringing social diseases or other troubles to each other.

I would like the women to take responsibility for guarding and respecting their bodies. Do not be easily be tempted by a sophisticated, but not necessarily evil, man. A woman, after spending many years with a man sexually abusing her, suddenly start to cry about it; she will make him an enemy, try to punish him and bring a very unhappy ending to the whole situation. Spiritually, at the beginning, the woman was wrong. How much financial compensation can one get in court over such a matter, and does court or financial compensation actually help? What women continue to do wrong is to think that men should be responsible for it. I am not going to condone this mutual wrongdoing.

I advise my women students to guide themselves well and not create any opportunity for a sexual relationship that they do not understand. Do not begin any sexual relationship that you do not wish to continue. If you still do it, it will be inviting a bitter experience that you do not want. If at the beginning you let a man treat you sexually like a prostitute, afterwards you will not like it. Or when a man acts like a prostitute by having too many relationships, you will not want to accept that reality either. A person should not have too many relationships with others at the same time. That would become a reason for the opposite side to want to punish you emotionally. It is also a shame to punish or take revenge on the other's sexual conflict instead of just walking away.

I stress and repeatedly advise my women students as well as my men students not to put themselves in a sexual relationship that is not proper. Do not even begin. Improper sexual relationships can lead to jealousy or disappointment when one's wishes are not fulfilled, such as finding out that the other has additional partners or purpose; then it cannot be a healthy relationship. You are responsible for whom you sleep with, and must consider if you are jeopardizing yourself by the action. Women continue to seek legal redress. The reality they should be seeking instead is self-responsibility, self-love and self-respect.

Please do not be upset as you read these commentaries. Suppose you were my dear daughter; I would like you to be smart enough to guard yourself and be responsible for yourself. I do not want to see you cry. This instruction comes out of my love and concern for my beloved students, not disrespect.

Student: Should women have orgasms?

Master Ni: Generally yes. A man in our tradition is trained not to have an orgasm in order to refine the energy. But, physiologically, women are different. In any event, I do not suggest that she has sex too frequently. When she does, she should have complete sex (with full release); otherwise it does not help. We have a special term called energy adjustment for the purpose of having sex. You are not adjusted if your sex is incomplete in any way.

Student: Then how does a woman transfer and refine her energy?

Master Ni: That is a different practice. Some women choose that practice and live without a man. If this is the case, apt guidance is given. Some live with a man without having sex and are able to do the subtle transformation. Usually this is more difficult for several reasons including age, the food they eat, the social environment or the personal nature of the individuals involved. Some people have more sexual need than other people. Some men or women, without proper sexual satisfaction, would become crazy; if this is the case, they had better have sex! If their minds are stronger spiritually than their bodies, then they can manage it very well and I think it is possible to transfer the energy.

Not everybody can achieve a higher spiritual state; different people have different levels of fulfillment. I am pointing out that the achievements of different people are not equal, but simply different. For some women, their sexual desire is naturally strong, and without sexual satisfaction they would become crazy. In that case, these ladies better have a boyfriend or something to maintain the balance of the body and the mind. Some people have spiritual energy that is already higher than their physical energy, and I don't think those people should engage in sex because they become unhappy every time after sex and complain. Those people should be more concentrated on spiritual achievement.

One cannot say whether one way is higher than the other. On the human level, if a person lives a balanced way, and all their relationships are harmonious, this is great! I do not say that the one who has lots of sex is a bad person or the one who does not have any sex is a special high person. Not at all. The spiritual achievement is different, and both are achieved if they have attained balance.

However, at this moment I am not going to go into the special refinement necessary to attain achievement. At the level I am speaking, both types of achievement are equal. Sexual fulfillment is different according to different ages, needs, etc. The highest sexual fulfillment, which is hardly the ordinary way, is getting along with people. By this I mean, a man and woman can be together without going to bed, and not having a fight between the soap water and the soda water. The sexual fluid of men and women are different, just like two kinds of water fighting together. They can, without touching, if they have a good friendship or care for or like each other, naturally be fulfilled without becoming physically involved. Men in middle age who live alone usually die earlier; I am talking about ordinary people without spiritual cultivation. The internal intercourse of the spiritual and physical energy of the individual is the most beneficial one. The other high form of sexual practice, sexual energy exchange, does not necessarily happen in the bedroom on the bed; it can happen anywhere; one can get what one needs, because the spiritual level is very subtle. People who live in monasteries or nunneries can be incomplete because of denying this. Energy intercourse means new creation. Looking at the existences in the universe is to know that it is the intercourse of different energies that bring about different things and different lives. That is the basic performance of the universe; otherwise it would be a dead lump of wasted energy.

Generally speaking, this talk was inspired by the modern problem of some psychologists, healers, teachers or religious leaders who abuse women. This is a warning for all my good female students who join any sort of group practice. While you may experience the benefit of group practice, you are, at the same time, exposed to temptation; there are lots of strong, handsome young men. You need to learn how to manage yourself. Also, learn how to choose the right man for yourself. According to the information I have given you in different books, conduct your sexual matters properly. Do not cause trouble and become like the ancient type of spiritual people who were afraid of sexual connection. Why were they afraid? Because they found that it was more trouble than fun. This is how people became discouraged and programmed special, extreme spiritual practices. You are responsible for maintaining the integral path within your life without allowing immature or irresponsible behavior to cause any disturbance. I do not wish such behavior to happen in the group practice I promote.

Student: I just do not know how to keep a man. Invariably, they take my energy and then leave me.

Master Ni: Your point would be that you do not want your boyfriend to have another woman. The man also does not like his girlfriend to be involved with another man. Thus, change always happens. There is nothing wrong with that. I do not advocate a rigid way that dictates no divorce or never changing relationships, but one important principle is: proper conduct and behavior means that even if you change your partner or divorce your wife or husband, it is not done for sexual or irresponsible reasons. If it is motivated for the mutual benefit of both people, one can make a shift without harm or damage.

Let us talk about energy being taken. I have frequently heard someone say, "Somebody else took my energy," especially sexually. Can a man take a woman's

energy?   Practically, if a man is overly strong and has
a high desire for sex, and a woman is at a time when
she does not need sex or is at low energy, but if out of
a certain temptation she does it anyway, it is harmful
to the woman.   If the man takes advantage to satisfy
himself without giving due consideration to the woman's physical or emotional condition, even if the man
does not take her energy, this will also destroy the
man's energy.   Perhaps the sex helped to balance him
in some way, but it is not good sex, and it does harm
the woman.

If a woman is strong and needs lots of sex, and the
man is weaker, and they attempt to have sex, then the
woman takes the man's energy.   There is no technique
or rule for who takes energy from whom; it is just that
disharmonious sex can do damage to one or both sides.

Some people today do not believe this, but I would
like to make a point of it.   On the deep spiritual level,
if a woman or man do not guard themselves, their
energy can also be taken by a ghost or a demon.   It is
not suitable for a women to sleep in the nude or sleep
face up on the bed.   A woman should not expose her
breasts or the middle of her chest on a beach, in public
or any place else.   At nighttime, it is dangerous if you
live alone; demons or ghosts can take energy from you
without the need for dreams; they just transform into a
small insect.   In the daytime, some dirty spirits can
turn themselves into an insect such as a butterfly, and
can touch you and take your energy.   It is not necessary for them to go to the organs, because the human
body has several centers.   For women in particular, the
point between the nipples is the energy center.   They
come and take that energy.   I do not especially promote this knowledge, but I warn all my female students to dress and sleep decently.   The most important
observation is to have decent thoughts, because improper sexual thoughts will invite sexual dreams or
invite different ghosts to come to a person.   Trouble
happens because people do not know how to guide
themselves well, especially sexually.

Student: In a relationship where a couple is living together and one person is not as sexually strong as the other, and the second one wants to have outside sexual relationships, does that not, first of all, bring about the spread of disease, and secondly, affect the home relationship? I have heard that it can either be beneficial or destructive to the home relationship.

Master Ni: I would say that sexually, if there is not enough restraint or a good way to transfer your energy to a higher sphere, if one side is weak and the other is overly strong, the strong side should not seek or over-extend into that kind of satisfaction. If there is some harmony or the relationship is based on love, they should be contented. It is like, how much money do you have to have before you feel rich? How much sex do you have to have for you to feel satisfied? This is a matter of personal emotion and psychology. Many people do not have a well matched mate. One should nonetheless respect their fortune, even if it is not an excellent fortune. If you have some sex already, you can do something more beneficial for yourself with that extra energy.

In ancient times, man was more aggressive and women were more passive. It is ancient guidance that a woman should be faithful to a strong man. If a man has another healthy sexual involvement, the woman should not use this issue to break up with him. She might break up with him and go to another man, only to find that the other man is the same way, and it never ends. A couple cannot be equal all the time. I do not promote this as an example, but this is for your better understanding.

Such matters are always influenced by local custom. Tibet, for example, accepts that a woman have several husbands, and in other places, a man can have several wives. If this suits these men and women, I do not think it is disagreeable in this circumstance. Whoever likes to expend their energy in this way has their own personal understanding of life, which is fine, as long as it does not damage other people.   It is like a person going to a restaurant and ordering three special meals for himself to eat at one sitting.   Another person may only order a small meal and eat lightly.   It depends on the individual.   The quantity is not a cause for guilt.

Student: How do things like childbirth, abortion, hysterectomies or removal of breasts affect a woman's energy?

Master Ni: It is affected.   In some cases, Chinese herbal medicine can assist the energy restoration or revitalization with good effect.   Chi Kuan or energy transformation practice can help too.

4
To Male Spiritual Students

Today's world and society is still dominated by men.   Ask the men if they're any better off than the women.   That is questionable!   Men exercise dominance in worldly affairs and society.   However, what security can they offer their women and children?   In the Middle East, there is a lot of warring; who starts wars and keeps engaging in them?   Have you seen the women and children lying in a pools of blood?   Is this done for any true reason?   All wars come from man's testicles.   Men are managed by the secretion from their testicles.   When men fail to control the secretion from their testicles, they become warlike and cause destruction.   External religion does not itself start wars, but it is often the fuel for wars, small and big.

The situation in the world will never change until you learn how to refine the secretion created and produced by your own testicles.   When you learn how to refine yourself and find your internal harmony, there will be no war in the world.   This is one basic practice in Tao.   I suggest that all men learn sports and martial arts, especially the type of martial arts presented by the College of Tao.   It is not martial arts in a combative sense; it is a style of movement known as the School of Internal Harmony, because, by practicing it, you combine secretions of all the different glands, in both the lower and upper levels. They can evenly and effectively support your life being without causing you physiological or chemical imbalance. Imbalances cause you to think wrong and do wrong. Do not be proud that you have testicles, but ask yourself if you can manage them. This is the first thing that I would like to tell my men students, to learn to manage their testicles. If you join the group practice you can learn the movement of my tradition called Internal Harmony.

The second thing I tell my young students is to value the opportunity they have of attending school. In many regions children cannot go to school, but instead must join the labor force, working in the fields at a very young age. It is great to be supported by your family to go to school; and you should, therefore, respect the hours you spend there and learn well. Do not ever learn to rely on the money your parents give to you. If your parents have something to give to you, it is best considered as a bonus, an extra gift of life; do not let that money poison you. Many highly educated young people today have as hard a time achieving as commonplace people of ancient times. In ancient times, the difficulty came because people lacked basic material support and education in their youth and so could not achieve as much. Today's young people, however, have support and education, and are still undeveloped. Their vitality and impetus is killed because of their parent's money, and so they cannot achieve.

Thirdly, when you are young, you are like a young tree or a young plant. Do not hurt the root of your being by early sex. If you hurt it, you will not enjoy full growth of yourself. When you are in your middle years, you will become impotent or hen-pecked because you have made yourself sexually weak by having excessive fun when you were young. If you respect your life, you should not have early sex. At fifteen or sixteen a man starts to have semen, but according to the ancient record, if a man can handle himself well, around thirty is the right time to have a family and children; women at twenty. However, if you marry late after having excessive sex in your youth, your children will be weaklings because your semen has become weakened and is no longer strong.

Today it is easy for you to have lots of fun when you are young. People say that America possesses many good things; but there is one good thing lacking; there are no virgins because people have sex when they are young. This is not a serious statement! This is just to express the general trend that there are not many women who respect their body and the clean and chaste spirit of life. In fact, nowhere in the world do men or women know how to value their bodies.

Another very important thing, my young beloved friends, do not make bad friends and join gangs. That may bring excitement when you are young, but finally it will cause you to ruin your life because of the wrong connection. If you connect with somebody wise or virtuous, you can study and develop yourself more. Be discriminating: look for and associate with people who can help you develop more. Associate with a person or group who can be an example for you or be a model for your own growth.

When you become an adult, you need to remember two things; first, you must have responsible attitudes toward life. The second is the right and responsible sexual practice. With an irresponsible sexual attitude, you may leave a woman pregnant; would you like to be responsible for having fatherless children who rely on social welfare? Fatherless children generally do not grow up with a healthy psychology; so you create second-class or third-class citizens in the world. This irresponsible sexual behavior is degrading the quality of people in the world. Irresponsible sexual attitudes cause women to be hurt; they weep or cry secretly, with a feeling of misery or helplessness. In this situation, I do not think that you could get good sex from women. It causes prejudice, hatred or other suffering in their minds.

If your woman is pregnant, you must consider the seeds you are bringing into the world. What is the mother's emotion? It is not only a womb that supports the child; the entire being of the mother is the womb which nurses a good baby, before and after its birth.

Sexuality is mainly an energy adjustment. You must think about the level and quality of the woman you can find, and not just do something irresponsible. For example, some men, for their sexual purpose, rush the process of getting a woman to have sex with them. If, however, they were to spend a little more time with her, they might see that inside she is full of negative experiences; consider then what spiritual energy you can get from her.

You may think that Master Ni is unfair, charging you with being irresponsible with women. Fair or not, any man or woman who is involved with life affairs should consider that theirs is the main role with the main responsibility. You are not a person being made demands of as a servant or a slave to do things for other people. So make your choices carefully and responsibly.

My beloved young friends, when you go to school you can learn something by which to express yourself, so do not drop out of school. Only stop if you have a better opportunity to learn a special trade, skill or profession. Even farming; it does not matter whether it is an old type or new type of skill, if you think that work can help you express yourself and you can live on it. Do not rely on social welfare as your bank. Some people never learn to improve themselves, find a skill or the right work or a good position; they work half a year, then quit, rely on unemployment for six months, then start again, repeating this cycle. Such people are wasting, killing their time; when they are old, they will become homeless people on the city streets because of their irresponsible life attitudes.

To be responsible, first learn some useful knowledge. Do remember that this is a means, not an end. Some people learn many things intellectually, but may still be irresponsible because they have not learned the important things about life. Life is in all skills; not only in the one aspect of reading books. We have seen many young men pursuing spiritual learning, not for the pure purpose of spiritual growth, but participating in spiritual groups as an excuse or means to keep from confronting the embarrassment of an unsuccessful worldly or professional life, because they do not have any proper thing to do. I do not encourage this if they not are really spiritually interested or achieved. Their gathering is a group of dependents and useless people in the world, and does not improve the world one bit.

5

To Both Male and Female Spiritual Students

Sometimes young people can be impulsive, which can invite negative events. It is good for those young people who are intelligent and have the possibility of reaching wisdom to become interested in attaining some training which can help them form and assist their good, long life. The human learning process itself is very long, especially when compared to simple animals.

Spiritual learning is the most essential learning of life. When you are a child, you are taught to respect your parents, teachers and elders, but you do not learn how to respect yourself. However, respect alone is not enough to develop the scope of the sense of life. As you live your life, things will come and things will go. You will see people with different manners and different ways of doing things; if you are aware, you slowly learn certain laws or universal standards that are practiced among successful, prosperous and also virtuous people. However, prosperous and successful people are not necessarily virtuous, so their seeming success or prosperity is not the true flower of life. Success without virtue is artificial; it is like using a strong acid fertilizer to hurry up the growth of a flower, killing the plant. So you must be careful whom you use as your example for success. A person with deep intelligence will not trade the beneficial qualities of his or her personal character for temporary success or prosperity.

The spiritual learning of the integral way does not entitle a person to rigidly commit to a certain religion. It does not encourage a person to stay in a monastery to become an artificial saint. Those who stay in monasteries are similar to the worldly, unvirtuously successful or wrongly prosperous people, because they are without deep understanding of the natural spiritual reality; neither group work on their deep natural spiritual condition. That which is superficial becomes artificial. The focus of life should be what is basic to life: the organic vitality of a natural life. This is what should be maintained. It is important to safeguard your spiritual potential and flexibility from damage by worldly pressure or worldly fashion; do not be changed to a worldly way. A person, by living an everyday life and not leaving the world to head to a monastery, has a better and more effective way to attain genuine spiritual growth. For example, a person cultivating spiritual growth who is interested in politics will not sacrifice his moral principles for artificial success in a political career. Similarly, a person of spiritual growth will not damage his spiritual root to become rich in business. Spiritual learning is not something organized for only a few people living in confinement, setting themselves aside as models. True spiritual learning is to learn the spiritual essence and attainment of the ancient developed ones, and to realize that essence to assist and benefit your own life. In this way, without going to church, visiting a holy land or bowing to divine beings, you can do two things: firstly, manage your own life well; then secondly, utilize your spiritual learning to radiate your beneficent spiritual quality to your surroundings wherever you find darkness. The ancient, unhelpful type of spiritual learning was accomplished by going into seclusion and avoiding temptation; this is not true achievement because in such a place there is no way to help true spiritual growth. True spiritual benefit comes through self-cultivation, by nurturing the spiritual vitality within one's root. One cultivates a light that will shine forth from one's own spiritual expansion and growth; there is no suggestion here that people be tempted to withdraw from life to achieve themselves spiritually. That would be only an escape.

In the world, people learn to live conceptually; they learn to barter their bodies and minds in exchange for a living. However, that is not what life is all about. The most important thing is to learn a complete and integrated way of life. One must understand the difference between the essential substance of life and peripheral aspects of life. The essence is to live. The side is to work and receive a reward. If you consider your life to be separate from your work, you still live in darkness. Why? Because, as far as small things are concerned, it does not matter what you do. It does not matter what you do to help people, make a living or do as a means of exchange to get what you need, as long as it is done in a good way. Whatever you do is the expression and reality of your life. Life itself is not a form; life is a process, a continuing process. When you are working, you are not killing time; you are experiencing and expressing the essence of your life. When you work, your life is proceeding through each minute, hour, day and night, month and year, going further and further. When a person has this understanding in their cultivation, their work becomes their realization of the spiritual in ordinary life. At the same time you are doing, you are giving. One's reward is in finding the correct way of doing meaningful work. You may believe that the work that you have to do is not meaningful in the world; but what you do not see is that even if it is not meaningful to you, it is meaningful to someone else. The attitude taken toward work today is to separate it from the touch of the mind and heart, and perform it with the superficial, partial attitude of making a living. People who are spiritually developed are not just money-making machines; they find meaning in their work, or find more meaningful work to do.

Many people are not spiritually responsible. They do only what will get them money; that is because they do not understand that the value of life cannot be measured by money.

So when a young adult comes to join group practice, he first learns to examine the tendencies within that push him in an unhealthy or self-destructive direction. Then he learns the discipline needed to protect his own welfare. A person who is not looking for spiritual cultivation should not join a group to satisfy social needs. The true benefit of group practice is in learning to nurture your spiritual root and advance the integrity of your character. This learning will assist you to develop continually and nurture the essence of your life.

At the College of Tao, we offer knowledge of different aspects of life. A basic training in spiritual discipline is outlined in our book, *The Heavenly Way*. Energy training like the Eight Treasures and Tai Chi Chuan is given in classes. We also offer information on nutrition and other practical aspects of life through books and classes. The most profound spiritual knowledge can be found in my written work. Through group practice, those things can be organized and learned, one by one, to assist you in your personal development and understanding. The teaching of the Great Path of the Integral Way is not any one person's external creation; it is the internally proven truth as it was discovered by the ancient developed ones. When you first touch upon something that is new to you, it may feel as if it comes from outside, but with careful study, you will notice that the descriptions and guidance originate with you, because all life is one life. All life is a good life. All life is the expression of the normalcy of the reproduction of universal life. After hearing this description of all life being one life, you may ask, then what is there to learn and why should we learn? The reason we learn is because you have lost your connection with the Universal Nature; you extend yourself in the opposite direction by acting on what you think. You lose yourself because you have lost the source, so you become trapped in the mind.

Your development is uprooted and disconnected and will never extend far without change. This is why we need to learn and develop ourselves spiritually.

I am a person who has love for man and woman equally. The stage of the matriarchal or mother-centered society is past and I do not think that the present patriarchy will change to make things equal for both men and women in society. The men are constructed to do the tough, physical work. I wish that men could learn to do the tough work positively, and not through war or killing.

In line with the principles of the I Ching, we are always looking for the balance of the yin and yang energy, because the different energies assist each other. The world is made of males and females. Many men are only penises; many women are only vaginas; though this is not how it should be. It is not a complete life. A complete life would include spirit and mind. It is important to develop different aspects of your life. Some schools of psychology make sex the center of life. Sex may be the center of life at its lower level, but human beings have already evolved and continue to evolve beyond that point. It is possible to develop a good mind and to refine and transmute these low spheres of energy to a high level of energy in spirit; in this way, one can enjoy the completeness of human life.

Remember my beloved young friends, youth is an asset, not a disadvantage. When you are young, you do not have the privilege of being foolish. You do not have the privilege of being ignorant. You must be responsible in study, following the footprints made by the sages and moving forward in cultivating a good life. Because you are young, you follow your social leaders into wars and die on the battlefield like rats on the highway. Do not be used unnecessarily by ambitious and evil social leaders in political maneuvers to destroy each other by evil means. China is an example of this, where Mao Tse Tung used young people not only to defeat a political opponent but to ruin a cultural heritage of 5,000 years. Damage unprecedented in human history was suffered. To be young is an asset; you need to protect it by yourself, through studying the wisdom of the sages who cherished universal love of heart and who can guide you to safety and natural growth. This will keep you from being misused by the blind, impulsive social leaders or the impetus of social trends.

My beloved young friends, do not speed when you drive. You have all the time to reach anywhere you need to be. On the freeway, the most accidents occur to youngsters. Your life is precious. You have come into the world, why are you in a hurry to depart your life so soon just because of something wrong in your brain? Is it alcohol, drugs, emotion or sex? Guide your life always in the direction of good health and self-mastery.

My beloved young friends, do you complain about your destiny? Do you admire good fortune? Let me tell you the reality of good fortune. Given the every-day thoughts you inherit or collective values you have received from society, you are inclined to think a person has good fortune who has a father with lots of money, a mother with lots of love, a sister who is supportive and a brother who is helpful. All your relatives would love you and after you grow up, you would have a wife who is very beautiful, helpful, understanding and tender. Good fortune also means that your friends would all be kind; when you do business, everyone would let you make money, and in the world, no one would ever try to cheat you or take advantage of you. This is the perfect image of good fortune that all people would aspire to. Also, in my understanding, there is nothing wrong with these inherited thoughts about good fortune; they are all correct. I agree one hundred percent with the traditional, conventional thoughts about good fortune.

You see, we all would like all aspects of our life be easy and supportive. But let me tell you, if you wish to have a good father, then I suggest you be a good father too. If you wish your wife to treat you tenderly,

I suggest you take the time to educate your daughter to be that way too. If you wish to meet people in the world who do not cheat you or cause any mischief or harm, be a person like that yourself. If the entire world truly understands good fortune and lives like that, then there would be a world of good fortune. There would be no more problem. Fortune is decided by people themselves. If you have misfortune or you see somebody with misfortune, you need to recognize that misfortune is the result of irresponsibility at some level. The person has not been aware. The lessons become harsher and more visible so we can learn from the subtle law. Thus, good fortune simply means to be a good son, good father or mother, a good brother or sister, a friend and a person with whatever connection or contact. Good fortune can be realized in the world, starting with your cultivating goodness within yourself. You cannot unearth good fortune anywhere. It can be found only in your fundamental being.

It is important to have that awareness. Let us have good fortune and be people of good fortune. Maybe on some occasions, we are cheated, tricked or mistreated; and that is bad fortune. But the person who mistreats you, tricks you, or steals something from you, is he a person who expects good fortune through his doing those things? Blessing is equal to good fortune. It is pitiful that people create religions, but they do not teach the understanding of self-responsibility for the manifestation of good fortune and blessings. Let each of us be a responsible person; let the entire world turn towards a world of good fortune, starting with each individual. We are responsible for the creation of a world of blessings, a world of good fortune. Then all misfortune will go away, because we will be aware of what we ourselves expect at the deepest level. In a very few circumstances, people are mistreated by nature. If the trouble is caused by nature, it is almost always escapable. However, one hardly ever escapes from the suffering or trouble caused by other people, or what you suffer from your own doing.

Student: Do you mean that when you start becoming a good person, then other people also change to be good, or that when you start becoming a good person, that the not-so-good people will no longer really be interested in you, and good people will become your friends?

Master Ni: I cannot give you a guarantee because the world has turned out to be very unfortunate.   Educationally, I think that everybody should understand that.   The realistic way, as I described, to have really good fortune begins by having a deep awareness.   For example, in a family, you expect your parents and everybody else to be supportive of you, seeing yourself as the center; but do you ask yourself if you are being supportive of them?   From this small scale of family, we can move into to the larger scale of society and the world.   It is unreasonable that you, without making any effort or doing anything supportive of others, make yourself the center, like the kings of old who demanded that the entire world serve them.   Misfortune can also be a reflection of the world rather than the person. I believe most of my friends are good people and do not trick or deceive others.   We would rather be tricked than trick other people.   And sometimes we do not guard ourselves well and find we are cheated by others.   But we must maintain firmness and not lose the stability of our virtue, because those people who steal from others never really have good fortune.   They suffer more in the long run.   But even if you have something stolen from you or are cheated, you are better off; you can have good fortune within.   The thieves, the impostors and the person cheating are forever in misery within themselves unless they change the internal quality of their personalities.   You do not need to punish them.   You do not need to expect God to stand up to say "They are wrong" and punish them. Their punishment is their own negative character. They have lost the contentment of an upright, healthy personality.   With this understanding, we must learn to manage our lives practically and cultivate virtue within ourselves.

When we have sympathy, we still need to guard against the people who have never learned compassion. When you have kindness, be cautious; your kindness could be returned by unkindness; one needs to develop the capacity to protect and defend oneself as well. You need to learn balance in worldly life. I would like to tell this story as an illustration:

Once a young spiritual student went on an important errand for his family to buy some valuable cultural things in another part of the country. He took a large sum of money and went to search for the meaningful books and scrolls to mail home. After he was finished, there still was a large amount of money left in his pocket. He was on a crowded street; a flood had occurred in another part of the region and many people from the flooded area had walked into the city. This young man had lots of compassion for those who had suffered and become homeless due to the flooding. In his life he had been encouraged to be compassionate to others. But as he went on his way, walking to the post office to mail the money back, his unconscious feelings of sympathy made him vulnerable to being pickpocketed and thus the money was stolen. He was a young man who had also learned to be alert, cautious and prudent in doing things. But because of the sense of other people's difficulty, his mind produced sympathy and he forgot one important principle: when you have compassion for others, you must guard yourself at the same time, too. Such precautions would not be necessary if all people were achieved, of course; clearly, this is not the way of today's world.

Another very important thing is that when you like another person, be careful. If you do not truly understand the other person, there could be a pit that you fall into. An illustration of this is when, during a certain time, there were two travelers who went on a trip to another country. As you know, when you go to another country, the currency is different and you must exchange it at a certain rate, which these two travelers did. After they finished their shopping, they needed to exchange the money that was left back to their original currency because they had exchanged too much. As they were preparing to leave the country, the travelers hoped to find someone who could exchange it for them. They spotted a group of people who were money changers at the roadside and made arrangements for the money changers to go to their hotel to make the transaction.

Well, what happened was this: each side counted their money, putting it into separate envelopes and exchanged them. However, after the money changers had left, the travelers looked in their envelope only to find that there was almost no money there. They had briefly let down their guard and the money changers substituted another envelope.

When you do business, you may like the people and think they are honest. It may be that the other person is young and pure and seems like someone who would not do anything wrong; however, they may have someone older at their side who is impure who guides them in the wrong direction. So do not let your personal preference for someone or your trust be the sole factor that makes your decisions. When you do business, never think emotionally. You can like or dislike them, but watch the business with a clear mind. If you like or trust the people and do not watch the business, you can still fall. This is a valuable caution. My beloved young friends, do not trust even your own thoughts. Sometimes what you think is good fortune sent by God could be a demon in disguise. God is rarely disguised as something really beautiful or attractive when you need help in a circumstance; it is usually the devils who are disguised like a god or look like an angel. So never have a preconception about whether something is a blessing or not; such a preconception is a pitfall that you create for yourself.

In the last story, the young people were religious, so when they conveniently found someone to change the money back, they thought it was help from God.

Sometimes people value religious emotion. Religious emotion is not necessarily effective or healthy. It can, in fact, be harmful to human life. Many young people do not like the rigid structure of modern society and go to the East looking for religion. They especially travel to south Asia, looking for spiritual inspiration or to learn some wisdom from the heritage of that region. Most of them come back sick; some people die from carrying parasites in their livers or other organs. In this situation, their religious emotion was harmful because they did not have true knowledge of whether they should go or not. We have seen, historically, many people become martyrs, sacrificing themselves for religion, because they are influenced by unhealthy religious emotion within themselves. Fueled by this religious attraction, they sacrifice themselves, thinking that dying is the way to become holy. That is non-sense. Some religious people become overly fervent and burn their fingers or body parts, or inflict other damage to parts of their body purposely as a sacrifice to show piety toward what they believe in. This was done in Buddhism and Hinduism, instead of doing something practical to improve their life internally and externally. But it is worse that people of different religions fight in so-called holy wars. They have all lost their sense and their true knowledge of life.

The ghost of religious emotion still lives in the world. Over a thousand years ago during the Dong Dynasty (618-906 A.D.), Buddhism came to China and became very popular. People earned admiration by burning off their fingers as an offering to Buddha. I do not know if Buddha likes it or not, but the people who did it thought it was a blessing. There was also a famous monk who took all the trouble of traveling to India to search for the old sutras and bring them back to have a better understanding of Buddhism. The person's spiritual piety was excellent and worthy of respect and admiration. But this kind of devotion represents only one aspect of human spiritual nature. You can examine numerous books in the vast collection of the Buddhist Canon. And if you examine them carefully with your natural intelligence, it not very hard to discover that most books are useless. From these experiences, you can see that people are often too ready to believe something and because of this, run into trouble.

I do not promote skepticism in human nature; but this kind of fervor is not our tradition. Over 6,000 or 7,000 years ago, beginning with Fu Hsi, our tradition looked for the understanding of nature, and did so until they discovered the principle of balance: of the mind, emotion and life. Up to today, we have not found any better principle to replace the discovery of the sages of ancient spiritual development.

So we have described good fortune and misfortune, using the illustration of two stories. Although their intentions were good, the people in both stories were affected by religious programming and training that proved to be inappropriate to the situation. Many people are also very engrossed in astrology and personal destiny. However, we cannot really utilize astrology or use the I Ching in our everyday management. The value of the I Ching resides in learning the principles that it offers, not in doing divination all the time and in all matters. Somebody who uses it frequently out of anxiety is another example of misapplication.

In conclusion, so-called good fortune is if you are the right person and meet another right person, you do the right business in an appropriate manner, and everything happens as smoothly and nicely as you expect. That is so-called good fortune. Thus, what is called misfortune is if you are not the right person, or you go to a wrong person, do a wrong thing with the wrong manners, attitudes, methods or strategy. However, after we come to understand so-called good fortune and misfortune, we find that it depends on people. It is the person himself that makes good fortune or bad fortune. How can you manage your good fortune and bad fortune? Firstly, be an upright person yourself. Accept and do what you can do, because you are an upright person. Then always have righteous company or an upright person. If the person is imbalanced - meaning, misfortune can occur - then you need to do the right thing, with the right method, manners and means. This is a very simple matter, and everybody can manage it. Unfortunately, many of us cannot even manage seventy percent of our lives because sometimes we are not upright people nor do we do the right thing. Sometimes we go to the wrong people or react incorrectly to the circumstance. So we have to attain more growth and develop ourselves more carefully, both spiritually and emotionally. If we are being managed by a circumstance, we can either become overly enthusiastic, overly cruel or just plain cold. If we are intellectually self-centered when we do something, we consider only our own benefit and usually lose the larger vision which includes the understanding of the opposite side. This one-sided mental development is usually expressed by overly selfish attitudes. So, never let your emotion become excessive in an expression of over-enthusiasm or over-skepticism. Do not let your mind blind you on an emotional level. Even if you have a deal with your parents, your sons or any other close ones, you must still see that when your happiness and your enjoyment becomes a priority over anybody else, you become selfish. So aim for the clarity and balance of your spirit. The natural quality of spirit is harmony, balance and integralness. This is the area one needs to develop more in order to be a person of good blessings and good fortune.

Young people are usually lacking in long-term vision, vision which reaches into the depth of life and everything connected with it, so they become easily misused and abused. Women also suffer from sexual abuse for the same reason, but for men it is worse, because society dyes and changes them to suit another's purpose; and because of idealistic or narrow-visioned ideas, they are persuaded to go to war and die. It is not the destructive wars to which you should offer your life; you should offer your life and energy to the living, because everybody has a time for being in the world; that has true value. You can conduct your life direction in a constructive way, you can treat your life to a better cause. Never let people abuse or misuse your life, or sacrifice your life to bring victory to some ambitious leader whose own development is incomplete.

Your life is precious. Learn to guide your life from a wider, more mature perspective. Everybody, men and women alike, must choose a direction in which they can offer their best energy to the world, not just to make oneself happy or to earn a basic living.

At one time in human history, a natural life was followed by a natural death; but now most lives suffer an unnatural death from bad medicine or a negative lifestyle. So many people die meaninglessly. This is because of racism, unhealthy patriotism or religious prejudice. Do not be seduced by the title of being a hero or a saint. People need to bring more value to their own lives and to all human life as one life. Young people need to learn patience and not rush into action or any situation involving life and death. Value your life, respect your life, and use your life well so that it can be as natural as it was meant to be. How can you attain that? You must integrate a healthy, natural program of spiritual unfoldment and development, not a partial or religious way.

This old tradition of the great path of integral truth offers you the way to come back to your own nature. It teaches you to learn about and know the value of your own natural life. When society has trouble, the wise ones offer themselves unselfishly to help those who are troubled. They also learn the balance between a life of natural value and a life of social value. Never let social values pull you away from the balance of your innate natural value. No one should live for himself only; no one should live for society only. We have seen some new socialist political parties that overvalue social life. In the end, they reduce all people to the role of simply being tools of society, with no individual value. It is also not the perpetual way of healthy human life. The perpetual way of human life pays attention both to receiving individual development and serving the world. Idealistic doctrines express themselves in extremes which cannot become true in reality. It is basically not truthful. Therefore, a person of natural balance is a person who follows the ageless model of human life.

6
Spiritual Immortality

Student: The information for a woman's and man's life was very helpful. Would you now please speak about how a woman and a man can cultivate themselves spiritually with or without the hope of achieving spiritual highness?

Master Ni: This question has two answers. One way is what I call middle attainment. This is where your goal is to someday exuviate from your body to become a respectful soul. If your goal is the middle attainment, then in your lifetime you need to be a respectful person and act accordingly. You must, therefore, pay close attention to your behavior and your life, which will either maintain the stature of your spiritual awakening or cause your spiritual sensitivity to become dull. Once you have lost your spiritual sensitivity, then you do not care about what you do, and you do things that are disrespectful or immoral. Actually, in reaching the middle attainment, you do not need to do anything specific but you do need to maintain your own virtue in your everyday life, by being respectful in all your undertakings, by having respectful thoughts and behavior. You do not offer yourself to make a great contribution of spiritual merit to the world that can benefit many people's lives for generations, but rather you simply maintain yourself spiritually and respectfully. That will be good enough. Surely you can attain the middle level of attainment and become a respectful soul.

Higher attainment is for the woman (man is included throughout the whole answer, also) who not only leads a decent life in her heart and her behavior by being respectful, but never lets emotion pull her down to do something insensitive to herself or others. Emotional matters usually harm her more than others. The kind of woman who is emotional continues to be a confused soul, and receives no benefit at all. She is like a decayed watermelon thrown into the river, bobbing up and down, following the current and being washed away into the ocean and disappearing. The soul of a woman who is awakening is different; she keeps studying herself, she keeps open to all possible channels so that she may attain high spiritual knowledge. It is not at all a matter of religiously looking for emotional dependency, for that is not achievement; it means that she sees through her own search, through her own study of wisdom, and learns to open the channels and make the connection herself. Wisdom has many different aspects in life that can be called channels. For example, some women can do very well in the home, but be very ineffective at doing other things. Some women can do very well at managing a business or career but be inadequate in their personal lives. In these two examples, some channels are blocked and some are open, but in both cases the women are not complete. Those women who wish to attain a higher level of spiritual attainment, work by studying and learning true wisdom; not by learning dependency on religious forms. As a rule, religious dependency is, at best, the middle level of attainment; a person of this sort maintains herself well, is alert, disciplined and does not let herself fall, but she does not achieve an inner spiritual reality or have the organics of spirituality. A woman, by opening more possible mental channels toward high wisdom, can be a developed soul within herself. Not only a respectful soul, but a developed soul. A developed soul is also respectful, but is higher than a soul who simply learned respect.

It is more complicated to talk about spiritual immortality, which means to reach the level of a goddess for a woman, or god for a man. The difference is that the respectful soul and the developed soul usually come back, but with a better chance of leading a more respectful and developed life.   However, they do not have mastery over their own soul; they still need to follow the universal flow of life, the current of life. The universal life is like a big current, a big ocean that continues flowing.   They have not jumped out yet.

The top achievement of spiritual immortality is not the top; there is not a single goal in spiritual achievement, because there are many levels of achievement. We are speaking about achieving immortality in general.   It has many requirements, through a highly organized process of cultivation.   For example, the person has to be born to a pure family.   Why is this?   Because the influence of environment is very important.   The negative influence of one's environment damages the soul, which generally makes the soul have more difficulty.   For example, if the soul is weak, it is much harder to learn and to achieve the breakthrough solution of all the problems.   The requirement is not that she must be born in a rich family, but a pure family, a pure community or a pure society.   Generally speaking, it offers her better control.   Once she has a chance to learn from a true master who possesses knowledge about achieving spiritual immortality, she can follow all the requirements.   The requirements are usually to follow good discipline, living in a quiet place, where she can keep away all infectious energies to keep her life energy pure and wholesome and growing higher and higher.   Then when the day of exuviation comes, naturally her new life is immortal, because she has attained self-mastery.   She is not pushed by the universal flow of life to come back to live in a shaped life, continuing the similarity of what she has been before. Before this is totally achieved, she is conditioned.   Thus to some people with good qualities of personality, spiritual immortality is conditionable and possible.

Spiritually, this is usually a reward, because if you have been a respectful soul and led a respectful life many times, and you have been a developed soul, then you know what you pursue.   Many people do not have an interest in spiritual immortality; they do not even know what it means to be a respectful soul.   They are emotional; they like to have fun and excitement; to make this moment be great. That is all there is for them, beyond which there is nothing to talk about. So I avoid talking too much. However, as a reward to the person who has already achieved a respectful soul and lived several respectful lifetimes and several developed lifetimes, they have the opportunity opened to them for spiritual self-mastery and the pursuit of immortality. The true freedom of life is not being bound to fortune.

Some people do not like to talk very deeply about spirituality; this is because the length and depth of that person's spiritual stage is limited, so their range is small. They might be curious about psychic energy, like somebody seeing things or knowing things about other people's fortune or past. Psychic energy knows what is under the ground, or the ocean, and what is happening at a far distance away or far off in time. This has been proven. There are different psychic energies. Those people who wish to attain psychic energy had better start early. If at three or four you are pure, and you have a good father and mother who live a decent life, you are protected and can quietly do the meditation or learn how not to scatter yourself. A good prenatal environment is also very helpful for the development of a child anywhere. With positive parental influences helping a child with the purpose of attaining it, the child's pure vision will develop. Such a child, with a few days or a few months of training, may possibly find that their spiritual channel immediately opens up, with no difficulty at all. Influence beginning when one is young will bring higher spiritual vision much easier than for an adult. If that person continues to develop themselves spiritually, it will be great. Generally speaking, if a child by chance attains some psychic energy, and the parents do not know anything about it, the child will forget. He will forget because he has not been put in a channeled life, but lives a scattered life like other people, and thus he loses the capability when he is older.

It is easy when you start early and not too old; then you can develop more. Also, people with psychic energy are liked because they can give some help to the lives of others. But it is still a partial development. Because psychic capability is still not spiritual development, psychic development is but a tool, as I described in another section of this book. However, it is all possible to achieve. Spiritual development involves a power over the spiritual realm, which enables a person to attain a more complete spiritual development. It cannot be used to get more money. Psychic power, however, reaches the sphere of physics and the sphere of the less subtle. It can see things, move things and take things. However, it cannot see the self. One can use it to work and receive payment. Psychic energy can be lost with aging or physical damage, and it ceases when the bodily life ceases. It is similar to the intellectual knowledge of any subject. Its source is the brain, while spiritual development is the development of the soul. Once it is developed, it does not fear exuviation from the flesh body. Instead, a new baby is born into the spiritual immortal realm.

To come back to your main question; can a woman achieve herself spiritually? Yes. It is not hard. Can a woman maintain herself very well, very purely, and value her spiritual chastity? It is usually hard for her. Women like to talk about social or other things and do not look for internal achievement. That is something in quite a different direction.

So achievement is possible. Achievement is also very hard for the person who does not pursue it with perseverance and constant effort to continue to develop herself. This part is especially hard in modern times, because almost all the good knowledge has been lost. It is also difficult in a conventional, religiously dominant society, because they do not know anything about it except the children's stories in Sunday school.

If you are not developed, you do not know if the spiritual achievement of immortality is real or not, so you never think about pursuing it. It is like going to a department store and seeing all kinds of fashions and clothes: you buy what you are offered. Spiritual things are so high for most people; because they do not see them, they do not want to buy. You need to develop yourself so that you have enough ambition for the achievement you like. Spiritual development is different from buying ladies' fashions. It is not a fashion. It lasts much longer than a fashion.

Student: You said that, through studying, one opens the channels in the mind. Where does one attain the books in English to do this? Your books are very helpful in this regard. Would they be enough or does one need to seek other knowledge?

Master Ni: I believe so. For example, in a wool sweater, once you find the end of the one piece of yarn, if you have the patience you can unravel the whole sweater safely, with no damage to the wool, and make a better one. Spiritual achievement is something like that, if you can find the end of the wool thread of the sweater. Do not waste time in irrelevant searches that do not come directly to the point or any books whose authors have never really experienced those things; by doing so you will use your energy to become a bookworm and have the achievement of a bookworm. However, you have to do some reading. If you do it with the goal of attaining development or immortality, then the whole blockage will unravel for you and the breakthrough will be achieved. It is an internal thing, not an external thing. It is as though the firewood is there, but you need a match to start the fire. One small match, that is all. The material comes from you, the realities you have been through in many lifetimes.

Frankly speaking, I do not encourage the highest attainment for most people; for them, the middle level attainment would be practical. Growth and evolution happen, step by step. A person cannot skip preschool, primary school or high school and just go directly to graduate school, except for a few geniuses. It mostly cannot be done.

Having psychic energy does not necessarily aid one in achieving immortality. It is not certain that a person with psychic energy is moral enough to avoid becoming somebody's tool for an evil or an immoral purpose.

I truly encourage all my friends to attain respectful and moral beingness, to attain the beingness of wisdom, to fulfill the wholesome potential for your further spiritual development. That is a very practical thing to do. Because I have talked about something higher, you might keep thinking about it and make it your fantasy. However, it is different than people fantasizing about winning the lottery. In a lottery, among the many people who enter, there is maybe one chance in a million for winning. Development, however, is very practical; every day you need spiritual evolution and refinement of your condition, and someday you will be there. Like traveling to a far place; you need an airplane, so you need to buy a ticket, go to the airport and take the airplane. You cannot fly away from your garage. But we are not going that far yet; we are still walking. I am earnestly answering the question and encouraging a practical pursuit.

You can pursue it, because everybody has a strong will, and it is the will that makes things happen. Practically, you should work through and learn the minimum attainment, the middle attainment and then the higher.

The basic foundation is the realization of *The Heavenly Way*, the small book that I produced. Most spiritual students only learn spiritual knowledge or moral knowledge intellectually, without actually realizing it in their lives. It becomes empty talk and is useless unless they can make those writings become the description of their very being. However, whatever their rank of attainment, they must have a basic spiritual discipline as a foundation; otherwise, attainment becomes an idealistic objective that can never be achieved. This is why we first talk about the respectful being and the developed being before discussing spiritual immortality; all those things can be realized and attained by learning and practice through *The Heavenly Way*. There are several important guidelines in *The Heavenly Way*. A student who goes to the group practices should learn to practice those foundations. Without the foundation, there is no middle attainment or high attainment and certainly not the highest attainment, because it depends on the person and how much she has realized those truths and virtues in her life. The ascertainment of the different levels depends on how much she realizes the truth of life in her personal life. However, more importantly, spiritual immortality sometimes involves some special spiritual requirement for personal cultivation. Some of the organized religious ways guide a person to become more self-interested, self-important, self-centered or, simply, a selfish person. Selfishness does not achieve spiritual immortality; it achieves nothing, because one's spiritual evolution is not complete. Only those who, by living their daily life, work on their nature and their virtue to realize heaven can realize spiritual immortality through their positive, effective way of life. Those special cultivations and special requirements become a supplement, but are not the main path. The highest goal of spiritual cultivation is still not a narrow sense of immortality; it is the union of Tao with the man or woman. It means to realize the universal nature and the nature of yourself as one. There is no division or separation between the two when you are alive. When you are in a physical body, the physical form gradually changes into a different stage until a higher, subtle form of life is achieved as a result of your internal work of sublimation or attained by your personal moral fulfillment. This spiritual goal does not rely on particularly living away from society to achieve oneself in seclusion. Nature can always be formed and can then dissolve the form. But the attainment of the union of Tao with man or woman is to realize the great universal life within your life. Your life continues to be realized by the life of universal nature. There is no limitation of time or space. With this complete understanding, a person, in any circumstance, takes each moment seriously, with great sincerity and with refreshed spirits and takes the challenge as the fuel or nutrition for working on their personal evolution.

7
Seeing the Light Again

About thirty years ago, at a small chapel on a South Pacific island, I was invited to support a friend, a new pastor, in giving his first important speech to the congregation. In the opening prayer, when everybody was bowing their head, I was suddenly enveloped by the shining snowy spirit of Jesus.

This morning, June 27, 1988 at 5:00 a.m., a dialogue took place between Jesus and myself.

I asked Jesus, "If you come back again, what would you support? Would you support the Catholic church or the Protestant church?"

His reply was, "The Catholic church stiffens me. The Protestant church distorts me. I support neither."

I asked him, "But in the gospels, once you were speaking to Peter (Peter in Hebrew means rock), and told him, 'My church will be built on you,' and that is how Peter started the Catholic Church."

Jesus answered, "Peter is a kind person, with not much wisdom, but he is a person with sincerity. I did not really assign Peter to build my church. It means, in a very straight or clear manner, my church or spiritual performance is built on the sincerity of any person. Sincerity is the foundation for spiritual learning or attainment. I did not mean Peter in particular.

"Also, once I said that the body is a temple. Each person's body is a church already. I do not particularly support anybody or any type of church that stiffens me or distorts my teaching. What I meant was to be close to universal spiritual nature, not to build anything to separate the direct relationship of an individual to the universal spiritual nature, such as churches or any creation of human ideas."

I asked him, "Will you come back again?"

Jesus said, "I did not go away. I did not die. However, the book that describes me is dead. All those books are dead. I am the universal spiritual nature. I am born in different ages, in different times, carrying different forms and different names. I speak different languages and manifest into different formations. In spiritual truth, life goes on. Life, itself, is life, not a dead thing. Books and language are already dead. They make things final. Thus, that is the dead language; I am universal nature; how can I be dead? I was Lao Tzu in China, I was Sakyamuni (Buddha) in India, I was Jesus in Israel, I was Mohammed in the desert of the same region, I was Zoroaster in the old Persian tradition. In different generations, I always need to learn a new language to teach people. I was not a particular person, but a whole person. I have carried different names when I appeared to the different regions; in each new generation and in each occasion I found a new shape for giving the message to the fellow lives. No names, no book and no language can directly be viewed as the whole truth. Books carry dead languages; none of them should be kept as a burden on new lives. New lives always need to look for new spiritual inspiration in their time and their life environment. It is not right for anybody, any book, any teaching or any language to cause a sacrifice of new lives. If it is that way, it becomes a burden.

"You asked me if I will come back, but it is not a spiritual question. This question comes out of the general conception and should not come from you. I have never died. Have you ever heard of universal nature dying? No. It is not possible. People die. The universal spiritual nature never dies.

"Also, you may find this difficult to believe or understand because physically I was crucified, but the crucifixion also was not an event occurring only at that one particular time. Each person has his or her own Jesus; by that I mean, each person has universal spiritual nature within them. At any time when they face temptation or anything that is temporarily important to them, they crucify me; they kill me, they poison me, they destroy me, they tear me apart in different ways. They do it all the time. I never die; but I can only survive within the person who embraces their spiritual nature. I am truly killed, sacrificed and crucified by the people who cut away the association with the universal spiritual nature. They kill me again and again. They crucify me again and again.

"So this is my answer to you. I live my life as you see. I am a spiritual immortal. I am immortal because I am universal spirit. I am spiritual universal nature, so how can I die? I live with all forms, but I can be killed many times by the form."

Then I asked him, "What about the relationship between the trinity: God the Father, God the Son and God the Holy Spirit?"

He answered, "Because I am spiritual nature, I was born into flesh life, I became the son. In each individual the spirit is God the father, the mind is God the son and the Body is the Holy spirit.

"In all flesh bodies there is a mind; mind usually is formalized by the post-natal life experiences, so that is the son. My body with its wholeness of body spirits, which function naturally to allow everything to keep going, is what is called the holy spirit. The spiritual nature in a person is called God, the Father. Spiritual nature is not an external thing. Each person has the god, that is their very spiritual nature. Each person has the son, if the mind aligns itself with the spiritual nature and with spirit. Each person has a whole group of holy spirits in which the body stores all natural and super-natural power. Further, if all the spirits follow the correct order of the trinity, it is an orderly universe. From this understanding, what is God? God, in totality, means the spiritual unity of all three in an individual and in the entirety of the living world.

"Because I told somebody suffering from his aggressive neighbors, 'If anybody asks you to walk one mile with him, you might walk two miles; and if anybody boxes your left ear, you should give him your right

ear, too,' you once commented to me about my statement.   By that, I was not promoting totally surrender-
ing.   I was promoting the spirit of yielding.   You see,
wars happen by emotional friction and the conflict of
two sides rigidly seeking benefit or profit.   If one side
knows how to yield, then wars, friction and further
damage can be avoided.   I would appreciate it if you
would correct that for me."

I asked him, "I accept what you say to me.   But
what about your teaching to the disciples?   When you
went to people and chased the ghosts away, saying 'I
do this in the name of Jesus,' - was it to establish the
name of Jesus?   You told people to pray in the name
of Jesus and you told them to chase the ghosts away in
the name of Jesus.   It seems that this was to establish
yourself.   Then how can you be somebody else when,
as you have said, you have been Moses, Mohammed,
Sakyamuni and other names."

At this point there was an interruption in our discussion.   The meeting happened when I was in my
meditation.   I got up from my meditation, but the
answer was not yet given.

At this point, I asked myself, what am I doing?
Am I doing channeling, which is something I am
against?   Then I slowed myself down and recalled
what my teachers had said: "A spiritually developed
person enters the universal spirits.   At the same time
you enter a spirit, the spirit enters you."   This means
that it is not that Jesus enters me or I enter Jesus, it is
both of us merge to make it a complete trinity, harmony, a complete communication or teaching.   I have
been taught this through many experiences.   Sometimes
when I write books, I look for advice from the high
and the developed spirits.   It is truly different than
general channeling.   During general channeling, other
spirits come inside your brain and squeeze your soul to
the lower part of the body and act as your person.
That is the weakness of your own spirit.   In this way,
because you are undeveloped yourself, you are a tool,
utensil or container for the undeveloped spirit or

demon you are channeling.   With achievement, you enter a sage spirit and at the same time the sage spirit enters you.   His life is your life and your life is his life, at least at the moment when you are in communication.   This part I needed to clarify so as not to confuse people.   I do not encourage people to do channeling, but I do encourage people to achieve themselves and have true contact with the high spiritual beings, not only to benefit themselves but also to gather confidence for living in the external world.

If you do not have such communication with high spirits, at least you can discover yourself from the elucidation in my work.   All my work is generated from self discovery; therefore, it is you.   It is not a description of somebody else, if you carefully read it. That is the quiet exploration that occurs when you read my books with good patience, a gentle approach and without stopping.   Continuing through the years, someday you will find that it is not hard to achieve the high spirit.   It is not a special gift or something given to one individual.   Everybody can do it: if you are open to universal nature, universal nature is open to you.   If you enter universal spiritual nature, universal spiritual nature awaits you.   The connection is already there between the father, son and grandson.   Body spirits are born by individual spiritual development. Thus, they come later; to spiritual nature, they are grandchildren.   To the mind spirit, they are children. The connection is natural.   This is why my tradition teaches that each individual human is a small model of the entire universe.   The vast, profound universal nature can enter the smallest thing in the world.   The smallest of spiritual universal nature can hold or wrap up the entirety of existence, without anything escaping from it.   Spiritual nature is very different from the material world.   Once you learn, you can know it and prove it, as your development takes you to a new range of experience.

"So why have you established one name to fight all the other names?   How can this be possible?   How can I fix that?" I asked him.

After a long while, Jesus answered me, "You are still looking for an answer? Do you think I did not answer you?"

I said, "No, you did not answer me, because you did establish yourself. This caused prejudice and conflict with other thoughts and beliefs. Why did you not say that you are universal nature and give no name?"

"I have already answered you. I am all names. I carry no name, truly. I am universal spiritual nature. At that time, human communication was very distinct from one region to the other. Different communities used different languages. That was the circumstance. No one should hold onto a name, it has nothing to do with people reaching their spiritual nature. I know your concern for the spiritual unity of human beings. There has been an abuse in the overestablishment of different names and different teachings. Looking at it broadly, one can see that it is truthful that the one universal nature has many expressions, which indicate the expansion of universal nature. Rather than having many unsuccessful ways of reaching universal nature, it would be more effective for humans to have one broad way. Religions, or spiritual forms of worship, which attempt to establish human social forms rather than reach universal spiritual nature would be abolished if people achieved adequate spiritual growth. It is not hard to see that external disunity exists today because of the abuse that occurred when different names and different teachings were established, which created a splintering from the universal spiritual nature. Thus, the different names are only ways of speaking of and describing universal nature. They have become a barrier within humankind's mind, making it unable to perceive the truth directly. Thus, people's teaching has been unsuccessful in reaching universal nature. Any useful way to reach the universal nature also needs to be objectively examined and held up as an inspiration for help, as an educational approach.

"Nothing can be held as the truth. New life is new truth. The universal capability of human life always looks forward, and does not always stumble because of the past."

The above was the dialogue in my meditation. Then the early summer sun rose. The strong energy was attracted to my head area; the communication interrupted. The early morning energy, before sunrise, is milder and usually can reach the holy beings. But my thoughts continued.

"I would like to tell my Christian friends and all churches to open up to the real Jesus in plain clothing. Open up to the direct teaching of universal spiritual nature. If you can really open up, you could find the real root, the real messiah in you. Otherwise, you are making a hole in your lifeboat and that of the world. You make your spiritual life and the world sink and are responsible for the damage of the unity of the natural universal nature. All the churches and temples in different regions of the world should open up to see new light and accept a new language which is not from any one person but the universal spiritual nature. It is the light directly radiating out from universal nature itself."

8
To Mentors

Student: Master Ni, there are teachers in different places teaching your work. In what way should I accept a teacher of your tradition?

Master Ni: I adopt the word mentor to title the volunteer teachers and helpers; I call them the Mentors of the Great Path of the Integral Truth. The mentors and teachers of the natural integral truth are those who are aware of their own responsibility for their personal spiritual growth. With this awareness, they do not choose to leave the troubled world to pursue the enjoyment of personal spiritual attainment, but extend their helping hands to people unaware of the total spiritual growth of the entire human society as one life being, as it is revealed by the Integral Spiritual Truth of the universe. Their help is not offered because of big material ambition; however, reasonable support can be provided them through their teaching and service. It is agreeable to this tradition that mentors and teachers charge for classes, services and the expenses of running centers. Any decent manner is acceptable, such as accepting donations given with a clear or pure mind, but not tithing people. Most importantly, good spiritual work must be protected from greed in material amassment for selfish interest, involvement in confused sexual relationships and unnatural power pursuits.

The teaching and the center of a mentor is the exhibition of his or her spirituality, as are his or her personal life, behavior and habits of speech, hidden psychology and submerged emotional reefs. He or she takes total responsibility for organizing his or her work, business, life, personal attitude, cultivation and virtuous fulfillment. While there is a unified goal and unified guidance for everyone, spiritual development is personal and cannot be made into another person's responsibility.

However, any student who joins a Mentor of the Integral Way in order to learn should accept his or her teaching and discipline. Otherwise, the meaning of a group educational program is lost. This is another way to receive external help.

Student: I have attended classes of different teachers who are all students of yours. They talk about the same subject differently, yet each of them insists on what you have said. I am not sure to whom I should listen.

Master Ni: You are learning from each of them to see which one guides you to the truth. You must listen to what each one says, because you are still growing. Anyone who quotes me from their own experience, rather than from my books, describes his own understanding or view of the situation. This understanding may not be the total truth, but it can be used as an answer. Correspondence written by my students also presents the student's understanding of the matter asked.

I encourage your own spiritual cultivation so you may understand matters directly, yourselves, through the help you obtain from repeatedly studying my books in great depth. This is what was in my mind when I wrote them.

Student: Master Ni, some of your students say they have helped you write these books and that they know more about your teaching than others.   Should I trust them?

Master Ni: In my eleven years of work in the west, some students participated in the program of learning through working, and they did offer help in polishing, editing, typing, designing and assembling these books, which present the Integral Truth and the Integral Way of life.   Some of them dropped out halfway, believing that getting information was everything.   Some of them have stayed longer.   However, they obtained the information and guidance as any other readers of my books do.   With them, as with everybody, true spiritual benefit still depends on personal spiritual self-cultivation. For the teaching to benefit them, they must have cultivated a higher quality.   Otherwise, the benefit will be lessened accordingly, by their own limitations, such as the emotional blockages they hold.   Therefore they end up only getting intellectual information from working on the books.   Nobody achieves spiritual advancement by merely intellectual experiences.

Student: Master Ni, can you recommend a Tai Chi teacher for me who has learned from you?

Master Ni: I offered a Tai Chi class for people interested in improving their health and as part of their personal self-cultivation.   It was an on-going, open class.   Now it is continued by Dao and Mao, my sons, with the same purpose.   This class is more of a social service than teaching an art.   No individual correction nor special instruction is made to any individual.   No tests for progress are made. It is taught with the purpose of developing the observation and absorption of each individual student and gives no limitation in molding them in one rigid formation like soldiers on parade.

Although there are teachers who have been in my class, they cannot seriously be considered as having been my personal students who would represent me, even if they have been given certificates. Nobody can represent any other person. Even a real student still cannot represent the teacher. I have not adopted any private student or given serious training in the martial arts nor qualified anyone as a representative of my art. I do not take as a student of Taoist arts anyone who lacks the basic qualifications for learning them.

Taoist movement includes Tai Chi, whose specific focus is the refinement of internal personal energy. None of my contacts have achieved it. I ordain people to become mentors of the integral way in support of their kindness and virtuousness in helping the world.

Tai Chi is an art. All art is a personal achievement. Personal achievement cannot be put in a frame as a certificate from an authority. Yet, I support those teachers' practice as it pertains to their personal goal, and I support promoting Tai Chi in a moderate and humble manner. Even in this limited manner, these arts can benefit the public.

Student: What is a Mentor of the Great Path of the Integral Truth?

Master Ni: A Mentor of Tao is a teacher, an organizer or a coordinator of a group study and practice. He or she is a person who has nurtured high spiritual awareness of his spiritual responsibility to himself and the public.

A Mentor is a student of Tao. (This word "Tao" stands for the Great Path of the Integral Truth.) He or she is a person who makes no excuses but improves his personal spiritual condition and gives his spiritual support to someone who likes to do the same.

A Mentor of Tao is a person who spiritually disciplines himself and avoids all unnecessary confrontation with people.

A Mentor of Tao is a person who gives up aggressive force toward his fellow people but develops his own spiritual tenacity.

A Mentor of Tao is a person who knows how to live effectively, work effectively and manage his emotions healthily.

A Mentor of Tao is a careful student who, through spiritual progress, can appreciate the work of the ancient achieved ones, such as Lao Tzu, Chuang Tzu and others.

A Mentor of Tao is a careful student who is ready to actualize the truth of his natural organic being in his personal and public life.

A Mentor of Tao is a person who may be treated by other people unfavorably in circumstances of the conflict of competition or in small worldly matters, but who always treats others fairly in all circumstances.

A Mentor of Tao is a person who discovers more valuable things to learn in the process of achieving himself and has less to argue or to brag about in making progress.

A Mentor of Tao is a person who can organize his energy of body, mind and spirit in useful, serviceable channels instead of becoming scattered or wasting it.

A Mentor of Tao is a person of Tao. A student of Tao needs no push from others. He is one who actualizes from the impetus of his own life into an honest realization of spirit. I have pointed out how to develop yourself physically, mentally and spiritually to reach the spiritual mission as Mentors of the Integral Way.

Next, I would like to describe the spiritual mission of all the Mentors of the Great Path of the Integral Truth. This includes:

The Spiritual Mission

1.   To guide yourself and others to live a spiritually centered life in a secular living environment.

2.   To guide yourself and others to use discipline in actual cultivation with your knowledge of its benefit.

3.   To guide yourself and others to be unafraid of mistakes but fearful of a lack of improvement or unconsciousness concerning what has been experienced from mistakes.

4.   To guide yourself and people to worship God, the spiritual unity of your personal energy that enables your entire being to attain all spiritual fulfillment.

5.   To guide yourself and people to embrace one another's spiritual nature, as it is the great all-in-one spiritual nature which would be variously entitled and worshipped as the God of Universal Unity, the Great Path of the Integral Truth, and the Universal Subtle Law, granted the mutual assistance given in the positive spiritual evolution of all people.

6.   To guide yourself and others to be sincere spiritual beings within and without in everyday life.

7.   To guide yourself and others to clearly see the mistake of conventional worship that limits one's nature to an illusory racial or tribal conformity or superiority, which only creates spiritual disharmony between oneself and others.

8.   To guide yourself and others to wash away the tendency to separate into small broken pieces of human spiritual relatedness with others and to enable each individual's energy to attain a new birth of great spiritual reunion with all people.

9.   To guide yourself and others to learn the main prayer that is:

"The Integral Truth of Universal Life, the Subtle Law and All Gods of Universal Love, uplift me from the small center of myself, my family, my friends and my race to the center of One Great Universal Life. Enable me to know to strengthen myself with my daily plain good food and spiritual study, and enable me to provide an opportunity for others to earn their daily meal too.   Enable me to survive safely and let me learn to let all others survive.   Let me learn to respect my life as well as the life of all others.   Let me learn not to use my faith in you as a personal tool to attain my selfish purpose.   Help me learn to live with no debt and pay any debt I have.   Let me learn to forgive other's offenses and to live a life without the need to beg pardon from my own conscience.   Let me raise the well-being of all levels, spiritual, mental, emotional, physical and financial.   Let me know that I live a life of universal nature.   This is my sincere prayer."

10.   To guide yourself and others to realize the truth of the Universal One Life by daring to step back when you are aware that you have offended universal harmony and offer surrender to universal rightness.

11.   To guide yourself and others to examine internal and external learning in everyday life and find a way to retreat from a disharmonious situation without aggravating the problem.

12.   To guide yourself and others to utilize the teaching of the ageless and limitless integral way, to integrate the pulls from the different forces of worldly life which keep people living in a split state of spiritual, mental and emotional life.

13.   To guide yourself and others to receive the true salvation of the world, following the religion of universal harmony, the spiritual direction of the integral way,

and the goal of spiritual development of all of human-kind.

14.   To guide yourself to know that it is the model of your normal plain life which helps others, it is not the long lectures, argumentative discussions or anything extra that needs to be done to your own plain, honest spiritual nature.

15.   To guide yourself to attain freedom and spiritual enjoyment in each day's life and also accomplish the highest spiritual achievement in the ordinariness of your own everyday life.

With the above, I have given the basic cultivation and mission of the mentors and students of Tao.

CHAPTER EIGHTEEN

IN WHAT WE BELIEVE

The following material records the spiritual activity of February 14, 1988 in the Shrine of the Eternal Breath of Tao in Malibu, California at the New Year's celebration and Ceremony of Spiritual Refreshing.

I.   Maoshing Ni gave a humorous opening.

II.   Daoshing Ni performed the ceremony.   All people followed his instruction in the ceremony.

Salutation   "Let us offer our salutation to the invisible essence which generates the rotation of all Heavenly bodies to let us small human people enjoy a yearly great return.

"Let us offer our salutation to the wisdom which has been passed down from generation to generation as wonderful beams of Subtle Light to guide the forward and upward growth of all of us.

"Let us offer our salutation to the great universal life-being which contains the three great spheres of physical matter, universal mind and universal soul, which are joined together and shared by all of us."

Reading   Communion with the Jade Emperor, the Universal Pure Realm.

"Your sublime energy envelops all heavens.
It is the wonderful and mysterious Source of energy
        rays which extend throughout the universe.
Your divine authority
            over this purple and gold shrine
            makes it the most glorious palace on earth.

You are the Primal Energy and the most exquisite
        of all beings.
You can be measured only by infinity.
You are the Source of subtle light, purity, quietude
        and impartiality.
You support all dimensions
        through your virtuous example.
The sacred Shiens are the extension
        of your subtle energy.
Your comprehensive wisdom is quiet,
        pure and profound.
Your calmness is sublime.
To settle arguments through argumentation
        is not your way.
Your way is simplicity, and sincerity is your power.
Your paternal energy sires selflessness.
Your maternal energy gives birth to kindness.
You extend to the fullness with emptiness.
With the completeness of your virtue you support
        those incomplete in virtue.
You choose no measurement to appraise individual
        beingness.
You use your absolute comprehensiveness
        to contain all existence.
You are the essential result
        of the highest sublimation.
You are the eternal guide of the unfolding universe.
You are the creator of the eternal Way.
A thousand beautiful cultures of humanity
        seek you and attempt to describe you.
You set order to the untamed world
        with your subtle formulas.
You preserve the truth on the physical pathway by
        combining physical with spiritual.
The Purple Tower Palace in the highest heaven is
        your residence.
The coarsest places of the earth
        are also your workshop.
You ride on the white energy horse,
        running on the channel of time and space.

The most mysterious shrine of all is where you are.
You communicate with all beings
in all realms of existence.
You reside not only in the yellow and gold Source
of the highest heaven,
but also in the lowest places of the earth.
You contain all beings
within your boundless nature.
You are the unruling ruler
of the profound vastness.
Your younger brother/sister and son/daughter,
with my body, mouth, will and whole heart
return to you.
I will follow the ultimate Tao for all eternity and
never tire of this exaltation."

At the end of his service, he guided everyone to do the salutation by saying:

Salutation "Let us offer our salutation to the Shrine of the Eternal Breath of Tao which is an extension of the spiritual expression of all of us.

"Let us offer our salutation to all universal-minded teachers and masters of the past, present and future who are like a torchlight in the dark, shining upon each of us.

"Let us offer our salutation to all students of Tao past, present and future as we firmly join in the Life of the eternal truth of Tao."

III.   Marc Chessler read Master Ni's work, the Ever Green Spiritual Life of Human Spiritual Development as the Goal and Cultivation of All Students of Tao:

THE GOAL AND CULTIVATION
OF STUDENTS OF TAO

While the learning of Tao is first and foremost a useful life endeavor, its application is multi-leveled, thus it can also serve as a belief system.

The human mind has reached a stage of intellectual power that is capable of creating the most powerful and destructive weapons in history; the entire human race could easily be destroyed with no great effort. This is due to the great imbalance between the intellectual progress we have made and the spiritual progress of mankind as a whole. The teachings of conventional religion fall far behind man's intellectual achievement, and it is very likely that human life may be swallowed up by this undisciplined intellectual force.

Because individual development through personal spiritual cultivation is such a gradual process, I would like to introduce you to the "believing of Tao." Belief is a human power that can be applied to anything. When people believe they are right, they will fight against others in order to impose their beliefs on them; they will not hesitate to harm someone in the name of their right belief. I believe we can all see the conflict and confrontation that has come about through strongly held beliefs.

It is true that faith and belief can bring strength to one's life, but such strength can be either positive or negative. Many years ago I taught in a public school where all the teachers lived together in a dormitory. One of the teachers, whose room was not far from mine, was a young, handsome, joyful person. One year, after a routine physical checkup and x-ray, this young man was told that he had tuberculosis. At that time, TB was as serious as cancer is now, and when the young man learned that he had the disease he suddenly lost all his strength. Overnight he became a totally different person. His energy changed, and he had no more life strength. He was soon faced with losing his job, and he suffered even more.

Just before he was about to enter a sanitarium for tuberculosis patients he received a notice that his name had been written in error on the lab report. He did not have TB! At first he doubted the notice, because he actually had felt the pain in his lungs, but after checking carefully with the hospital, he found that he was perfectly healthy and became his old self again.

Since his room was so close to mine, I was able to observe how powerfully affected he was by his belief.

What we believe is very important. However, there are two kinds of belief: some are truthful and some are false. There are a number of examples that illustrate this.

Among the famous students of Confucius was one named Tsen Sen who was a kind and ethical person, trusted by all who knew him. One time Tsen Sen happened to travel to a place called Fe where someone else named Tsen Sen had killed a man. Word traveled quickly that Tsen Sen, the student, had killed a man. His old mother, who had known and trusted him longer than anyone, had unshakable faith in her son's good character and knew that he would not kill anyone. Another person came to tell her the news, and she still remained firm in her belief in her son. When a third person came to her, however, she finally began to doubt. Beloved friends, your psychology sometimes leads you to make mistakes. As the Chinese proverb says: From three people's talk, you trust there is a tiger coming.

Not long ago, in the Western Hemisphere, people believed that the earth was the stationary center of the entire solar system. In the fifteenth century, Nicholas Copernicus discovered that the earth does move, revolving to create day and night, and orbiting the sun to create our yearly cycle. His discovery was rejected, however, as disrespectful to God because of the religious beliefs of his day.

In this century, Bertrand Russell, a British philosopher who was an English voice of Tao, described the wasteful struggle between scientific and religious belief in his book, "Religion and Science." This struggle has been going on for generations and is still not over. In world culture, religion can pull back the legs of marching science, but science is never permitted to assist the development of religion.

The tradition of Tao is a totally different situation. In Tao, belief is the result of the teamwork of religion and science. In Tao, scientific achievement only serves as the explanation for all the spiritual advances one makes in learning Tao. Thus, the religion of Tao is not overshadowed by science and does not need to suppress scientific achievement, because all scientific achievement serves the learning of Tao to some degree. Tao expresses the entire achievement of nature and the human race in all generations, past, present and future.

In these past eleven years I have attempted to explain to you the different aspects of learning Tao, and you now have eleven books, each with a different function working for you. Now I simply present Tao as a system of truthful, helpful belief that I hope will mean something to all of us and to our society.

A person of Tao believes that he or she is on the path of continual growth, betterment and development. He or she does not believe themselves to be perfect; thus they remain open to wisdom from other sources.

A person of Tao believes that all pressures in his life, internal and external, are opportunities to strengthen himself; thus he does not try to escape to somewhere else or try to be someone other than he or she is.

A person of Tao believes that wherever he or she is, is Heaven. Not a static, imaginary Heaven stripped of all creativity, but one that offers room for more improvement. A person of Tao can also distinguish supportive elements in a negative situation and use these as tools to develop himself or herself above whatever is a cause for suffering.

A person of Tao believes himself or herself to be sufficient and capable in all aspects of life. Richness is a state of mind, and self-sufficiency relies upon good management. There are rich people whose minds are tightly wound, whose personalities are dried up, whose emotions have gone sour, and whose hearts have turned to stone because they do not experience sufficiency in their lives.

A person of Tao believes that he or she is unconditionally happy, because happiness is merely a state of mind. If one's happiness is conditioned by the circumstance, one can be deprived of that happiness by a change of circumstance and, as we all know, circumstances are always changing.

A person of Tao truly believes that he or she has a great life and that he or she is no greater or less than anyone who has ever lived.   If one becomes very successful and respected, he or she knows clearly that circumstances have allowed him or her to express their innate good qualities.   If life circumstances do not allow free expression of those qualities, a person of Tao knows that those good qualities are still undefeatedly within them.   Their truth is not dependent upon being expressed.   Even if other people do not think you are successful, you still have a great life because your good qualities are there.   The qualities which need circumstances to express them are relative, not the absolute spiritually.

A person of Tao believes that he or she is a good person at all times and in all places.   Even if society or life circumstances influence one adversely, he does not stop believing that he is a good person and cannot be bent against his own natural morality to harm himself or others.

A person of Tao believes in simplifying his or her unreasonable ambition or desire, curtailing unnecessary activities, and restraining unimportant contact with others in order to gather the essence of his life.

A person of Tao believes that a good place to be in life is not where he or she is cheered by many, but where he or she can diminish the ego and quietly serve others.

A person of Tao believes that good friendship is formed naturally by his or her own good nature and by treating others fairly, not by making demands on other people.   A person of Tao can thus maintain spiritual independence in all relationships and not be pulled down or influenced by a change of circumstance in the relationship.   He or she is able to enjoy something without drowning in it.

A person of Tao believes that the world is his home and that his contribution is to make it a safe and enjoyable place for people to be. In his personal life on earth, however, the world is only his lodging and he must keep himself bravely moving along the way.

A person of Tao believes that everything, including the understanding of truth, makes room for more development. In his personal life especially, he never hesitates to correct and improve himself and the situation. Without a moment's hesitation he can decide to start life over, fresh and new, especially spiritually. This is the light that enables him to constantly correct himself.

A person of Tao believes in the direct practice of personal development. This means improving one's own conceptual, psychological, physical and social condition and being open to whatever can fulfill one's continuing development. This is not like following rigid standards set by someone else. One can certainly follow the guidance and principles such as those expressed in the *I Ching* and the *Tao Teh Ching*, but all teachings and beliefs are open to further development and understanding. The life of a person of Tao can be expressed by words, but words are not what he should live by.

A person of Tao believes that his life carries the truth of life itself. He seeks no personal glory, therefore, but merges his life with the great life of the developing universe and his soul with the great soul of the evolving universe to live forever.

A person of Tao believes that he is a tunnel through which everything moves, thus he keeps nothing for himself. He is not a channel or medium for the voice or tune of one person at one time; to be a tunnel is a spiritual achievement. A tunnel is something through which things pass, good and bad. A person of Tao remains receptive and does not become attached to the things that pass through his life because, if things accumulate, the tunnel becomes blocked. The life of a person of Tao keeps moving; it does not stop; thus it is healthy. A channel can only channel a specific voice, like a channel on a television set which can only channel one program at a time. A person of Tao is not limited to a single channel with only one voice or program on it. If you are a tunnel, you will be above all life experience and your soul will not become stuck to any of it. All people's lives are tunnels, actually, but they do not believe it.

A person of Tao believes in spiritual immortality. All of nature is one big life that never dies but circulates without end. An achieved soul can always ride on the flow of natural life and refresh itself with the essence that connects and directs the eternal flow of all life.   The practical goal of spiritual self-cultivation, therefore, is maintaining the well being of one's own self.   If everyone did this, the well-being of society would be assured, because the well-being of human society as a whole is assured by the achieved well-being of each individual.

Health, longevity and emotional enjoyment are side effects of the belief in spiritual immortality. First, one should have the goal of no sickness. There is a saying in Chinese, "Bai beng po sen," which means literally "No hundreds of illnesses happen to you." In order to maintain "Bai beng po sen" in your life you have to watch out for yourself. You have to work on yourself and keep your life moving. In the physical sphere of life, for example, when you discover a little illness, you should immediately treat it with natural herbs and a holistic approach so that it will not become big. You should also watch out for the possibility of becoming sick. A common cold can become the cause of many troubles if it is not properly treated. When someone does become ill, the good results of his spiritual cultivation can help him overcome the illness. You should all know this.

If you should become very ill and your organs or body fail you, it is then time to gather your spiritual energy and prepare yourself to withdraw from physical life. Life has cycles: spring is the time to sprout; summer is the time to grow; autumn is the time to harvest; and winter is the time to withdraw your energy to the root and wait for another spring to bring about new life. In the winter of human life you withdraw to your subtle root, your spiritual energy; however, deathless life can be attained by spiritual cultivation. You shall know more as you develop yourself more.

When your life has a physical shape, you need to serve your physical being. You need to gather support for it and provide for its needs, wants, and even luxuries. All this is limited to the physical level of life. Once the great life of spirit is achieved, however, you are no longer limited by the small life of the body. Once you attain spiritual life, which means transfer from the stage of physical limitation into the stage of unlimited spiritual purity, you no longer need to serve or work for your small bodily self any more. You no longer have the inconvenience and obligation of physical life. After you have uplifted yourself to the level of universal life, you become a great life that is subtly helpful in assisting and guiding all lives. You no longer need to maintain the small life of form.

A Student Asks: Does this only refer to when the physical body dies?

Master Ni: There are two ways to utilize this knowledge. When you are alive, you can still extend yourself from your limited physical being, and your mind and soul can embrace the entire universe. If your body fails you and you cannot go further, you need to be able to ascend with no attachment, no looking back, and no struggling. By just being ready to go, you can withdraw to a sphere where there is no limited, small life. An achieved soul will naturally become a soul of the great life of the universe.

In the cultivation and teaching of Tao, the ancient achieved ones discovered that human life is a small model of the universe. In your lifetime you can develop, see and experience different spiritual agents within your own body. At the physical level, some of these are related to the faculty of enjoying eating and some are related to the faculty of enjoying sexual activity.   An achieved person, however, is not pulled down by a small group of spiritual faculties, because his or her destination is not the fulfillment of physical desires.   Neither are they the tools of psychological ambition.   To a person of Tao, the physical body is an instrument of the soul which continues to develop until it becomes one with the great life of the universe.   A person of Tao is not his or her head or feet, penis or vagina.   He is not the finger which only wishes to touch something smooth, but rather the great mind that gives all other life faculties and instruments their creativity and virtuous fulfillment, whether in formed, physical life or in unformed spiritual life.

Student: So then you evolve to become the spiritual head of your life being?

Master Ni: You are now the spiritual head or "soul" in your body.   At this stage, however, you are not necessarily the leader or master, because you are influenced, pulled or enslaved by many factors, internally as well as externally.   At this stage of physical life, although you are not called a slave by society, you are still a slave of physics.   An achieved soul is not a slave of physics.   It is a master of physics who can utilize his or her own sexual, mental, physical and emotional energy in positive, helpful, serviceable ways that bring happiness in one's own life and the lives of others. This can be achieved while you are still living in a physical form, but if you do not do it before the physical form fails you, you should not look back but gather your spiritual energy to transform to a higher stage. The goal of a person of Tao is union with Tao.   Unfortunately, our lives are not only dualistic but multiplistic.   People have cut themselves into so many small, unimportant elements that their soul, which should be the leader, becomes lost and uninfluential.   When one's soul is weak, life becomes disordered and filled with upset.   Thus the need for cultivation, restoration, refreshment, rejuvenation and regeneration.   A person of Tao believes in having a strong, effective soul.

Now I would like to extend our discussion of the big life and the small life. A "small life" means serving only your physical life: you feed yourself; you get yourself a mate; you provide yourself with a dwelling. All these things serve your physical being. The "big life" is not limited to your physical self, but can expand to embrace other lives, including the great life of the universe itself. In your lifetime, you already communicate with the soul energy of the universe; spiritually you already connect with the great life, the great soul, the great spirit of the universe; you do not communicate with other small lives only. Life is not a physically limited, individual circumstance. Therefore, a great life is not something unattainable or unachievable. You can realize union between Tao and your personal life being the moment you start to dissolve the demands you place on yourself.

A person of Tao believes in extending kindness, sympathy, love and patience to all lives, especially those which are undeveloped. For example, with enough spiritual awareness, you know that there are many undeveloped spiritual elements or agents in your body. A person of Tao does not negatively try to block them out in an ascetic way; instead you work to harmonize them. In cultivating Tao, you give all things a chance for development, not just the small tiny soul which shares so many spiritual agents or faculties with the body. In general, when the hour of death comes, separation and disintegration occur and there is no union. The soul ascends and the other spiritual faculties descend and scatter into water or air or stay in the trees because you abandoned them. This is the result of the old type of religion. A person of Tao believes in bringing the "whole family" together through internal unity. A company of spiritual faculties or agents is forged during the course of your life. Then, as your company expands, this is called the union of Tao and the life-being. Once you are internally and externally fulfilled, the process is the same, and you ascend. If you do not have patience, tolerance and sympathy towards the undeveloped spiritual elements within yourself, it will be ridiculous to think you are helping the world, because you are not even helping yourself. You are not achieved. If you ignore the undeveloped spiritual agents within you, how can you claim to be helping other people? This is an incomplete, undeveloped level.

A person of Tao follows the way of union of Tao with his or her own life being. This achievement is the achievement of all being, not the achievement of a single soul. Other religions have attempted to isolate your head as Heaven and leave the rest of the body in Hell. Tao does not cut your head off from the rest of your body and call it Heaven. In learning Tao, one learns the teamwork of the whole being and thus brings about the great harmony and completion that is truly Heaven. That is the great knowledge of this tradition.

A person who already has incurable trouble inside may believe it is too late, but he still has a chance. Although his spiritual elements cannot be gathered completely, the mind can produce the essence which transforms to be different spiritual energy. That energy can be gathered, and the person can safely withdraw from the body with a certain completeness in spiritual life.

The teaching of all developed ones of ancient times is not for the achievement of a single, individual soul. Conventional religious faith says that if you do something that pleases God, you do well, and God will reward you by taking you to Heaven and giving you a seat next to him. It is not that way in this path of spiritual development. There is no ascension of one single life element by renouncing life and following an ascetic way that sacrifices your sexual energy, your mental desire and so forth, without using a proper way to transform it to be a supportive element of your spiritual development. That is nothing more than cutting off the head and throwing the body away, or picking a flower instead of tending the whole tree for its fruit. The cultivation of Tao is the art of growing the whole tree, not just the enjoyment of cut flowers.

There is no real achievement in single matters, only the fragmentation of wholeness. When you choose a piece of silk to make a blouse from, you cannot separate the softness of the cloth from the silk. Spiritual development values wholeness and allows each part to serve and support the entire life-being. Can a head live all by itself? That is the trouble with religions that talk about the head without mentioning the harmony of all the parts. Their picture may look very angelic, but there is no reality behind it.

In your very shape I see the beauty of God. Not just in your body, but in your entire being I see an angel. That is the point of learning Tao. Other religions have that expectation, but in practice they cut themselves up into too many pieces that cannot be put together. In our daily lives we cannot ignore our emotions or our intellect or our physical impulses or our rational mind, otherwise we would become a tool of one or more of them. Likewise, spiritual matters cannot be singled out from one another. A lotus flower cannot exist without the mud at the bottom of the water. Its beauty is the product of its whole existence: the pond, the water, the leaves, the stem, the sunshine and the air. You cannot take a pair of scissors and cut the head off from the stem and call it the religion of Pure Lotus.

A person of Tao believes in a living religion of wholeness called the Great Path of One Complete Truth which teaches people to live completely, wholly, happily, enjoyably - embracing the entirety of all lives and all things. Narrow religious practices are like looking for fish eggs in the tops of trees. They all insist on very definite pictures and rituals without ever looking at the reality of total spiritual achievement.

A person of Tao believes in changing and improving his personality so that he can give sweetness and kindness to the world rather than poison. This is called moral health. Very few people harm others for the sake of personal benefit. Most people want a good life and are willing to take responsibility for themselves

and make the effort to earn a good living. Those who
do not and who work instead at finding fault with
others are morally sick.

A person of Tao believes in rational health. Many
things are done out of rational sickness. For example,
when a man loves a young girl without looking to see
whether she is the right person for him, this is rational-
ly sick.

Physical, moral, emotional and intellectual health
are all connected, and an error in one area can bring
about problems in the others, so you need to check out
each one in yourself. You especially need to examine
your relationships and notice whether they are sick or
healthy. Is the relationship with your parents normal
or not? Do you join your friends in morally sick activities without encouraging them toward spiritual
achievement or without discouraging them from the
use of drugs? You should also examine the relationship with your siblings and your fellow workers.

Do you treat the man or woman with whom you
live fairly, or do you take their love for granted without appreciating it and without fulfilling your own part
of the relationship? If you are a woman, do you always expect the man to fulfill you without consideration for your part in the relationship? When
your man is suffering or angry, can you stay quietly at
his side? Can you be emotionally supportive or do
you laugh at him and say it is his problem and walk
away?

A person of Tao believes that relationships should
assist personal growth and spiritual development. If it
is not positive and helpful to each side, is it not better
for everyone to live separately in peace, without the
trouble of having a relationship? Relating to another
person can help one's spirit if the occasion, no matter
how difficult, is utilized in that way. Whatever else
you gather from the relationship, such as softness or
sweetness or gentleness, is nearly not as important as
the spiritual benefit and wisdom you can gain from the
situation.

Gloomy, unreasonable moods are emotional sicknesses.   Stubbornness, aggression and extreme subjectiveness are intellectual sicknesses. Self-righteousness and self-love are moral sicknesses. Obsession with an idea or untruthful belief, jumping to conclusions or indulging in wild, unjustified fancies and foolhardy actions or baseless talk are rational sicknesses. Treating another person unfairly or exerting a harmful control over someone is the sickness of relating. Lao Tzu has said that to not know what is sick is truly sick; to know what is sick and correct it is the development of a sage.

These are all examples of "Bai beng po sen."   A person of Tao believes in not being troubled by disease or sickness, because wholeness is what the person worships.

A person of Tao believes that the first important guidance of his or her own spiritual self-cultivation is to channel one's own spiritual energy rather than scatter that energy or channel the energy of a confused ghost. Someone who can channel someone else's spirit to give a high spiritual teaching is no higher than someone who can channel his own spiritual energy correctly. There is no need, therefore, to channel someone else's spirit.

A person of Tao believes that the highest achievement of spiritual cultivation is to channel the universal spirits or wholeness of the universe and that channelling the ghosts of others is spiritual sickness and abnormalcy.

While Tao is truth, it can also serve as a belief system that expresses the truth of the spiritual nature that is within oneself. Spiritual truth is not something outside yourself. Most religions are the result of spiritual sickness - whether they are Indian or African or Christian - because people do not know how to channel their personal spiritual energy correctly. Anyone who can channel his own spiritual nature is wise and can guide people directly and make beautiful things happen in his or her own life without making it into a circus sideshow. It is time to recognize and stop the misleading mistakes that have been passed from one generation to another. Those who are seriously looking for spiritual achievement for themselves and for others need to look to their own discipline and cultivation within themselves and elsewhere for truthful, effective spiritual guidance.

A person of Tao believes in learning useful, effective and healthy practices, methods and skills that support the development of his or her own being. He or she also believes in using the learning of Tao to help other people who need to develop their own well-being. The development and practices of a person of Tao are not the conventional black magic that makes trouble in the world. Once people discover their own spiritual power, that power, like intellectual power, is affected by the mind and can be utilized for good as well as bad purposes. For instance, people in the United States have the psychic power to know when nuclear weapons and missiles are deployed by another country. People in Russia can utilize a person's psychic energy to do the same. That is not very different from the practices of black magic. Psychic energy is just a tool which can be used for good or evil. Protecting one nation could be harmful to another. A person of Tao learns methods from the great tradition of Tao which support his or her true achievement as a whole being, not just how to open the third eye or third ear or any other single organ. A sexual practice that benefits only one partner and not the other is not a practice of Tao and is not practiced by a true person of Tao. A true sexual practice helps both people. Black magic of any kind is a result of partial spiritual development, and it not only harms other people but also the purity of one's own spirituality. The profundity and vastness of Tao is an ageless tradition with countless skills and methods. I do not promote the practice of partial development because it will only make you partially blind. I tell you as my friends that this direction is worth your attention. Something bringing you good for yourself, while bringing bad things to other people, is not worth learning or achieving. If you have a chance, you should learn the practices and skills of the tradition of Tao stage by stage. If you don't have the chance to learn these helpful skills, then the basic guidelines of the most ancient developed ones are directly and adequately expressed in my books, so you don't need to feel disappointed that you have not learned the secrets. If someone is openly promoting something they call a secret, what they truly have to offer may well lead your personal development astray rather than fulfill it.

A person of Tao believes in adopting nonsexual disciplines at different stages and situations in life. Such discipline is natural because it is a matter of personal growth, not of moral restraint. In the tradition of Tao we do not make a point of advocating marriage, nor do we support undisciplined, undeveloped sexual freedom. Sexual contact without the development of personal knowledge brings no benefit. The tradition of Tao advocates co-existence of the sexes - in the family, in society, in any circumstance at all. There is no reason for women to reject men or vice versa. There is no reason for men and women to pull each other down; instead, they should assist each other. One of the most helpful situations in spiritual cultivation is a couple who can assist each other's development with or without sexual contact.

IV. Master Ni ordained the Mentors.

"The New Year's celebration of the combined solar and lunar cycles' calendar serves the yearly spiritual renewal ceremony for appointing new spiritual workers; it also serves as the conjoint birthday of Heaven, Earth and Mankind. The age we live in on earth is counted by the beginning of the joint natural cycles. This calendar was arranged by the Great Yu (who reigned from 2205-2197 B.C.), the one who gathered the ancient spiritual power and manpower successfully to overcome the problem of the great deluge, the big flood on earth. He made the first day of the new cycle as the Day of

Heaven, the second day as the Day of Earth and the third as the Day of Mankind. He was the one who preserved spiritual achievement even before the Yellow Emperor (who reigned from 2698-2598 B.C., and was himself an earlier great model of high public spirit and fulfillment, and, also, of spiritual achievement, like Great Yu himself.)

"Today, I ordain some of you as Mentors of the great path of the integral truth as the Taoist Global Mission to take the example of the Yellow Emperor and the Great Yu, who had high public spirits balanced with personal spiritual cultivation. All of you should serve as examples for other people. You are authorized to teach and do spiritual work in global society. Mentors, including masters and ministers in Tao, are people authorized to teach classes or lead study groups for new students of Tao and guide them by your achievement. Mentors can create centers to serve people according to each individual's qualities and capability. Mentors also perform different ceremonial activities. On the New Year in different centers and places, a New Year Spiritual Renewal Ceremony can be done with a gathering of friends and family, or an individual, by following such a model as is given today.

"For a group gathering, a convenient day for everyone should be chosen, such as a Sunday close to Spring Day of the new solar cycle, or the first day of the first lunar month. It is often impossible to have it on the actual day. A gathered celebration can be lead by a master, a minister, a mentor or a mentor candidate when he or she is the only worker available.

"In a group or individual Spiritual Renewal Ceremony, the shrine should be newly lighted and scented with good quality incense. A personally chosen invocation is read, such as "The Goal and Cultivation of a Student of Tao" or "The New Year's Resolution of My New Ever Green Life."

"Now, the chosen students of Tao, please come forward in front of me to be ordained. Your names will be kept in the records of the Taoist Order of Global Mission."

"Now I have ordained you as the Mentors of the Integral Way. Do not discount your qualification in any circumstance. This is a Yellow Dragon year. In every twelve year cycle, there is one dragon year. In every sixty year cycle, there is one Yellow Dragon year, as a milestone in the time channel. I would like to see success in promoting universal harmony through personal spiritual development of each of you. Thank you."

V. Master Ni guided the Mentors and all those who participated in the meeting by reading "The Resolution of My New, Ever Green Life."

"The purpose of my life is to continue the ageless ever-green wisdom of Tao.

"My life activities are the activities of universal natural truth.

"My life will be the continual unfoldment of the universal subtle law.

"My soul continues the evolution of the universal soul.

"My life is the unlimited exhibition of the integral truth.

"The condition of the world is the condition of my physics. I must work to reach its well-being, because the well-being of the world is the good support of my soul.

"It is sinful to keep looking for my personal salvation alone. Such a thing does not exist as long as others are suffering.

"It is sinful to keep searching for my personal individual delivery alone; such a thing is unreal until the wisdom of all the world's people is improved and until all people live in the Subtle Light.

"Physically, I have outgrown the shape of my childhood; spiritually, I have found the truth that inspires me for endless growth. I have purified all narrowness and prejudice from my conventional, non-fruitful and backward religious education.

"I cannot abandon the world to enjoy my spiritual life only. I am one of worldly life. The world is part of my life. I uphold my share of responsibility to bring flower and fruit to all lives. Without the well-being of the world, one individual's prosperity is only a false paper flower.

"As long as I dedicate my life to the welfare of my own person and of all other human people, I will continue to grow.

"I dedicate my life to the limitless spiritual development of myself in order not only to serve myself better, but also to serve the world better. The world has helped me develop, thus I am also going to help the world develop.

"I dedicate my life to the common goal of total global progress without prejudice or discrimination. That is Tao.

"I dedicate my never-tiring life to the learning of Tao. Then I can bring good life with development of all three spheres to myself and all my fellow people.

"Finally, I dedicate my life to bringing goodness, beauty and truth to myself and all other lives."

TO THOSE INTERESTED IN ORGANIZING
A STUDY GROUP

This material was contributed by Frank Gibson and his respectful study group in Atlanta, Georgia. Here we quote from his letter: "Many of the students at the Center of the Integral Truth may be able to establish a group as has been done here."

The gathering together of people to further their spiritual development and share in cultivation is an excellent opportunity for growth. A centered discussion group can help students with self-cultivation and to understand the practical nature of the learning of Tao. Meeting and practicing with others can offer support through the exchange of wisdom gained through life experience.

The successful organization of a study group may be accomplished through patience and an understanding of the purpose, which is to provide an environment for a group of people to grow together, share life experience and maintain an open door for others to share in the development of the group. The growth and success of the discussion group is dependent upon nurturing the group and avoiding any difficulties which may arise. If difficulties are not discerned and avoided or corrected, the group may increase in size, but it will not mature. The most common causes of failure are pride, control and the loss of spiritual chastity through dilution and mixing of the teaching.

Group members sometimes perceive the person who initially organized the group or the person in whose home they meet as their leader and teacher. Their desire to find a teacher as well as failure to understand the purpose, format and method often lead them to passivity, which results in unrealistic demands on their perceived leader. As a result, the initiators can become too active while others become too passive. As the balance dissolves, the structure of interaction no longer encourages growth. They are merely discussing the learning of Tao and expounding information.

It is, therefore, very important to assist others to understand that this will be an independent group without a leader or teacher. The role of the initial organizer is simply to encourage the formation of the group.

Before taking the responsibility for this work, reflect on your spiritual maturity. Are you seeking emotional support? Are you filling a psychological need? Even if you are free from these difficulties, your desire to do well will lead you to do as much as possible and meet all expectations. It can be a trap. Pride can begin to affect the perceived leader as he or she tries to do more and more to maintain that role.

The second difficulty is the use of force to make the group grow. Intelligent publicity makes information about the group available to those interested in studying Tao. Yet it is important to maintain detachment from the outcome of the advertisements. Try to understand growth as maturation rather than as an increase in quantity, though both may have occurred.

The group may expand into a Taoist Center at some time through increased interest and the availability of a teacher trained and authorized to teach. This would be beneficial for all concerned. However, this is not the purpose of a discussion group. If a center does eventually develop, it should be from a strong foundation built at this level. Put your energy into the groundwork. Don't be anxious to add classes and jump into large scale projects. Follow the examples of other successful groups. Let friends gather and nourish the growth of the group, just as the individuals nourish their own growth and development.

The third difficulty is maintaining spiritual chastity. The group's purpose is to study and discuss ancient Taoist texts and the modern works, as are available in the works of Master Ni, Hua Ching. Comparisons with religions and comments about other teachers are sure to arise. However, these may be non-beneficial. Combining the practices and teachings of other traditions will result in an eclecticism based on what currently seems true to members of your group. The attempt to understand a tradition new to oneself by drawing on what is familiar may be well-intended. But frequently it results in the loss of the opportunity to develop self-understanding through direct experience with the new tradition. The resulting eclecticism tends to mirror what is already in the students' minds.

How can these difficulties be avoided? Try to remain aware of them and discuss them, emphasizing the importance of equal participation by all members of the group. Also emphasize the importance of examining motives, especially motives to start a group, teach or lead. Encourage all members of the group, but especially those who carry a formal responsibility to carry it lightly, to move within the group naturally rather than try to control it.

Creating a Group

Initial Publicity Begin by advertising for people interested in forming a Taoist discussion group. Do not schedule it and do not present it as if it has already started. The goal at this point is to enlist the assistance of a few others. By only making contacts at this time, you will be able to explore various meeting places, expand your distribution points, and also encourage the group spirit of cooperation. It is most beneficial to gather several people to become involved in the development of the discussion group. This foundation of unity and shared responsibility will continue to be more valuable as other projects develop.

Spread news to meet interested people through stores and organizations which may attract those likely to be interested in the learning of Tao. Bookstores, natural food stores, and martial art schools are good sources. Meet with the owners and staff personally, discuss your plans and ask them to assist by directing people with an interest in the learning of Tao to you. They may let you post a notice in their location. Vegetarian organizations, chiropractors, acupuncturists and massage therapists have newsletters and mailing lists which may be obtained. In addition, local papers and radio stations have public service sections where announcements are cost-free.

Even if you have several friends who want to help, it is beneficial to also meet people from out of your immediate group of friends and contacts. This will expand your opportunities and offer a broader view.

The Organizational Meeting After several people have responded to your notices, schedule a meeting to clearly outline the goals, method and purpose of the group. At this meeting, discuss the following:

Purpose Discuss the purpose as outlined previously. Be sure all members understand the nature of the group as that of an independent study group without a leader or teacher. The role the initiators have is simply to encourage the group.

Method The method is that of independent self-development.

Goal The goal is to provide an environment and place for people to grow together, share life experience and create opportunity for others to join.

Meeting Place From this group, an initial meeting place may be formed. Try to project your needs so the group does not have to change locations more than once. A home is a good place to have meetings. However, there are several points to consider: Are other family members or roommates supportive? Is there sufficient room as the group grows? Is the neighborhood likely to be disturbed by increased traffic? Is there adequate parking? Is the location convenient to main roads? Is it easy to give directions and find?

Sometimes public places may be found, such as bookstores or natural food stores. In fact, these may be good initial locations because of their exposure and location. As more people join the group, you may be offered a better location. Remain flexible, have no personal preference, and utilize the best meeting place for the benefit of the majority of the group.

Fees It is not recommended that a fee be charged for the discussion group. This often encourages people to visit the gathering.

Meeting Times Try to plan your meetings at times that do not conflict with the regular meetings of other important groups in your community. Their schedules should be published in the local newspapers. Avoid "social" evenings. Once you have established a time, do not change it. It is convenient to schedule gatherings for 7:30 or 8:00 p.m. so that there is adequate time for dinner after a workday. A good discussion runs about an hour and a half.

Contact Person It is most likely that your ads will contain only a phone number. One person should take responsibility for receiving and returning phone calls. Consider these suggestions: 1) The contact person may install a phone answering device to receive calls. 2) He should be at home to answer and return calls personally during certain periods, especially in the evening. This is the time most people want calls returned. 3) The contact person should be familiar with the purpose, method and goals. 4) A phone line may be installed just for discussion group calls if the group finds it necessary and can share the expense. The least expensive way to do this is to order a second residential line such as a children's phone (business lines cost more). 5) The contact person should fully understand his responsibility and be sure he can maintain this position. Once you publicize the contact phone number, it is not easy to change. It may be common to receive more than thirty calls a week.

Mailing When people call, always ask for their address and add it to your mailing list. Mail an information packet as soon as possible. This packet may contain a map showing your location, a list of Master Ni's books and information regarding the purpose, method and goal of the group. (A suggested information packet is available from the Center of Integral Truth, Atlanta, Georgia).

It is most convenient and efficient if the contact person does this mailing. However, another participant may be selected to do this. Try to mail out promptly.

Method and Structure At this meeting, establish the method and structure of the group clearly. The most beneficial method for the discussion group is the awakening method of guided discussion. This is designed to promote interactions within the group which nurture each member's self-reliance and confidence in their ability to learn. Interactions with an "authority figure" can replace interaction with the teaching itself and is rarely as fruitful. Three ways of speaking within the group tend to encourage the confidence and involvement of others.

One is to refer to the books first when responding to the questions or comments of another group participant. Then you can add your own comment. It is very important to assist people to know that they have the tools and information available to them. This will help develop their self-responsibility. This also encourages the independent nature of the group.

Second, when you do share your comments, speak only from your own personal experience. If you have only information to repeat, you are not sharing wisdom. You can best assist in the development of others if you understand information and wisdom are not the same.

Third, it is helpful to ask questions which are open ended, but still focused enough to guide discussion. Examples are: what has been the result of this practice in your daily life? Has anyone found this subject or related subjects in any of the books? Can anyone answer that question? Who else can add to this? What have you found in your daily life that relates to (the subject)?

Begin each discussion with a reading of *The Tao Teh Ching*. Let students rotate the responsibility for this. Always clearly state the purpose and format whenever new members are present. It is beneficial for members to volunteer to select and read from the books at the following week's meeting. It may also be helpful to rotate the responsibility for opening the meeting, explaining the format, and reading *The Tao Teh Ching* among members of the group.

The Cauldron
Thoughts for New Spiritual Teachers

In *The Book of Changes and the Unchanging Truth*, Hexagram 50, Ting (cauldron) represents several images and meanings. The Cauldron represents stability, indicates a large family and teaches how one can mature to ripeness and mellowness. As a symbol of a balanced life, Ting expresses the unity which extends from one's inner self to one's immediate family, to all of mankind and the entire universe.

Following the progression symbolized by the levels of the Cauldron can help one develop accordingly. It is a model for both group growth and self growth.

The discussion group may have no designated teacher. Yet, as a student of Tao, you are also a teacher of Tao. The group can present a good opportunity to develop teaching skills. Careful, slow development can help you develop these skills naturally. Knowledge and wisdom must be combined with the ability to correctly guide people.

Carefully examine your motivation and develop yourself to move away from dependency, emotional luxuries and psychological needs. At the practical level, you must be willing to develop virtue and sincerity. Offering your time and resources selflessly to organize beneficial activities is a good expression of virtuous service to the world. Improve yourself by eliminating all negative attitudes and habits. Your behavior and speech become the manifestation of your own spiritual attainment. And your daily life offers true teaching to all people selflessly, not out of any desire for self-aggrandizement.

A person of Tao is not ambitious to be a leader unless the responsibility falls to him. He fulfills the task that is assigned to him and then takes no credit and holds no attachment to it. He merely offers himself to serve others.

Attain spiritual maturity through true life experience in the world. Then spread your light to all and remain unattached, whether people accept it or not.

Help all people without discrimination, but let them realize they did everything for themselves. Good spiritual teaching helps people avoid making mistakes. It does not lure them away from their normal lives in search of extraordinary blessings. The normalcy of life is a blessing itself.

If you have begun to liberate yourself from the darkness of blind impulses, ignorance, stubbornness and aggression, you have begun to assist the whole world. The gathering of a few friends along the way can assist in reuniting all people with Tao.

For further information, you may contact the Center of Integral Truth, 5215 Green Oak Court, Atlanta, GA 30327. A group in Miami have used the same model for their study group and are located at The Tao Center of Miami, 20730 NE 8th Court, #102, North Miami Beach, Florida 33179.

BOOKS IN ENGLISH BY MASTER NI

The Complete Works of Lao Tzu

The works of Lao Tzu are considered the essence of human spiritual vision, expressing the natural truth in the simplest language and shortest form. In addition to the well known *Tao Teh Ching*, Lao Tzu's later teachings are also included in the rare classic, the *Hua Hu Ching*. 212 pages, 1979. Softcover, $9.50

The Book of Changes and the Unchanging Truth

The time-tested guidance of the *Book of Changes* has been unsurpassed by any individual spiritual teacher or tradition in any age for its broadness and usefulness in all circumstances of life. This translation also includes invaluable background material and commentaries from the ancient Taoist tradition. 732 pages, 1983. Hardcover, $35.00

The Way of Integral Life - *New Publication* - This work can help build a bridge for those wishing to connect spiritual and intellectual development. It is most helpful for modern educated people. It includes practical and applicable suggestions for daily life, philosophical thought, esoteric insight and guidelines for those aspiring to give help and service to the world. This book helps you learn the wisdom of the ancient sages' achievement to assist the growth of your own wisdom and to integrate it as your own new light and principles for balanced, reasonable living in worldly life. 408 pages, 1989. Softcover, $14.00; Hardcover, $20.00.

Enlightenment: The Mother of Spiritual Independence - *New Publication* - The inspiring story and teachings of Master Hui Neng, Sixth Patriarch of the Zahn (Zen) Buddhist tradition in the sixth century. Master Ni includes enlivening and deepening commentaries and explanations of the spiritual principles outlined by this spiritual revolutionary. People who learn from Hui Neng may find spiritual independence from undeveloped religious confusion and confirm their continual spiritual growth. 264 pages, 1989. Softcover, $12.50, Hardcover, $18.00.

Attaining Unlimited Life - *New Publication* - Presented in this volume are the thought-provoking and mind-expanding teachings of Chuang Tzu, the greatest philosopher and Taoist master who was one of the forerunners of the Taoist school. This is the greatest treasure of human life. His work has been expanded to relate to modern times and includes questions by students and answers by Master Ni. 476 pages, 1989. Softcover, $18.00, Hardcover, $25.00.

The Gentle Path of Spiritual Freedom - *Recent Publication* -
This book is a record of Master Ni's public talks and classes throughout the world and across the United States. It encompasses a wide range of topics from everyday practical life, with its psychological and emotional problems, to the most profound aspects of individual spiritual improvement and immortality. The guidance and practices that he offers in these talks can bring practical, positive change and happiness to the lives of his readers. 464 pages, 1987. Softcover, $14.50

8,000 Years of Wisdom
This two-volume set of informal talks and classes given by Master Ni over a five year period covers a broad spectrum of topics including diet, marriage, sex and pregnancy from the perspective of traditional Chinese and Taoist healing. Vol 1, 236 pages, Vol 2, 241 pages; 1983. Softcover; each volume $12.50

The Uncharted Voyage Towards the Subtle Light
In this book, Master Ni looks at the entire history of Spiritual development and human evolution. Throughout the maze of differences and conflicts, he subtle and skillfully traces the Great Awakening Path of all people: the path of universal and eternal truth that never changes and which underlies all religious efforts and traditions. 424 pages, 1985. Softcover, $14.50

The Heavenly Way
A translation of the classic *Tai Shan Kan Yin Pien* (Straighten Your Way) and *Yin Chia Wen* (The Silent Way of Blessing). The purpose of this booklet is to promote the recognition of truth, because only truth can teach the perpetual Heavenly Way by which one reconnects oneself with divine nature. 41 pages, 1981. Softcover, $2.50

Footsteps of the Mystical Child
This book poses and answers such questions as: What is a soul? What is wisdom? What is spiritual evolution? The answers to these and many other questions enable readers to open themselves to new realms of understanding and personal growth. There are also many unforgettable stories about real-life people and their internal and external struggles on the path of self-development and spiritual evolution. 166 pages, 1986. Softcover, $9.50

Workbook for Spiritual Development
Living with integrity is the basis of all spiritual growth. This book of daily practices and guidelines for living provides an excellent tool for self-development. 224 pages, 1984. Softcover, $12.50

The Taoist Inner View of the Universe
This presentation of Taoist metaphysics provides guidance for a long and healthy life, as well as information on spiritual development which can lead to the real possibility of immortality. 218 pages, 1979. Softcover, $12.50

Tao, the Subtle Universal Law
Most people are unaware that their thoughts and behavior evoke responses from the invisible net of universal energy. Understanding this subtle law can be personally transforming and lead to great harmony in life. This books tells not only why, but also how to harmonize with the subtle law. 165 pages, 1979. Softcover, $7.50

BOOKS ON TAOIST HEALTH, ARTS, AND SCIENCES

The Tao of Nutrition by Maoshing Ni, Ph.D., C.A. with Cathy McNease, B.S., M.H. - The healing and disease prevention system of traditional Chinese nutrition has evolved through generations from an ancient wisdom that honors food and diet as integral components of the expression of harmony and balance. While Western nutrition is based on biochemical analysis, the Tao of nutrition works with the energetic and therapeutic properties of food, weaving them into the context of body type, season, location and method of preparation. This book provides remedial diets for common conditions, meal plans, simple vegetarian recipes, and information on special Chinese foods. Softcover, 214 pages, 1987 $14.50

Chinese Vegetarian Delights by Lily Chuang
An extraordinary collection of recipes based on principles of traditional Chinese nutrition. Diet has long been recognized as a key factor in health and longevity. For those who are on restricted diets and those who choose an optimal diet, this cookbook is a rare treasure. Meat, sugar, dairy products and fried foods are excluded. Produce, grains, tofu, eggs and seaweeds are imaginatively prepared. Learn how to make Mochi, Honeysuckle Flower Drink, Azuki Bean Cake, Cereal for Beautiful Skin, and many more simple, unique Chinese vegetarian delights. Softcover, 104 pages, 1987 $7.50

Chinese Herbology Made Easy by Maoshing Ni, C.A.
The distillation of overwhelming material into essential elements, enabling you to focus efficiently and develop a clear understanding of Chinese herbology. This text provides an overview of Oriental medical theory, in-depth descriptions of each herb category, with over 300 photographs, extensive tables for easy reference, and an index of pharmaceutical and Pin-Yin names. Softcover, 202 pages, 1986 $14.50

AUDIO AND VIDEO CASSETTES

Tao Teh Ching - Cassette Tape
This classic work of Lao Tzu has been recorded in this 2 cassette set that is a companion to the book translated by Master Ni. Professionally recorded and read by Robert Rudelson. $12.00   Order both tapes and book for $20.00

Invocations: Health & Longevity; Healing a Broken Heart - Cassette Tape - "Thinking is louder than thunder." The mystical power by which all miracles are brought about is your sincere practice of this principle. Using the invocations on this cassette as a guide, you can strengthen your mind and integrate your spirit into harmony with your true nature. Every living being has its own healing system and power. These invocations can channel and conduct your own healing energy and vital force. By Maoshing Ni. $5.95

Chi Gong for Stress Release - Cassette Tape
This audio cassette guides you through simple, ancient breathing exercises that enable you to release day-to-day stress and tension that are such a common cause of illness today.   By Maoshing Ni. $8.95

Chi Gong for Pain Management - Cassette Tape
Using easy visualization and deep-breathing techniques that have been developed over thousands of years, this audio cassette offers methods for overcoming pain by invigorating your energy flow and unblocking obstructions that cause pain. By Maoshing Ni. $8.95

Eight Treasures - Video Tape (VHS)
These exercises helps to open blocks in a person's energy flow and strengthen one's vitality. It is a complete exercise combining stretching and movement. Patterned after nature, these exercises are an excellent foundation for Tai Chi Chuan. By Maoshing Ni. $49

Tai Chi Chuan - I & II - Video Tape (VHS)
This exercise integrates the flow of physical movement with that of integral energy in the Taoist style of "Harmony," similar to the long form of Yang-style Tai Chi Chuan. Tai Chi has been practiced for thousands of years to help both physical longevity and spiritual cultivation. By Maoshing Ni.
$49 each/$90 set (I hour each)

Crane Style Chi Gong - Video (VHS)
The most popular Chi Gong exercise practiced in China. It is an energy enhancement exercise that promotes healing, releases stress, increases vitality and is practiced for the purpose of longevity. By Daoshing Ni. $49

ORDER FORM

Newest Releases:	Hardcover	Softcover	
_____ The Way of Integral Life	$20.00	$14.00	$_____
_____ Attaining Unlimited Life	$18.00	$12.50	$_____
_____ Enlightenment: Mother of Independence	$25.00	$16.50	$_____
_____ The Gentle Path of Spiritual Progress		$14.50	$_____
Other Favorites:			
_____ The Book of Changes	$35.00		$_____
_____ The Complete Works of Lao Tzu		$ 9.50	$_____
_____ 8,000 Years of Wisdom, Book I		$12.50	$_____
_____ 8,000 Years of Wisdom, Book II		$12.50	$_____
_____ Uncharted Voyage towards Subtle Light		$14.50	$_____
_____ The Heavenly Way		$ 2.50	$_____
_____ Footsteps of the Mystical Child		$ 9.50	$_____
_____ Workbook for Spiritual Development		$12.50	$_____
_____ The Taoist Inner View of the Universe		$12.50	$_____
_____ Tao, the Subtle Universal Law		$ 7.50	$_____
Taoist Health - Arts & Science:			
_____ The Tao of Nutrition		$14.50	$_____
_____ Chinese Vegetarian Delights		$ 7.50	$_____
_____ Chinese Herbology Made Easy		$14.50	$_____
Audio & Video Tapes:			
_____ Tao Teh Ching Cassette Tape		$12.00	$_____
_____ Tao Teh Ching Tapes and Book		$20.00	$_____
_____ Invocations Cassette Tape		$ 5.95	$_____
_____ Chi Gong for Stress Release Cassette		$ 8.95	$_____
_____ Chi Gong for Pain Management Cassette		$ 8.95	$_____
_____ Eight Treasures Video (VHS)		$49.00	$_____
_____ Tai Chi Chuan Video (VHS) ($90/set)		$49 ea	$_____
_____ Crane Style Chi Gong Video (VHS)		$49.00	$_____

U.S., Canada and Mexico, Postage/Handling:
Books and cassette tapes: $1.50 First Item,
$.50 Each Additional item.
Video Tapes: $3.00 each tape. $_____

California Residents Only, Add 6-1/2% State Sales Tax $_____

TOTAL $_____

- -

Please make checks payable to the Union of Tao and Man. Mail order to:
117 Stonehaven Way, Los Angeles, CA 90049. Please allow 3 - 4 weeks
for delivery.

Name_____

Address_____

City_____State_____Zip_____

SPIRITUAL SELF-STUDY
THROUGH THE COLLEGE OF TAO

The College of Tao was originated by the Union of Tao and Man according to guidelines from origins in the ancient past. The College does not offer an ordinary academic program in which the student follows a planned and scheduled curriculum, but assists and instructs the student in self-cultivation so as to help develop virtue and self-awareness. The purpose of the College is to further an integral way of life through the spiritual development of its students. At the present time, the College is directed and sustained by Master Ni Hua Ching who offers this unique treasure in education wherever he goes.

Although most educational institutions emphasize intellectual achievement, but the College of Tao focuses on providing its students with the foundation for cultivating a spiritually centered and well-balanced life, a person obtains the correct knowledge with which to properly guide himself or herself, he or she can then become more skillful in handling the experiences of daily life. In this way, individuals are then better able to help themselves and their families, and the world becomes a more peaceful, compatible and enjoyable place in which to live.

To promote this goal, the College adopts Master Ni's written work as its basic teaching, thus the curriculum includes all the fundamental aspects of life, with the primary focus being the discipline and self-cultivation outlined in the *Workbook for Spiritual Development of All People*. In addition to studying Master Ni's books, you may submit three to five year reports on the changes and progress in your life, along with photographs and reports on real-life activities. Students are also encouraged to further their growth by offering some form of service to the College. This ancient practice will allow the College to become better acquainted with individual students and at the same time offer the student an opportunity for more personalized instruction and guidance.

You can accept the support and guidance of the College of Tao as a lifetime student wherever you are and whatever your spiritual or educational background happens to be. Only those students who choose to attend classes in special techniques, and who are accepted to do so by the College, are required to pay a tuition. Since it is the assimilation of good guidance in one's practical life that brings about the different stages of spiritual development, the College of Tao is a school of no-campus where students can enjoy an education of no-boundaries.

- -

_____ I would like to enroll in the College of Tao as a lifetime student.

Name:_____

Address:_____

City:_____State:_____Zip:_____

INDEX

NOTES

NOTES

NOTES

NOTES

NOTES

NOTES

NOTES